Exchange of Expertise:
The Counterpart System in the New International Order

A Westview Replica Edition

This book is a Westview Replica Edition. The concept of Replica Editions is a response to the crisis in academic and informational publishing. Library budgets for books have been severely curtailed; economic pressures on the university presses and the few private publishing companies primarily interested in scholarly manuscripts have severely limited the capacity of the industry to properly serve the academic and research communities. Many manuscripts dealing with important subjects, often representing the highest level of scholarship, are today not economically viable publishing projects. Or, if they are accepted for publication, they are often subject to lead times ranging from one to three years. Scholars are understandably frustrated when they realize that their first-class research cannot be published within a reasonable time frame, if at all.

Westview Replica Editions seem to us one feasible and practical solution to the crisis. The concept is simple. We accept a manuscript in camera-ready form and move it immediately into the production process. The responsibility for textual and copy editing lies with the author or sponsoring organization. If necessary we will advise the author on proper preparation of footnotes and bibliography. The manuscript is acceptable as typed for a thesis or dissertation or prepared in any other clearly organized and readable way, though we prefer it typed according to our specifications. The end result is a book produced by lithography and bound in hard covers. Edition sizes range from 300 to 600 copies. We will include among Westview Replica Editions only works of outstanding scholarly quality or of great informational value and we will exercise our usual editorial standards and quality control.

Exchange of Expertise: The Counterpart System in the New International Order

edited by Irving J. Spitzberg, Jr.

The vision of the New International Order emphasizes justice and equality. It also raises profound questions about the nature and future of the relationship between postindustrial and Third World countries. The counterpart system describes one aspect of this relationship: an expert from a postindustrial country teaches a special skill to a Third World national. In this collection contributors draw on political science, economics, education, sociology, history, and communications theory to illuminate the forces that shape the nature of the exchange of expertise between postindustrial and Third World countries. Each author raises theoretical points and offers practical observations about the future of this exchange--a critical point of contact--in the New International Order.

Irving J. Spitzberg, Jr., is dean of the colleges at the State University of New York at Buffalo. He was previously a fellow at the Institute of Current World Affairs in New York City, founder and chairman of the Program in Policy Studies at the Claremont colleges, and consultant in adult education to the government of Kenya.

Exchange of Expertise: The Counterpart System in the New International Order

edited by Irving J. Spitzberg, Jr.

Routledge
Taylor & Francis Group
LONDON AND NEW YORK

First published 1978 by Westview Press

Published 2018 by Routledge
52 Vanderbilt Avenue, New York, NY 10017
2 Park Square, Milton Park, Abingdon, Oxon OX14 4RN

Routledge is an imprint of the Taylor & Francis Group, an informa business

Library of Congress Catalog Card Number: 78-19221

ISBN 13: 978-0-367-01786-6 (hbk)
ISBN 13: 978-0-367-16773-8 (pbk)

Contents

This paper examines the counterpart relationship as a dyad in relation to a number of support systems. The organizational context of the counterpart syad is viewed as an important variable in the evolution of the relationship in the context of the New International Order.

Adult learning is one of the outcomes from the exchange of expertise. As a way of understanding some of the factors that affect learning, this chapter examines some basic adult learning principles and discusses the implication of these to cross-cultural interaction and counterpart relationships. Other topics included are: learning environments and the conditions that help to bring these about; learning with a time a frame and the concept of time; the dyad and triad in the counterpart relationship; and linking the basic principles of learning to some of the goals of the New International Order. An argument is made that any contract that brings about an exchange of expertise is in essence a learning-teaching contract and hence is a kind of non-formal education. Perceiving the relationship in terms of learning helps to identify indicators for assessing behavior change and the achievement of educational goals.

Preface

This book has grown out of the interest of a number of scholars and practitioners in the relationship between experts and local nationals in the development process. The exchange of expertise is viewed as the ideal which should govern the so-called counterpart relationship. Many of the papers included in this collection were written in first draft for the World Conference, in Amsterdam, of the Society for International Development. The encouragement of Mr. Andrew Rice, then the Executive Director of the Society, contributed to the panel discussion of this issue in Amsterdam. Since that time, the original authors and a number who have joined us in our endeavor have cooperated extensively in preparing this multidisciplinary analysis of the counterpart system in relation to the proposed New International Order. A number of persons and organizations have contributed to the further development of this project and deserve credit for the contributions included here. Ms. Barbara Kaufman, Secretary to the Dean of the Colleges, State University of New York at Buffalo, helped type a number of the original drafts. Ms. Kate Scherer, my graduate assistant, has served a critical editorial function in helping me prepare the manuscripts for publication. And Ms. Doris Gettings, secretary in the Council on International Studies of the State University of New York at Buffalo, has typed the final manuscript. The Council on International Studies, in addition to approving Ms. Gettings' services for us, has also, through the good offices of its Director, Professor Albert Michaels, supported in spirit this undertaking.

Although all of the contributors and those who have provided editorial and typing services deserve credit for the accomplishment, the Editor must acknowledge responsibility for all errors of fact and value in this commentary.

Irving J. Spitzberg, Jr.
Dean of the Colleges
State University of New York at Buffalo
March 15, 1978

Exchange of Expertise: The Counterpart System in the New International Order

Introduction

Irving J. Spitzberg, Jr.

This book is about an important point of human contact between the post-industrial and the developing societies. There are, of course, a number of different institutional settings for the exchange of expertise: schools, colleges and universities, public debates, and other media of communication between at least two people. All of these forums, as well as the mass media, have been used for purposes of exchange between the post-industrial and the Third World, and all deserve careful scrutiny for purposes of evaluating their impact and effectiveness in this exchange. However, the focus of this book will be on a particular setting for the exchange of expertise: what is called in many places "the counterpart relationship" between an expatriate adviser and a local national advisee. This particularly intimate setting for the exchange of expertise is one where every major political, social, economic and psychological question about humankind arises but where the focus of past analysis has been on the one-way transfer of expertise, or as it is usually called, transfer of technology or knowledge. In this collection of essays, we hope to provide more balanced analyses.

The Counterpart Relationship

The counterpart relationship is generally that involved when an expatriate expert enters a Third World country in order to undertake a particular professional task as well as to train a local national in the pursuit of the professional role in which the expert claims his expertise. The traditional paradigm is that of an apprenticeship system, where the master craftsperson is an expatriate from a post-industrial country and where the apprentice is a Third World national. Around this core, one finds a number of examples which include the following permutations and combinations. For example, an expatriate national will come in as director of an agency, and he will have under him a number of junior officials drawn from the Third World country who will assist him in carrying out the professional goals of the agency, but will also be expected to learn from the expatriate manager through both instruction and example. Another is where the expatriate expert plays an advisory role to a local government official. In this case, the apprenticeship characterization becomes less apposite. The cooperative solution of problems facing the agency is supposed to allow the local national to draw on the skills of the expatriate and learn many of them himself. Finally, there is the professional colleague relationship which one often finds in the universities. In addition to the teaching of local national students in the classroom, there is a learning process through observation of the example of teaching and also through the professional interchange of colleagues about professional issues. This professional interchange also may go on in other counterpart settings when expatriate experts organize professional conferences as a mode of insuring communication.

All of these modes of counterpart relationships often share some important characteristics: they occur within a project where the major goal is an action and/or output, not primarily the exchange of expertise; there is usually a lack of preparatory training for both the expatriate expert and the local national; and there is very little, if any, provision of support systems for the exchange of expertise. Also, there are some important differences among various counterpart relationships. For example, those which occur in the setting of multinational aid--e.g., UNDP--differ from those which are bilateral. The political psychology of the multi-national may be in some ways quite different than that of the bilateral. But in most cases, regardless of the permutation of the paradigm apparent in a particular example, the differences are far outweighed by the similarities.

In this introduction, I shall only briefly identify the parameters of the counterpart relationship, which will be analyzed in greater detail in the essays which follow. The political parameter of the counterpart relationship is very real and immediate although generally neglected. Both the local political setting involving conflicts of personality and tribes or ethnic units and the international parameters of a political relationship between post-industrial and lesser developed countries are realities that impinge directly and immediately upon the relationship itself. The understanding of techniques of skill sharing and learning--that is, the educational aspect--constitutes a critical parameter if a project is to have an educational result as well as an operational outcome. The social class setting--which transcends differences of salary and economic system--of both the local national and the expatriate constitutes the critical parameter to this interaction.

The cultural setting of the counterpart relationship with its distinctive claims on the professional role--particularly the cultural discontinuity between most expatriates and local nationals--creates an important element of conflict which is necessarily a part of all counterpart relationships. In addition to issues of cross-cultural communication, there are real problems of cross-cultural action, which are endemic to the counterpart system. All of these aspects of the counterpart relationship impinge most immediately upon the core interpersonal contact which is central to the paradigm of the counterpart system. The role of personality conflict and differential adult development in various cultures and between different people constitutes a critical variable in the operation of the exchange of expertise. The multi-dimensional character of the exchange of expertise in a counterpart setting creates the need to draw on a number of alternative analytical perspectives in order to begin to understand the dynamics of this relationship.

Much has been written about the transfer of technology, technical assistance, and the role of education in development. However, surprisingly little has been available for general publication which looks explicitly at all of the parameters of the so-called counterpart relationship. A focused examination of the economics, politics, sociology, interpersonal relationships, and other parameters of this critical person/political contact between the post-industrial and Third Worlds has been sorely neglected in the general literature. There do exist individual project studies in the classified files of a number of development agencies, and there are one or two more general studies offered by units such as OECD and UNDP. But the present standard of research about this critical personal relationship in the international order has been generally weak. Therefore, this collection of essays must be viewed as a rudimentary beginning in the process of providing a multidisciplinary, critical analysis of this crucial international point of contact. And we undertake this exercise at an historical moment when the norms guiding the international order are fast evolving from a period of decolonization to a period with a goal of emerging equality. Therefore, we must ourselves undertake a critical evaluation of standards by which we can conduct an appraisal of the counterpart system in particular and the exchange of expertise in general.

The Essays--A Preview

This collection of essays grew out of some early research by the editor on the counterpart system in Kenya. An initial article was published in the International Development Review (1) and provoked strong response. Out of this response there emerged a group of scholars with interest in the counterpart relationship based at the State University of New York at Buffalo but involving a number of other persons in other institutions. This Counterpart Group prepared a panel discussion for the Society for International Development World Conference in Amsterdam in 1976. From this core has emerged this collection of papers. Most of these essays are original and offered for the first time to the general scholarly public in this collection.

At its best moments, a multidisciplinary undertaking is extraordinarily difficult in that it requires that the disciplinary analyst communicate his observations with his immediate research peers in a language which they, who share a common interest but not necessarily a similar background, can understand. The enterprise of multidisciplinary analysis is itself in its infancy and in regard to international issues perhaps even a neonate. For that reason, we do not pretend that we offer an interdisciplinary evaluation of the counterpart system even at this rudimentary level; we only offer alternative perspectives from different disciplinary backgrounds on the issues at hand.

Because of our base in the United States, we have not involved scholars in the Third World in this undertaking to date. Although all of our number have lived and worked in the Third World and at least one of us is originally a Third World national, we view this lack of dialogue in the preparation of this volume a severe handicap. And we invite our Third World colleagues to begin serious participation in this analysis of the exchange of expertise through critiques of these essays and also by participation in the research and work of the Counterpart Group.

This collection is divided into four parts. The first section provides context for the discussions of particular issues and the contributions of particular disciplines which follow. My essay explores the various parameters of the counterpart system and provides a view from the perspective of post-industrial society about the impact of the New International Order* on these relationships. John Spencer's analysis of the background of the counterpart system puts the following discussions into historical context. Philip Altbach's argument about the neocolonial role of the exchange of expertise through the counterpart system provides a sobering introduction to the following analyses.

The second section of the book draws upon communications theory, sociology, learning theory, and economics to explore the contributations which different disciplines make to an understanding of the problems of the exchange of expertise through the counterpart system. Graham Kerr, a sociologist and communications theorist, engages in a critical analysis of the concept of counterparts and relates it to the literature on change agents and the sociology of change. Russell Stone, a sociologist with experience in a number of Middle-Eastern countries, analyzes the relationship between organizational context and the interpersonal relationship which is central to the exchange of expertise in the counterpart system. The contribution which the growing, though still young, literature on adult learning can make to the understanding of the counterpart system is the central issue discussed in James Draper's paper, where he approaches the counterpart relationship as an environment for learning. Mitchell Harwitz and Abraham Haspel, two economists, take their technical tools to the decision which every government must make about the mix of environments for the exchange of expertise and develop a linear program for modeling this example of public

* Discussed later in this Introduction

choice.

The third section of this collection includes two case studies and two more general papers which look at two very different institutional contexts--science and the military. Arye Globerson's study of the interaction between experts and counterparts in six French-speaking African countries provides an analysis based upon the most extensive collection of data presented in this collection. Dr. Mabel Jesse and Mr. David Smith have drawn on their analysis of a mission in Thailand to raise very general questions about the components of successful environments for the exchange of expertise. A study of engineering education in India has allowed Thomas Eisemon to explore the role of the exchange of expertise through the counterpart system in establishing scientific communities in developing countries. The difficulty of using the exchange of expertise as an occasion for transmitting values from post-industrial to developing countries is the interest of Claude Welch in his essay about the weak role of counterparts in the establishment of civil control of the military in Africa. These latter two essays specifically focus upon the role of value discontinuity in the exchange of expertise.

The final chapter in the book includes a critical essay by Dr. Khairy Kawi, a person born in the Third World who himself lives in the United States and has served both as a counterpart and as an expert. He has participated in the exchange of expertise on both sides of the North-South divide and offers a critical commentary on all of the other papers in the collection as well as a consideration of the relationship between the form of technical assistance and the expert/counterpart paradigm.

Finally, Professor Graham Kerr has developed a bibliography of materials about the counterpart system and the exchange of expertise which we publish as a contribution to further research for others with an interest in this important area of international relations.

The Setting for the Exchange of Expertise

One must view the exchange of expertise in the context of the evolving relationship between post-industrial and Third World countries. The relationship now characterized by the concept of exchange has in the past been viewed as a one-way transfer from a post-industrial expert to a Third World learner; this is what one would expect given the colonial heritage. It is colonial history that continues to dominate the post-industrial and Third World development of means of sharing knowledge through the legacy of a mature international capitalist system. The colonial tradition assumed that the Western rulers had the knowledge which the colonial ruled needed. Although the liberation movements of the late 1950s and 1960s changed the political relationship, skills transfer became a means of continuing social and economic domination. (2)

It is a matter of debate whether this domination has been part of a post-industrial conspiracy or the necessary development of mature capitalism, but the effect of it is readily apparent. The major change in the mid-1970s has been to recognize the power of this expertise in continuing the combination of the international minority over the majority and to begin to ask why and how this domination continues and to explore ways of moving from domination by expertise toward equality of exchange.

The language often used to discuss the problems created by this domination of expertise is that of changing the relationship from one of dependence to one of self reliance on the part of the Third World. I would argue that this language misconstrues the critical characteristics of the system of exchanging expertise which exists among the post-industrial countries and which will necessarily affect the relationship between post-industrial and Third World societies if in fact domination is to be changed to a relationship of equality. The real issues is how one can move from a system of dependence of the Third World on the post-industrial societies to one of interdependence between both sectors. The evolution of the relationship between the post-industrial and the OPEC countries in the last few years provides an interesting lesson in the development of interdependence. One would never construe the role of the OPEC countries as one which is self reliant, because the economic security of the OPEC countries depends upon the maintenance of the post-industrial economies. And, of course, the post-industrial economies are quite dependent upon the political will and material resource of the OPEC countries. The relation is clearly one of interdependence. This very interdependence and the recognition of it must become the model for the further development of international order, although the nature of this interdependence must shift from that of a few technological monopolies in relation to a cartel of those controlling natural resources to one of interdependence based upon respect and need.

A goal of interdependence instead of self reliance is a necessity if in fact the Third World becomes an equal partner in the knowledge system of the World. The major characteristic of modern science and technology, as well as, I might add, the contemporary humanities and social studies, is one where identifiable transnational communities of researchers, scholars, business persons, and government officials all share in the advancement of knowledge and the development of new approaches to social problems. The complexity of this system demands the free exchange of knowledge based upon a mutual respect for contributions to the advancement of the international order and in a particular area of endeavor. Certain countries and organizations play leadership roles in particular areas--e.g., the role of the British in radio astronomy, the American multinational corporations development of complex management systems, the Japanese electronic industry--but all of these leaders operate in a system which draws upon basic research and the applied experiences of transnational communities. This is the environment in which the Third World must operate if it wishes in the future to become a full-fledged participant: an environment which one must characterize as one of interdependence, not self reliance.

However, nothing that I have said so far can be construed as suggesting that a strategy for self reliance may be inappropriate for all countries as an interim measure. Indeed, some measure of self reliance may be an appropriate strategy for a medium term leading to the interdependence of equals. The point of this discussion is that the exchange of expertise must move from the colonial and the presently neo-colonial to one which is really an exchange in an interdependent international order.

The present point of development in the history of the international system is always a real environmental factor in the operation of the counterpart paradigm. The counterpart system is the personal manifestation of the present state of international affairs. Therefore, the norms set in the international system will establish standards for the counterpart relationship.

The New International Order

The norms of the international system are now

being shaped by the debate about the New International Order. It seems safe to say that the ideas of the New International Order will certainly be a major influence on the development of the exchange of expertise through the counterpart relationship. The ideological environment within which the exchange of expertise occurs has moved from the explicit imperialist system of the 19th century, the omnipresent colonialism of the first half of the 20th century, through the liberation movements of the 1950s and 1960s to the norms of the 1970s which are evolving out of the debate about the New International Order. Therefore, insofar as we begin to analyze the present and future of the exchange of expertise, we must do so through a process which is enlightened by an understanding of the rhetoric and the reality of the evolving New International Order.

The impartial observer would have to suggest that at present the New International Order is more rhetoric than reality. This is in no way meant to be a criticism but only a recognition that in considering the New International Order we are considering goals not achievements. This recognition allows us to focus our attention on the rhetoric in order to provide a critical view of the web of objectives which constitute the New International Order.

Much of the rhetoric about the New International Order has come from discussions of what was originally called "the establishment of a New Economic Order." The U.N. General Assembly on 9 May, 1974 adopted Resolution 3201 (S-VI)--Declaration on the Establishment of a New International Order, which proclaimed the U.N.'s determination ...

> to work urgently for the establishment of a new international economic order based on equity, sovereign equality, interdependence, common interest, and cooperation among all states, irrespective of their economic and social systems which will correct inequalities and redress any existing injustices, make it possible to eliminate the widening gap between the developed and the developing countries and insure steadily accelerating economic and social development and peace and justice for present and future generations...

This invocation of every national virtue was based on the fact that developing countries which constitute 70% of the world's population, "account for only 30% of the world's income." When one reads all of the items in the declaration, one quickly sees that the emphasis is upon redistribution of resources and opportunities from the developed to the developing world. Section 4C provides the crux of the principles of the New International Economic Order:

> Full and effective participation on the basis of equality of all countries in the solving of world economic problems in the common interest of all countries, bearing in mind the necessity to insure the accelerated development of all the developing countries, while devoting particular attention to the adoption of special measures in favor of the least developed, landlocked and island developing countries as well as those developing countries most seriously affected by economic crises in natural calamities, without losing sight of the interests of other developing countries.

Although the conception of justice implicit in the New International Economic Order is not articulated explicitly for purposes of subjecting it to criticism, it is quite clear from the rhetoric of this U.N. resolution* that the conception of justice is one which focuses on redistribution of resources for the purposes of insuring greater equality among nations.

The documents themselves do not address the issue of justice and equality within countries, although many other commentators have raised this as an issue. No metajustification is provided for the conception of justice which focuses on redistribution and, implicitly, equality of results, although elements of a contractarian analysis as offered by John Rawls (3) offer a very similar conclusion (see Spitzberg, p.25).

*There are many other documents emerging from international governmental and non-governmental bodies. Especially see the deliberations of UNCTAD and other more recent U.N. debates, as well as the conclusions of _Restructuring the International Order_, edited by Professor Tinbergen.

There are, of course, elements in the U.N. resolution itself which are contradictory: for example, Section 4A focuses on the sovereign equality of all states and their rights to non-interference in their internal affairs and Section 4E focuses on the full permanent sovereignty of every state over its natural resources and all economic activities. Both of these sections are used to justify the rights of the developed countries to maintain their position of privilege without the interference of a New International Economic Order. The conflicts in the rhetoric are very real.

Although there are many inconsistencies in the rhetoric of the New International Economic Order, there are certain inconsistencies which are not intrinsic to the analysis itself and which have been overcome in the writings of more enlightened proponents of the New International Economic Order.

Mahbub ul Haq is one of the most articulate spokespersons for the New International Economic Order. In his writing, one clearly sees a recognition of the need to be explicit about the conception of equality and justice used to justify the operational principles of the proposed new order. He writes:

> ...the Third World must keep stressing, as often as it can, that the basic struggle is for equality of opportunity, not equality of income. The Third World is not chasing the income levels of the rich nations. It does not wish to imitate their lifestyles. The Third World is only suggesting that it must have a decent chance to develop, on an equal basis, without systematic discrimination against it, according to its own value systems and in line with its own cultural traditions. The Third World is not asking for a few more crumbs from the grand tables of the rich. It is asking for a fair chance to make it on its own.(4)

The mechanism which ul Haq suggests for accomplishing the restructuring of the international economic order does not look to a continuation of the existing programs of assistance from the post-industrial to the Third World. Instead, he suggests,

> ...the most important principle underlying a new framework must be a clear recognition by the international community that the trans-

> fers from the rich to the poor nations cannot continue to remain as voluntary acts of periodic generosity: an element of automaticity must be built into such resource transfers. (5)

The general conception of justice which seems to underly ul Haq's statement of the objectives of the New International Economic Order rests on a very traditional conception of justice which looks to opportunity and desert. He makes this point implicitly in his quotation of a speech which he once made at an international gathering addressing the objections of one Mr. Polanski to his demands for the automatic transfer of resources from the presently rich to the presently poor. Because of the scope of his remarks, I repeat them extensively here:

> I argued from the experience of India and Pakistan that, when we were associated with Britain in a partnership of the 19th century and the British had this slight problem about financing their industrial revolution and their structural transformation, we willingly brought out our gold and our diamonds and our agricultural produce for nominal prices and told them to go ahead and not lose the opportunity for technological breakthrough. We cheerfully stayed on an agrarian economy and applauded the industrial strides of our partner. In the modern terminology, such a thing would be called a transfer of resources, but the world was such a happy community at that time that we never even dreamed of such terms or asked for performance audits.
>
> Mr. Polanski, unreasonable as he is, wanted to know the magnitude of the transfer and I mentioned an off-the-cuff figure of 100 million dollars--a modest estimate for which I may be disowned by my fellow economists in subcontinent. I cannot confirm to him whether this amount was 1% of our GNP at that time. Anyway, I argued that this amount could be treated as a voluntary loan, at 6% interest, which has been happily multiplying over the years so that it would stand at 410 billion dollars today. I also explained to him that since the amount is

> doubling every twelve years, at this stage it is an advantage to leave it with Britain, as it will be 820 billion by 1982. We can always draw this amount whenever we need to finance a bit of our own delayed structural transformation. But Polanski, who does not understand the basic principles of sound international finance, kept on insisting that we must call up the loan immediately. I tried to reason that Britain is in no position to pay, and, being equal partners, we are in no position to collect. If we insist on quick repayment, the international community may have to do a bailing-out operation. I also told him that in matters like this, we ought to be more generous and at the very least, undertake the standard debt rescheduling exercise, for instance, we could forget the 10 billion and only ask for the remaining 400 billion.(6)

The question raised by this justification which focuses upon historical desert is whether what is being requested by reference to desert is the creation of equality in the allocation of economic resources. Ul Haq's statements about the commitment to equality of opportunity instead of equality of income do not clearly and consistently relate to his emphasis upon the automatic transfer of resources from the rich to the poor. Insofar as he is talking about redistribution of the world's economic resources, then one must say that he may be talking about equality of resource result and not just equality of opportunity for access to resources. However, this position must be moderated by a recognition of the fact that there is some minimal level of transfer of resources and, indeed, of maintenance of minimum income which may be a necessary condition for real equality of opportunity and equality of access.

Since most of the rhetoric of the New International Order has come out of the debates about the redistribution of resources and changes in the terms of international trade, the overall focus has been upon a New International Economic Order. But in recent years, the debate has been enlarged to a discussion of a New International Order which not only looks at the importance of redistribution in regard to economic resources but also to the overall political balance of power and the development of a new constitutive system for purposes of making critical value judgments which affect all countries in this interdependent world. The world has now moved to a discussion of a new political order, although the implications of this broadening have not been clearly worked out.

Technology and the Exchange of Expertise in the New International Order

One example of the broadening of the discussion can be seen in an aspect of the debate about the New International Economic Order which could not be addressed within the constraints of a discussion of the redistribution of natural resources: What is called the discussion of the transfer of technology. In the U.N. resolution itself, in Section 4P, there was a discussion of access to technology:

> ...giving to the developing countries access to the achievements of modern science and technology, and promoting the transfer of technology and the creation of indigenous technology for the benefit of the developing countries in forms and in accordance with procedures which are suited to their economy.

This analysis of technology transfer and the right to it as predominantly an economic issue misses the role of technology transfer in developing the political relationships between the developed and the developing worlds and thereby affecting the whole concept of development in the Third World. This point is clearly understood by Dennis Goulet in his new book, The Uncertain Promise: Value Conflicts and Technology Transfer. (7) He suggests that technology, as a resource and the creator of new resources, is a powerful instrument of social control, bears on the quality of decision making to achieve social change, and constitutes a central arena wherein new meanings could be created to counter alienation to the antithesis of meaningful living. (8) Goulet recognizes that what is viewed as technology indeed constitutes the capability of inventing the process of invention throughout social life. He comments on those who suggest that there is a technological force which determines development and which necessarily establishes certain sorts of power relationships between the post-industrial and Third Worlds and within developing countries. Technology construed broadly is powerful, but we are able, as Dennis Goulet suggests, to make decisions to control that power:

> A few moderns may, it is true, remember that Leonardo da Vinci refused to communicate the plans of certain inventions (e.g., submarines) to princes or to develop working prototypes after his designs had been perfect. They may also praise the wisdom of ancient Chinese rulers who chose to use gunpowder not for warfare but merely for fireworks on ritual days. In past centuries, however, technology had not yet become the object of a near idolatrous social cult. Thus "technological imperative" is traceable not to anything intrinsic in technology but to the infatuation of contemporary human beings with their own creativity. (9)

His point is that the transfer of technology, or, as we use the term in this book more broadly, the exchange of expertise can have prodound impact on those who exchange it, both giving and receiving. Yet, we are capable of making certain judgments about what that impact ought to be and then controlling the exchange for those purposes. This decision about control must be self conscious. And it is not a decision just about an economic relationship. But instead it is a judgment about the ethics of human interrelationships and the role of knowledge in them. So, insofar as one talks about controlling the transfer of technology or the exchange of expertise in the New International Order, then one must, if he is consistent, use a standard of justice to appraise any given transfer or exchange. This then is the force of the New International Order when one begins to consider its political impact as well as its economic use in the exchange of expertise.

When we consider seriously the exchange of expertise in the New International Order, then we not only ask questions about whether or not there has been accomplishment of the goals of a particular project or even whether certain technical skills were given by the post-industrial expert to the local counterpart, but, more importantly, whether this relationship provided an opportunity for a more equal exchange of knowledge. Will this contact primarily benefit developing societies and also contribute to a growing sense of equality and equal participation in the international system which is the important ideal illuminating the claims of the New International Order? It is an interest in this appraisal which informs our collection.

Conclusion

All of the authors whose essays are collected in this volume clearly acknowledge the tentative character of their arguments. We all intend to pursue our own research and would welcome opportunities for cooperative research endeavors with post-industrial and developing countries. One of the major problems in advancing our knowledge about the role of the counterpart system in the exchange of expertise is the lack of systematic data in the public record open for scholarly debate and analysis. Therefore, we propose three research priorities which we hope may grow from our work and research in the archives which are relatively hidden in the files in international agencies throughout the world: first, the publication and organization of all existing studies of various institutional settings for the exchange of expertise; second, the development of joint research projects between post-industrial and Third World scholars, drawing upon the theoretical foundations of modern social science in order to explain the variables which affect the exchange of expertise in the emerging New International Order; and third, the development of alternative models of the exchange of expertise which reflect a value commitment to equality and justice, accompanied by a commitment to implementation as well as a thorough plan for evaluation of the success of these models. All three research priorities can be undertaken by interested scholars and practitioners working together throughout the world. But the success of the pursuit of any one of the priorities will be dependent upon the political recognition of them by all of the participants in the international order.

This necessary understanding of the importance of the exchange of expertise does not assume agreements among its authors, drawn from a relatively narrow universe of potential scholars, which is characteristic of the present state of knowledge and discussion of values relevant both to the counterpart system and the New International Order. However, this collection proves, in the elaboration of arguments about the counterpart system in the New International Order, that one can begin to generate very useful knowledge both for the theorist and the practitioner. It is in the spirit of serving both the scholar and the person in the field that we have undertaken our research and share it with you. For this research to proceed, our individual interests will not suffice: only with the development of a suitable knowledge base for a New International Order through a commitment by those of us in the post-industrial world and those in the Third World will knowledge be advanced and the present order be changed.

NOTES

1. Irving J. Spitzberg, Jr., "The Counterpart System: Some Suggestions for Change," Focus: Technical Cooperation, Vol. 3 (1975) p. 3-9.

2. See Philip Altbach and Gail Kelly, "Introduction, in Kelly and Altbach, eds., Education and Colonialism (New York: Longman, 1978) p. 1-53.

3. John Rawls, A Theory of Justice (Oxford: Clarendon Press, New York, 1972).

4. Mahbub ul Haq, The Poverty Curtain (New York: Columbia University Press, 1976) p. 167.

5. Ibid. p. 207.

6. Ibid. p. 141.

7. Denis Goulet, The Uncertain Promise: Value Conflicts in Technology Transfer (Washington, D.C.: IDOC/North America, Overseas Development Council, 1977).

8. Ibid. p. 12.

9. Ibid. p. 25.

Part I Alternative Analytical Frameworks

1. Some Thoughts About Counterparts: The Political, Ethical, and Educational Aspects of the Relationship

Irving J. Spitzberg, Jr.

Much is now said about the dawning of the new, international economic order -- a vision and demand that all participants in the world economy have certain rights to a minimal allocation of resources and a claim to be given economic independence commensurate with national claims to political autonomy. The specifics of the vision and demand are still being worked out, but the outline is clear; the unequal distribution of resources and its concomitant inequality in economic power is fundamentally unjust and all international economic arrangements -- both private and public -- must be restructured to respond to these claims of right. (1)

It is important to recognize from the outset that we are dealing with a claim of right that does not look to what is but is necessarily based upon a vision of what ought to be. In its simplest terms, it is a claim of right to a redistribution of economic and political resources which requires a complementary obligation on the rich to give up some of what they have. (2) In the economic order at any moment in history, the game of distributing resources has a zero sum. Although the demands for a new economic order do not accept the limitation of the present historical moment, it would be naive to expect the rich countries to view long term benefits as outweighing short term gains entailed by the maintenance of the present system. If there is to be a restructuring of the present economic order, it will require the burden of change to be placed upon the shoulders of the benefitting nations without reliance upon the philanthropies of the rich. This is the essence of the strategy for change which lies behind the demands for the new economic order: establish the claim, but do not expect the obligations to be met; be prepared to enforce rights through active participation in the international economic system in the manner of the OPEC nations. (3) It is in this context that one must begin a discussion of counterparts.

The counterpart system has firm roots in the colonial past of world history. Although the styles of skills transfer varied (particularly between the Anglophone and Francophone colonies), there was a historical recognition of the need to establish a bourgeois indigenous class in all colonies to assist rulers in maintaining their power and to act as the interface between the colonized and their masters.(4) The general task of class construction was viewed as one for formal educational institutions, built on the model of the colonizing system, usually at least one generation out of date. (5) But the problem of transferring specific skills (those necessary to keep the trains running on time, at least figuratively) was usually met informally without much thought about the manner of transfer. The colonial civil servant related to his indigenous assistant much as the medieval master to his apprentice. No thought was given to the manner and context of skills transfer; it was assumed only that at some point, the indigenous apprentice should be competent to implement the policies of the colonial officer. (6)

During the post World War II decades of formal independence for former colonies, a great deal of attention was directed toward the creation of competence for self-government, although the legacy of accomplishment left by the colonial powers was notable in terms of its paucity not in regard to its excellence. However, the discussions were usually in terms of developing minimal skills quite similar to those idealized in the colonial master, with no understanding of the changes required for the future in the context of national pasts (with some exceptions, i.e., Tanzania). (7) The formal educational systems continued to be images of the colonial powers although the demands being made on them were for technical competencies which were seen to be better provided by the model of the American land grant college and comprehensive secondary school. Colonialism was essentially supplanted by neocolonialism in the spirit of _Pax Americana_ or, to a more limited degree, _Pax_ "_Russiana_" or "_Siniana_." The formal educational systems were (and are) being constructed according to the plans of outside architects. (8)

At the same time that mini-Western educational

systems were being constructed throughout the Third World, the pattern of relationship between the colonial civil servant and the indigenous bureaucrats continued but in a different context: the relationship between the "expert" from the rich nations who brought the skills viewed as necessary for economic development and the newly educated bourgeois bureaucrat who was supposed to learn these skills through an informal apprenticeship system and then replace the "expert" in the life of the Third World country. This relationship became institutionalized in the counterpart system in the public sector and a less formal "nationals replacement" system in the private sector. The latter was brought about through the operation of multi-national corporations in response to local laws demanding the economic involvement of nationals in their own economy. (9)

Regardless of the sector, the counterpart model shared important characteristics: the view of the learning relationship as a one way street -- from the expatriate expert to the national apprentice; the educational process as incidental to the delivery of technical services to the donee country; the time scale of any particular relationship as limited in duration although nothing is undertaken to evaluate the learning experience at the end.

All of the characteristics of this arrangement flow from the political realities which surround the counterpart relationship: the power of the donor to terminate its donation, and ability of the donor (or multi-national corporation) to use its powers in other spheres to affect the donee country (and most immediately concerned nationals). Without recognizing this reality (and the unlikelihood of this context changing in the foreseeable future), one will be unable to provide a helpful analysis of the counterpart relationship and positive suggestions for change. These characteristics must be evaluated in political, moral, and educational terms. Once evaluated, they can be addressed in terms of possible policy changes justified in regard to the moral claims of the new economic order and the political and economic realities of the present and likely futures. The tasks of this paper are threefold -- to provide a conceptual framework for analysis; to offer the outlines of an evaluation of the three primary characteristics of the counterpart relationship already identified; and to suggest directions for policy changes.

Conceptual Framework

In order to analyze the counterpart relationship, we need to be clear about our mode of analysis in the areas of politics, ethics, and education. In order to clarify the core concepts to which I shall refer in my evaluation of the paradigm of this relationship, I would like to outline my understanding of them.

First, when I refer to the political parameters of the counterpart relationship I shall be simplifying the complex interrelationship between power and authority which is the essence of political questions. For purposes of the macro-analysis -- that is the relationship between the genre "counterparts" and the rest of the political order -- I shall have in mind the power relationships between nations and the implications of such for counterparts. I believe that the concept of authority is so weak in international matters (because of the tortuous connection between the consent of an individual and the operation of the international order) that it is essentially useless in evaluating the political parameters of international problems. This is not to say that one cannot challenge the authority of a participant in the international order, it is only to suggest that the challenge can better be discussed in terms of the total ethical dimensions of international problems rather than an evaluation of authority based upon a judgment about the consent of the governed.

Although I rule out authority questions in terms of macro-political issues, I believe that inquiries about authority can usefully be made in terms of any particular political interaction in a specific counterpart relationship. Political authority in this context may be just as relevant as power, because if the participants in the counterpart relationship do not view each other as legitimate participants in the role as judged in the context of their respective political orders, the relationship itself will be affected. And the exercise of brute political power in this relationship will be the exception more often than the rule. Also, when power is exercised it is quite likely to operate in a manner which contradicts the macro-political relationships -- that is, the indigenous national is likely to use his political connections to rid himself and his country of an especially repugnant expatriate expert. (10)

The ethical parameters of the counterpart relationship focus on a central question in human relations which has become the moral cornerstone of the claims on behalf of the new economic order: justice. The historical tradition of debate about justice is lengthy and profound. In the context of this essay I would wish to avoid the intricacies of the debate but at the same time I would like to highlight some features of the concept of justice without necessarily buying the total analysis of that concept which any particular school might require. Recent writings in political philosophy have picked up the discussion as conducted by Plato, (11) Aristotle, (12) J.S.Mill, (14) and Karl Marx, (15) and rephrased certain essential characteristics of the concept of justice which might be quite helpful to the debate about the new economic order and more particularly about counterparts.

John Rawls, in his THEORY OF JUSTICE, (16) pretends to offer a comprehensive analysis of the concept of justice which resides in the tradition of the social contract rather than in the utilitarian or Marxist schools. Even though I do not believe that Rawls has succeeded, I believe his rephrasing of the contractarian view offers a brief statement of the concept of justice which would allow us to evaluate the justice or injustice of the counterpart relationship without buying his total contractarian argument at the expense of Utilitarianism or Marxism. (17) In its simplest form, Rawls asks the person making a judgment about the justice of an institutional arrangement to assume the role of a party to a contract vis-a-vis that arrangement, who has no knowledge of the future development of the social context of that institution or of his particular role in that institutional arrangement; Rawls asks that one further assume self-interested judgment on each person's part. (18) He then argues that if one were willing to prescribe that institutional arrangement, knowing that he was equally likely to play any one of the roles in it, then one could fairly call that system just. (19) In other words, the central ethical question to ask about counterparts is whether, if one did not know if he would be an expatriate expert or an indigenous apprentice, would one prescribe the counterpart system as the approach to deal with the problem of skill transfer? If so, which characteristics are consistent with this standard? If not, what changes must one initiate to make the system just?

One could object that the Rawlsian analysis of justice is inappropriate to account for the rules which are to be used to evaluate the character of the relationship between different nations or, as manifested in the counterpart relationship, between nationals of different nations. Those who make this claim suggest that the nationals from different societies have very different social frameworks for the social contract imagined in the Rawlsian analysis. I would suggest that such an argument tries to particularize the general force of any analysis of justice, Rawlsian or otherwise. It is quite true that in any particular counterpart situation it would be fanciful to suggest that the national of one country could imagine himself playing the role of a national of another; this fancifulness is emphasized when one is talking about a representative from the industrialized West in comparison to the indigenous national of a developing country. But the force of a Rawlsian analysis is not limited by the so-called unreality of the present particular fact; instead the so-called unreality is a testament to the inequality of the particular relationship being viewed. (20) If one is to attempt a general evaluation of justice, then one must of course acknowledge the limitations of the particular case, but should not be bound in terms of the analysis to a so-called present reality of unequal power relationships. The injustice of the real cannot be cited as an objection to the analytical framework which allows one to identify that injustice. Indeed by highlighting the injustice of the relationship between the expatriate expert and the Third World national in the counterpart system, the Rawlsian analysis tends to support the helpfulness of that analysis, not denigrate it.

One should argue that the intrusion of a national from one society in the affairs of another by his very presence commends an analysis of justice but is not limited to the view of the parochial society. Although one may not claim the consensual basis of a contractual relationship between societies, one might quite correctly identify an act of intent by the intervening in the Third World (the national from an industrialized country) and also the consent to social relations by the Third World country in the acceptance of the national as an intervenor; the social contract in this relationship is more than figurative. The point is that all parties to a counterpart relationship have agreed to participate in an unusual society -- that of an institution built between two nations. Justice should be just as relevant here as in consideration of a single national society.

The educational questions involved in the counterpart dyad are an amalgam of the political and ethical considerations with central issues in epistemology and learning theory. Indeed, the concept of education itself is so complex as to defy brief statement in the context of this paper. For my purposes, I would only wish to highlight certain characteristics of the concept of education and to refer to one line of debate in the analysis of educational issues. Once again one has long tradition of discussion beginning at least as early as Plato in the Western heritage. (21) We do have in hand the analysis of contemporary scholars which draws on the tradition, but which approaches it in an analytical manner and which might be helpful. Professor R.S. Peters of the University of London has suggested three necessary criteria for the concept of education: that it be worthwhile, in that one would prescribe it according to moral norms (e.g., to teach one to murder would not be "educational"); that participation in the process be voluntary; that the particular learning experience provide cognitive perspective (that is, place the particular learning in a more general context and thereby transform the perspective of the student). (22) These criteria can then be used to evaluate particular models of education to decide whether these pretenders are actually educational. Peters himself offers a model of education as initiation. (23) I shall later suggest that an alternative conception -- education as the complex interrelation between guide and tourist in a new land -- is more consistent with the criteria of education. (24) For present purposes I only wish to indicate the moral component of the conception of education, which Israel Scheffler has identified as its "programmatic" character (25) -- the relationship between a conception of education and a general program for social change in the context of which a person is educated. The logical connection between education and ethics is important to understand in evaluating the counterpart relationship. (26)

One debate in the history of education is relevant to an appreciation of the concept of education and an understanding of the counterpart system. Philosophers have tried to distinguish between teaching and training; education and learning. The central points in this debate are the characteristics which distinguish the rote learning of behavior from an understanding of ideas which inform that behavior. The classic example used to illustrate training is learning to swim; the classic manifestation of education is learning to debate the meaning of cause and effect. (27) For our purposes we need not indulge in the philosophical game of counting the number of educational angels on the end of the counterpart pin; we need only recognize that we must clearly distinguish the tasks we assign to the counterpart relationship. If we wish to use the concept of skill transfer in a technically correct philosophical manner, we shall not be talking about education, at least not directly; however, if we expect the participants in the counterpart relationship to emerge with more than technical skills, then we shall be setting a different (and perhaps "higher") standard which must be informed by criteria not unlike R.S. Peters'. And in both cases, we must understand the socio-psychological processes of learning which provide the context for any conception.

An Evaluation of the Counterpart Relationship

Before taking my conceptual framework to the counterpart relationship for purposes of evaluation, I must make clear in greater detail my understanding of the "is" of the counterpart relationship: therefore I shall sketch the paradigm of the interaction between expatriate expert and national apprentice. Then I shall draw from my conceptual analysis a statement of standards by which counterpart relationships should be evaluated.

The picture of the counterpart relationship presented here will be a paradigm abstracted from any number of variations which will border on a caricature; nevertheless the picture itself will approximate reality in most cases.

The expatriate expert will likely be assigned by a public national or international agency or multi-national corporation to serve in a less developed country for a one to three year period. This expert's primary mission will be to provide the service which his skills allow him to offer. But incidentally, he will also be asked to supervise some local persons in the carrying out of his duties, one or more of whom will be expected to replace him at the end of his tour of duty. That expected national replacement will be the expert's counterpart. Most of the interaction between the expatriate and the LDC national will occur in the delivery of services associated with the expatriate's skill. The LDC apprentice is usually picked by his government on the basis of the formal educational training he offers in comparison with the qualifications of other nationals. And, of course, local political factors are important as well -- e.g., in Africa, tribal affiliation will be as important as educational credentials. And the standard of educational preparation enjoyed by the local national rarely approaches the standard which the expatriate expert is expecting.

The expatriate expert is selected on the basis of his educational credentials and work experience in relation to the particular task or tasks facing the country to which he is assigned. Since the expert service is the product expected, little or no attention is paid to the qualifications of the proposed expert in regard to his ability to share his knowledge through either a formal or informal educational process. The task set for the expatriate expert is usually one of program creation with an implicit educational assignment; but the reality of implementation always focuses upon the immediate delivery of services, with little or no allocation of resources to the task of sharing skills.

This caricature of the counterpart relationship may do injustice to a limited number of enlightened programs; however my experience and, to the degree that it exists, the literature both suggest that this template would provide an accurate outline of most counterparts. If this is the reality, then our conceptual framework will help us evaluate it and make suggestions for change.

In terms of the macro-political relationship, the inequalities of the reality should be minimized but not disregarded. As long as an American national works in East Africa, for example, the power disparities between the U.S. and Kenya or Tanzania will continue to be a factor in the relationship between the two sets of nationals. Indeed, the existence of the need for the counterpart relationship is in part the result of this disparity. However, although the reality of the disparity will affect counterparts in their generic roles, both sides should self-consciously minimize the effect through the mutuality of respect and effort in a cooperative venture which provides the usual spirit for most counterpart endeavors. The reality demands a self-conscious effort to compensate for the disparity. But this compensation should not assume an abdication of judgment on the part of the donor powers. The power of the donor carries with it the obligation to make specific judgments about the effectiveness of the support given to and by the local national counterparts and to require quite clearly the development of a counterpart program as part of the delivery of expert services in development agreements.

At the micro-level, issues of legitimacy become quite important in analyzing the political relationship of counterparts. It is critical that each participant in the counterpart system view the other as legitimate, at the very least in the context of each person's own national system. At the threshold level this legitimacy will depend upon the paper qualifications of the counterparts: the documentation of competence of both parties. At the second level the legitimacy will depend upon the perceived capability of both parties to deal with the tasks put to them; there will be differences in degree of skill between the expert and the apprentice but not of kind. Finally, both counterparts must be open to the virtues and vices of the interacting cultures. Too often the transfer of skills is perceived as culture independent -- anyone can learn to correlate statistical variables. Usually this insensitivity to culture is a problem of the expert more than the local apprentice. The expert does not appreciate the learning opportunity which he has and the resources which the apprentice offers. Indeed in every counterpart context, the mutual respect which mutual learning could afford is an invaluable component of the political relationship, which establishes the conditions under which the counterpart relationship will develop or die. The typical counterpart relationship seldom provides this mutual sense of legitimacy.

The ethical standards implicit in the Rawlsian account of justice may appear to be trivial in the context of any particular counterpart relationship. Indeed, the standards may be nothing more than another way to put the golden rule. However, viewed generically and also in the context of the justice or lack thereof of the societies interacting, questions about justice phrased in Rawlsian language may be useful: whether or not the arrangement is one that the participant would prescribe if he did not know his particular role is the issue. This question may provide a tool of some sharpness for testing the impact of the counterpart relationship on those most immediately affected by it and on the rest of the country. Viewed in itself, if the counterpart relationship is strictly one of the expert making the professional judgments without consultation with the counterpart, and with the counterpart doing little more than providing the paperclips for connecting the pages of the expert's work, then the arrangement itself is unjust by Rawlsian standards.

Also, if the counterpart relationship seems to draw on a limited population -- say all experts are white, Northern Europeans, and all indigenous apprentices are from a single tribe or section of the local country -- then equality of educational and economic opportunity will be denied the participants. This denial of equal opportunity is a clear injustice which must be avoided insofar as the constraints of power relationships allow. Indeed, one of the few benign uses of the inequities of power between donor and donee nations is for the donor to require equality of access as a condition for the provision of all aid, and particularly the opportunity to acquire expert skills. Justice between nations demands that the standard to be applied in the intervention of one nation in another's affairs must be that of fair access to the power which is being exercised. The present exercise of unequal power by the donor might, in the longer run, entail greater access to that power by all.

The issue of equality of opportunity in the standard of justice logically and necessarily raises the question of the quality of that to which all are to have equal access, which in turn necessarily requires that we articulate the standard of education which is to inform the learning process of both participants in the counterpart dyad. At the very least one should expect that the counterpart process will give to the local apprentice the opportunity to learn the technical skills which the expatriate expert uses in performing his technical role. In the language of the teaching/training distinction one should evaluate the counterpart system as one for providing technical skills. In order to evaluate the system, it must be compared and contrasted with alternative mechanisms for providing those skills in cost benefit terms. And in order to assure the effectiveness and efficiency of the counterpart relationship as a training system, one must understand the complex nature of adult learning, which depends upon an understanding of the interaction of adult development and cultural context, about which there is little systematic knowledge. We are beginning to accumulate a literature on adult development and adult learning; (28) also, there is material available on the effect of cultural differences on learning patterns, but little has been done to combine the two. (29) Insofar as one can articulate a criterion for evaluating the training through the counterpart system, one will have to establish certain behavioral standards which look to the uniqueness of the participating individuals and the sensitivity of the relationship to the cultural patterns of thought and performance of both members of the counterpart system. There is nothing in the counterpart paradigm to encourage such an approach.

If one is to expect more than technical training out of the counterpart relationship, then one is faced with the development of a conception of education by which to evaluate the quality of the counterpart learning experience. I am not at all certain that one ought to set an educational criterion in this sense for the counterpart system. However, as a standard of excellence, it is still worthwhile to have in hand a conception of education. The history of thought about education is replete with a large number of alternative models -- Locke's tabula rasa (30), Rousseau's noble savage (31), John Stuart Mill's growing tree (32), and the more recent R. S. Peter's model of education as initiation. (33) Instead of surveying and comparing each of these models in terms of its appropriateness for application to the counterpart relationship, I would prefer to offer briefly my own model which draws upon characteristics of all of these models.

My model is derived from Wittgenstein's observation that the learning of mathematics is something like the experience of learning about a foreign land: one stumbles about and finally discovers the sights and sounds and best pathways among them. My model is that of the stranger and his guide in a new land. The process of education is one of discovery for the stranger but assisted by the cues and conventional wisdom of the guide. But the learning process is not a one way street. Many of the most exciting discoveries have occurred from the fresh perspective of new eyes, and the goal of education for both the stranger and the guide is to discover new paths and new places through mutual cooperation. This conception of education as supported exploration ascribes independence and choice to both participants but acknowledges the wisdom of those who have prior mastery of the conventional and the insight of those who come fresh to an enterprise.

The equal importance of prior mastery and fresh insight cannot be overemphasized, because mutual understanding demands the respect of the equal importance of both characteristics. The mutual respect of this model of education if it informed the counterpart relationship might allow the learning in that context to transcend mere training and result in a learning experience for both participants which would reap many rewards for all involved. Such a process would likely meet the criteria set by Peter's concept of education with its demands of worthwhileness, voluntary participation, and cognitive perspective. Once again, however, except for certain serendipitous occurrences which have little to do with most counterpart relationships, the counterpart paradigm offers little to meet this standard.

Suggestions for Future Policies

The paradigm of the counterpart relationship is affected by, though rarely sensitive to, the macro-political considerations we have identified. Little note is taken of the impact of the colonial history and the continuing neocolonial relationships between countries, which affect the potential for effectiveness of the counterpart relationship. For example, the unwillingness of some governments to provide counterparts for expatriate experts may be a fear of the "brainwashing" and political cooptation which might result from the extended, close contact between the expert and the apprentice. Also, the process of negotiation which surrounds the development of an aid agreement or the establishment of a branch of a multi-national corporation is always informed by the power inequalities, but seldom is the power reality articulated and discussed in order to cope with it in the process of implementation. The most that one can expect here is recognition. The problem itself is very difficult to address and may be intractable.

The micro-political matters of legitimacy are much more complex and have a more profound effect on any particular counterpart arrangement, and may be subject to some solution. The "legitimacy" of most experts is given by their appointment by the donor: they are certified competent by the agency. However competent the expert may be in his field, he often soon loses legitimacy through ignorance of the cultural milieu within which he is working. By not recognizing the standards of behavior of the host culture, the expert, while still maintaining technical authority may in fact lose legitimacy by violating or not respecting the local standards. This is a problem created by the structural assumption that the expert is only the provider of knowledge and not a receiver. The source of legitimacy for the indigenous apprentice will be both his educational background and also political status in the local system. The former must at least be minimal both for the respect of the expert and also for that of the local bureaucratic system. And the second, political status of the local apprentice, is important. It is critical to the success of the local counterparts in their support role and in their future replacement function that the expatriate expert clearly respect his political position.

I observed a counterpart relationship in Kenya where an educational expert treated his counterpart with disdain, even though the counterpart was a man of clear accomplishment in the political realm -- he was a member of the dominant Kikuyu tribe and a land owner of substance in his native rural area. The counterpart was clearly legitimate in local terms and had real authority; something the expatriate expert lacked. If the legitimacy of both participants in the counterpart relationship is to operate, self-conscious efforts must be made to structure the interaction to enhance the authority of both participants. Occasions must be created to allow (require) the expatriate to see his local counterpart in activities which show him in a political milieu outside of the relationship.

There is little in the record of most counterpart relationships which indicates concern for justice in the initial design or actual operation of the relationship. Internal to the relationship it is critical that an atmosphere of mutual respect is entailed by the structure. Here some obligation on the part of the expatriate to learn about the culture and politics of the counterpart might encourage more justice throughout the interaction. In relation to the larger system, careful concern about the methods of appointment operating in both the donor and donee nations seems in order. Both parties to any counterpart agreement should study carefully the patterns of past employment. If one racial or ethnic or tribal group seems overly represented, the need for affirmative action on behalf of other groups should be addressed in the process of negotiation. For such an affirmative action program to operate, one may also have to be sensitive to the qualifications described and imagine alternative sorts of preparation which might be most helpful to the counterpart relationship.

One must be modest in his/her expectations about the possible impact of any counterpart policy changes on the justice of the relationship or on the justice or lack thereof of the society. And one must also admit the political difficulties of using standards of justice in matters of international negotiation, where the initial macro power relationships will be quite important. However, one can justify these concerns with justice, because the counterpart relationship involves all parties in the internal life of a country: it is a mode of participation involving the responsibilities of all members of the local society. No claim can be made that one or another participant should not "meddle" in the internal affairs of a country, because all parties are involved in internal affairs by participation in a counterpart arrangement.

If the demands of justice do not prohibit the intervention of one country in the affairs of another through the counterpart relationship, then the neo-citizenship obligations of the intervening expatriates must be interpreted in a manner to demand such judgments about the justice and equality of the counterpart relationships. This special sort of social relationship which one finds in the counterpart arrangement is one that is subject to the moral evaluation which one ought apply within the confines of an individual society. The supposed amorality of international relations is inappropriate when one is talking about the character of obligations exercised in the active participation in the individual national society. The donee society has every right to expect good citizenship on the part of the donor, and vice versa.

The policy changes implied by the evaluation of the counterpart arrangement from an educational perspective are sweeping and profound. At the outset one would have to consider quite explicitly the educational and/or training component of the counterpart relationship as important and central to the mission of all of those involved. Each aid agreement (or contract to establish a local unit of a multi-national corporation) should contain an extensive and detailed clause about the counterpart relationship and how it would operate and be evaluated.

Every counterpart relationship should be viewed as, at the minimum, an exercise in skill sharing and therefore training. This minimal learning criterion itself requires detailed attention to the learning background of all participants and also to the state of adult development of both members of the dyad. The ecology of the counterpart relationship must also be sensitive to the cultural differences between the expatriate expert and the local apprentice and the unique problems created by conflicting cultural styles. And finally, even just for training, a great deal more research must be done about the dynamics of informal learning, one on one, which is the essence of the counterpart arrangement.

In special cases one may wish to invest the time and other resources necessary to make the counterpart relationship truly educational. And, I might add, that in theory all counterpart relationships should be "educational" if the local counterpart is to actually have the same command of professional judgment which the expatriate expert supposedly brings and if the expatriate expert is to take away a greater understanding of the wisdom of his so-called apprentice's knowledge of the local culture and the way in which one accomplishes tasks within its framework. The most important condition for the creation of an educational situation within the constraints of the counterpart relationship is to break down the one way street of most counterpart interactions. The stranger and guide in the new land of the counterpart system must both recognize what each has to learn from the other and the relationship must be structured to provide occasions for both not only to learn but to be seen to be learning from each other. To return to the example of the educational expert and his counterpart in Kenya, the expatriate never mastered the local culture because of his attitude toward the lack of technical skills of the local bureaucrat and because of the expatriate's attitude, the local counterpart got little out of their relationship.

In order for either training or education to take place in the context of a counterpart relationship, both participants need a great deal of support from outside of the dyad. Both should have institutionalized support units to assist the counterparts. A unit specifically assigned the task of assisting counterparts in each country with such arrangements could draw upon the experience of adult learning systems such as the Open University in Great Britain (34) or the Empire State College in New York (35); or mass adult education projects such as those undertaken in Tanzania. All such units should be clearly under the control of the local governments, so that they would not be tainted by the macro-political inequalities which surround the counterpart system.

Conclusion

It is appropriate to conclude this paper by returning to its beginning; to remind us that our discussion of counterparts must acknowledge the international context of neocolonialism which is the reality of the relationship between the developed and developing countries. The conception of "development" reeks of a paternalism which sets the standards of the industrialized countries to be met by the rest of the world. (36) To make this observation is not to suggest that the counterpart system should be jettisoned because of this neocolonial affiliation; it is only to ask that the arrangement itself be made less a mirror of the reality which provides its context. The context should also make us sensitive to possible alternative approaches to the sharing of knowledge which might be less neocolonial in power relationships and probable implementation. This sensitivity to the neocolonial character of the relationship should not act as an impediment to donors in insisting upon the most effective and just counterpart system once this strategy is undertaken.

The counterpart system has accomplished much even though it has historically been muddling through. Think what might be accomplished by attention to this arrangement and the minimal investment of resources to make it more effective! The future of the counterpart approach must be such that it leads to greater justice both in its internal structure and its expernal effect. Only then will greater equality in the distribution of knowledge, which should be one of the most important goals of the counterpart system, set the stage for the first act of the new economic order.

NOTES

1. See Hugh L. Keenleyside, International Aid; A Summary (New York: Heineman, 1966) and Uner Kirdar, The Structure of An Economic Aid to Underdeveloped Countries (The Hague: Martinus N. Johoff, 1966).

2. Wesley Hohfeld, Fundamental Legal Conceptions (New Haven: Yale, 1964).

3. See article, "Algerian Says Oil-Buying Nations Conspire On Price," by Clyde H. Farnsworth, New York Times, Thursday, March 21, 1974.

4. Ali A. Mazrui, "The Impact of Multinational Corporations on Educational Processes and Culture Change: An African Perspective," unpublished

working document for the Experts' Meeting on the Impact of Transnational Corporations on Development and International Relations, convened by the Division of Applied Sciences of UNESCO for May or June, 1976 in Paris.

5. Philip G. Altbach, "Education and Neocolonialism", Teachers College Record, May, 1971, Vol. 72, No. 4.

6. See Archibald P. Thornton, For the File on Empire (London: MacMillan and Co. Ltd., 1968).

7. See Budd Hall, "Notes on Adult Education, Equality, and the Tanzanian Experience," working paper prepared for the XXth Annual Conference of the Comparative and International Education Society, Toronto, 1976.

8. Altbach, op. cit.

9. The experiences in Kenya and Uganda during their different Africanization programs provide cases in point. To the best of my knowledge, no analytical case studies of these exercises have been written because of the political difficulty of collecting data. If such studies exist, I would be very interested in reading them.

10. I saw such events in a number of contexts during my work in Kenya. The most vulnerable expatriates were those who were preceived to have some say over the grant making policies of aid agencies.

11. The Republic, trans. H.D.P. Lee (London: Penguin, 1955).

12. The Politics, trans. T.A. Sinclair (Baltimore: Penguin, 1969).

13. Social Contract, trans. G.D.H. Cole (London: Everyman, Dutton, 1959).

14. The Social Philosophy of J.S. Mill, Marshall Cohen, ed. (New York: 1961).

15. The Early Writings, trans. and ed., T.B. Bottomore (London: Watts, 1963).

16. (Oxford: Oxford University Press, 1972).

17. For commentaries see Robert Nozick, Anarchy, State and Utopia (New York: 1974) and Brian Barry, *The Liberal Theory of Justice* (Oxford: 1973).

18. Rawls, p. 11 and pp. 142-150.

19. Rawls, pp. 11-21.

20. Rawls, pp. 54-55.

21. Plato, *The Republic*, *op. cit.*

22. R.S. Peters, *Ethics and Education* (London: 1966).

23. R.S. Peters, *Education as Initiation* (London: 1968).

24. See IJS 3 and 4, Institute of Current World Affairs, 535 Fifth Avenue, New York, New York 10017, U.S.A.

25. Israel Scheffler, *The Language of Education* (Springfield: Thomas, 1960).

26. Peters, *Ethics in Education*, pp. 25-30.

27. Gilbert Ryle, "Teaching and Training," in Peters, ed., *Concept of Education* (London: 1967), pp. 105-120.

28. For an interesting example of this literature see Arthur W. Chickering, "The Developmental and Educational Needs of Adults" (unpublished paper).

29. For an analysis of some of this literature in the context of issues of equality in America, see Christopher Jencks *et al.*, *Inequality* (New York: 1973).

30. *Essay Concerning Human Understanding*. Book II, Chapter 1, Section 2 (London: 1960).

31. *Emile*, trans. Barbara Foxley, ed. Ernest Rhys (London: Everyman's Library, 1930).

32. *The Philosophy of John Stuart Mill*, p. 251.

33. *Education as Initiation*, *op. cit.*

34. *The Open University*, Bletchley, Great Britain.

35. Empire State College, Saratoga Springs, New York.

36. For a trenchant discussion of the concept of development see Colin Leys, *Underdevelopment in Kenya*, California: 1974, especially the chapter on "Development and Neocolonialism."

2. Colonial Antecedents of the Counterpart System in British and French Africa

John Spencer

This paper is an attempt to put the counterpart aspect of technical assistance in historical perspective. The argument here is that it is nothing new, that its roots go back into earlier centuries and that it began to take its present form, not with the midnight lowering of British and French flags in the early 1960s, but with the end of World War II, some fifteen years earlier.

To understand the direction colonial policy took after 1945, one has to know what happened earlier. Accordingly, the paper is divided into two parts. The first traces the evolution of British and French colonial policy from the New Imperialism of the 1880s to the depression colonialism of the decade before World War II. The second describes the post-War change of course that led to the counterpart system we know today.

Pre-1945 Britain

I

Let us look first at the British. Here it is useful to divide the pre-independence period into two states: pre-1914 and 1919-1945.

Britain, like France, had little interest in acquiring more African territory until the last two decades of the 19th century. She had footholds in Sierra Leone and along the coasts of present day Ghana and Nigeria and, of course, a large chunk of land at the tip of Africa at the Cape, but these were the results of her anti-slavery campaign, past commercial interests and the Napoleonic wars, not of colonialist expansion. This changed for several reasons; the rise in power of Imperial Germany, the pervasive spirit of aggressive nationalism of the time and economic competition with her continental neighbors. This led Britain to occupy Egypt in 1882 so that her life-line to India, the Suez Canal, would not fall into other hands. It was this move, many think, that precipitated the European "scramble" for African territory. (1) By 1914, Britain had greatly expanded her West and South African holdings and had moved into Eastern and Central Africa where only the German area (Ruanda-Urundi and Tanganyike) and Ethiopia kept her from owning a continuous strip of land from the Cape to the Red Sea.

The pre-World War I years of this century were ones of consolidation and pacification in British Africa. The partitioning lines drawn on the green baize tables of Europe enclosed areas that contained some peoples who did not yet know they were under colonial rule and others who knew it and resisted, like the Kisii and the Nandi in what was then the Wast African Protectorate, now Kenya. Above all, however, this was a time of administrative rationalization, for the new colonial subjects, both the passive and the resistant, had to be fitted into some sort of organized rule, more orderly and less corrupt than that of concessionary companies like the Imperial British East Africa Company that administered Uganda and the East African Protectorate until Britain took them over in 1895, and the ones in French Africa. Britain's best known solution to this problem was, of course, Lugard's system of Indirect Rule, which he pioneered in northern Nigeria.

To Lugard, the two essential elements of Indirect Rule were "decentralization and continuity," that is, a lack of interference with the man on the spot and the avoidance of rapid turnovers of personnel. (2) It was a system designed to lead the local people to eventual self-government, although Lugard himself said, "...the era of complete independence is not as yet visible on the horizon of time." (3) There simply were not enough educated Africans to replace the disinterested, yet concerned, public-school, prefect type of District administrator who was Lugard's ideal. Also, as Lord Hailey notes, for all Whitehall's talk of future colonial autonomy, "Unlike the terms 'responsible government' or 'dominion status', the term 'self government' had no precise connotation in British constitutional practice". The term was never defined in any authoritative policy statement.

In the second period, from 1919-1945, the theory

of Indirect Rule, in Lord Hailey's words, became "a religious dogma". (4) Paradoxically, this slow ossification occurred in an era when those who had survived the wholesale slaughter of World War I were questioning not only the utility, but the morality, of colonialism. As we shall see, the French response was increased control from Paris. British reaction was less severe. An overall colonial policy--perhaps "attitude" would be more apt--emerged, that of "trusteeship," under which His Majesty's Government acted as the protector of "native" interests. (5) Part of the change stemmed from the old British humanitarian tradition, and in part it was due to Britain's position as a League of Nations mandatory caretaker for the former German territories in East and West Africa. Like Lugard, the implementers of this trusteeship believed that they had an "indefinite time ahead." (6) Somewhere within this vague period Africans would be ready for self-government. Until then, it was the duty of the trustees to prepare their wards--by example for the masses, and by education of a select few. (7)

It was education on two levels. At the top, there were elite secondary schools like Achimota College in Ghana and the Alliance High School in Kenya, both of which were founded in the 1920s. On a lower level, there was the Booker T. Washington variety of trade education provided by institutions such as the Jeanes school in Kenya, and rudimentary training in the management of local affairs through the establishment of district advisory groups under the chairmanship of the District Commissioner.

One must realize, however, that in contrast to the iron grip of Paris on the French colonies there was a considerable amount of local autonomy in the British African territories. Particularly, the policy of what at the end of colonial rule would be called "Africanization" was at the discretion of individual governors. In the Gold Coast, for example, Governors Clifford and Guggisberg, just after World War I and in the 1920s, began to appoint Africans to senior posts. It was, in fact, Guggisberg's goal to have a Civil Service that was fifty percent African and fifty percent European. (8) But this was still trusteeship, with the aim of maintaining the Empire. As Guggisberg himself said, speaking about education, "This then is our immediate task--the provision of teachers, instructors and professors from among Africans.... In no other way shall we keep them permanently the loyal and working members of our Empire...." (9)

But he was a rarity among Governors. His conservative successors scrapped his plans. Their colleagues in Nigeria agreed that it was inconceivable that an African administrative service (e.g., African District Commissioners) could play any part in the country's eventual self-government. In the 1930s even a scholar of administration in Nigeria such as Dame Margery Perham was against the appointment of Africans as District Officers, Commissioners or their equivalents. "There is...one branch into which, I believe, Africans should not enter, and that is the Administrative Service". (10) With the marked improvement of the quality of British administrators after Sir Ralph Furse reorganized the Colonial Service's recruiting and training methods and, more immediately, with the Depression, this seemed as far over the horizon as before.

In sum, British policy in these interwar, precounterpart years can be viewed as a scaffolding around a slowly rising structure of African self-government. (11) The lower floors of this edifice, the clerks and messengers, were already filled with Africans in West Africa and with non-Europeans like Goans in the east and central African white-settler territories. The skeleton of this new building was the training, slow and sure, of Africans who would one day govern themselves. It was a policy that would weaken the future African states in several ways. The expatriate monopoly on top-level jobs meant that when the Europeans left there would be very few people with equal skills or experience to replace them. Also, while the education system was designed to produce leaders eventually, its immediate effect was to turn out low-level clerks for government and commerce. Only in the late 1930s did the Colonial Office give some thought to local post-secondary school training. Finally, the vast administrative difference between black and white in these interwar years led not only to feelings of inferiority and anger among Africans, but when they succeeded the departing Europeans two decades later, to their own continuation of British colonial class consciousness. (12)

The closest equivalents to the modern counterparts in this period were, on the larger scale, the ruler-ruled relationships of Indirect Rule and, on a lower level. Furse's cadet administrators fresh from their training in England, who would trot along behind a District Officer or Commissioner for a year or two before becoming a D.O. themselves. (13)

Pre-1945 France

Before 1945 it is helpful to divide French colonialism into three stages; pre-1871, 1871-1920 and 1920-1945.

It is a commonplace that in the decades before the Scramble there was little European interest in colonial expansion. This was particularly true in post-Napoleonic France. Certainly, her empire grew with the addition of Algeria in 1830, but the rest of her colonial possessions brought back too many unpleasant memories of Bourbon, Roman Catholic, and mercantilist comination to arouse widespread support. (14) Commercial and religious groups with interests in West Africa could often make themselves heard in government circles and, without doubt, the generals had an interest in perfecting their trade in pacifying North Africa. But these were isolated cases. In general, domestic and European interests pushed colonial matters to the side.

In 1830 the French Government decided to set up trade and refueling stations on the Gabon coast, although it was not until 1842 that the French Navy sent one of its officers to put them into operation. (15) The 1848 revolution led to no new overall colonial policy. Napoleon III's costly intervention in Indochina in 1859 and France's failure in Mexico reduced the appeal of imperialism even further. Finally, in these pre-1871 years, France had no central administrative direction for her colonies. The small colonial bureaucracy, the inconsequential Direction des Colonies, was part of the powerful Ministry of Marine that directed the Navy. (16) The main justification for colonies at this time was that the Navy would be meaningless without them, and without it, France could not look her rival, Britain, in the eye.

A crucial element in France's earlier 17th century expansion had been a desire for prestige. Richelieu's aim overseas was to enhance his king's *dignite*. French colonial policy in the second of the three periods, from 1871 to 1920, was based on a similar desire for national prominence, but of a new and urgent kind, stemming from France's defeat by Prussia in 1870. Until the first World War, except for a brief slackening of colonial fervor around 1881, French colonial policy was generally to grab as much African land as possible. Without doubt, both the politicians and military men responsible for her colonial policy in these years justified their actions on the basis of eventual commercial profit, but underneath it all lay the desire to regain national face, to be considered one of the great nations of the rapidly expanding world. It was a policy of amour propre blesse.

What is important for us here is that France's participation in the Scramble, her conquest of the western Sudan and penetration inland further south, was not accompanied by a coherent colonial administrative policy. Only in 1894 was a separate Ministry of Colonies established, ending the anomalous role of the Ministry of Marine.

The local administration of France's African territories was no more organized. In an attempt to remedy this, the Government founded a school for French colonial officials, the famous Ecole Coloniale, in 1890. It was the administrative embodiment of French colonial prestige. It was to train the senior officers of a great and unified empire, men who would be able to handle a variety of posts throughout it. (17)

The creation of the Ecole and of the Ministry coincided with the decline of military influence. After Fashoda and the end of France's dreams for the Nile, with the defeat of Samori and Rabih and the successful conquest of the western Sudan, the army lost its influence upon France's politique Africaine and the administrators took over. A decree of 1895 put the Ivory Coast, Guinee, and the Sudan under the control of the Governor General of Senegal. In 1904, after much discussion, the French Government created the French West African Federation. The AOF, as it became known, was made up of five territories-Senegal, Guinee, Dahomey, the Ivory Coast and upper Senegal-Niger--under a Governor General. Sixteen years later, Mauritania became a colony and joined the AOF and in the resulting administrative reorganization, the French created three new areas: the Soudan, Niger, and Upper Volta. In 1910, Tchad, Ubangi-Shari, Gabon and the Middle Congo were grouped together into the French Equatorial Africa Federation (AEF). (18)

To many Frenchmen, the pacification and the creation of these two federations gave an appearance of comforting Gallic order. France could now start making money from them. Jules Meline, Minister of Agriculture in 1809, stated it clearly. "(We should) discourage in advance any signs of industrial development in our colonies (and) oblige our overseas possessions to look exclusively to the mother country for manufactured products, and to fulfill, by force if necessary, their natural function, that of a market reserved by right to the mother country's industry. (19)

The general popularity of this approach led to the dividing up of AEF among large concessionary companies like those the Belgians had used so sucessfully in organizing the production of rubber in the Congo. After a Commission of Colonial Concessions had reported favorably on their use as developing agents, another scramble took place. In four months in 1899 the Government granted concessions to forty companies in the Congo territory alone. Despite its immediate popularity, the concessionary system was both a humanitarian and economic failure. In 1905 a newspaper article describing the companies' brutal treatment of Africans led to a trial of two officials, which, in turn, revealed further abuses--sanctioned by the companies. (20)

After a February 1906 decree (the Clementel reforms), the Government sought to take them over. Their investors' initial hostility to any official intervention quickly decreased when they discovered that the companies were losing literally millions of francs. In 1907 there was a fall in rubber prices, and this brought the brief era of the concessionaires to an end. (21)

If they had helped write one of the uglier chapters in African history, the companies had at the same time helped provide the beginnings of an economic infrastructure in AEF. But it was at a great cost. When the French Government cut them down, the ivory and rubber trade, in fact, trade in general, was in a state of confusion and the population of the area had been severly reduced. This episode and the very questionable gains from it led to a period of disillusionment with the whole colonial process that lasted until World War I.

As Hubert Deschamps has noted, "With the Treaty of Versailles, France reached its greatest extent as a colonial power."(22) In addition to the Maghreb, Indochina, her island territories, and the three governments-general in Africa--AEF, AOF, and Madagascar--France now had mandates for Syria, Lebanon, Cameroon, and Togoland. In the pre-World War I years the French had come to view their colonies as sources of manpower for their armies. Literally hundreds of thousands of Africans had fought against the Germans; 181,000 Sengalese, 175,000 Algerians, 50,000 Tunisians, 41,000 Madagascans, 34,000 Moroccans and 2,000 Somalians had served in the French Army. (23) It was, in part, due to them that

Deschamps could say, "After 1919, Waterloo and Sudan had finally been avenged." (24)

Pre-World War I French colonial policy was characterized by the concept of assimilation, an idea, like that of prestige, that went back to the 17th Century. By the post-World War I years, this had officially become "association," which on the surface of it, seemed to mean that the colonies would stand on their own feet, still ruled by France to be sure, but each with a definite identity, with its own recognized needs and policies. In fact, the opposite took place. The interwar period was one of increased, rather than lessened, central control, years when, more than ever before, Paris told the colonies what to do. The Law of Finances of July, 1920, codified this principle of centralization; instead of asserting colonial individuality, the new law repressed it. The goal was greater efficiency. The Ministry of Colonies itself became increasingly centralized in the hands of a few career civil servants. "The permanent officials are everything, the Minister...a subsidiary...." (25)

There was one exception to this, Albert Sarraut, who was Minister from 1920 to 19]4, and who, during these first two combat-free decades of the new French empire, supplied the only clear direction in French colonial policy. The title of his 1923 book, La Mise en Valeur de nos Colonies, described his goal. He set up a system of government guaranteed loans to the colonies that were used to create an infrastructure (roads, railroads, harbors) that would speed development and would support social projects such as schools and urban plans that were designed to bring Africans into the 20th Century.

The mise en valeur goal lingered after Sarraut, but factionalism in French politics and the Depression made any coherent and sustained colonial policy impossible. The socialist regime of Leon Blum was able to make a few improvements in working conditions and in the harsh summary justice system (the indigenat), but its main project, "a big program of small works," never got past the French Senate. After the overthrow of Blum's government in 1937, the Radicals again made a few changes, once more in labor matters. But on the whole the interwar period was one of stasis; there were no new directions in French colonial policy.

II

I turn now to the second of the two periods under consideration here, that from 1945 to 1960. It is ironic that what appeared to be two such dissimilar systems--France's assimilation of Africans, (under the guise of "association") often to the very highest levels of metropolitan politics, and Britain's policy of grass-roots development-- produced the same lack of trained senior officials at the time of Independence, the same need for the counterpart system of the 1960s and the 1970s. To see why this is so, let us look first at the British in post-war sub-Saharan Africa and then at the French.

Post 1945 Britain

Like many other post-World II changes, the shift in British colonial policy had actually begun before the war ended. (26) In our look at the background of the counterpart system, the post-War period begins in 1940 with the passing of the Colonial Development and Welfare Act, the first major legislative move away from trusteeship towards economic and social development. The force behind it was Lord Hailey. His giant African Survey (1938) and the report of his 1940 tour, Native Administration and Political Development in Tropical Africa, made him the leading colonial authority of the time. Native Administrations provided the rationale for Britain's post-War emphasis on the development of local government institutions and on Africanization. To Hailey, the colonies could only be self-governing if there were an adequate economic and social substructure to support the inevitable local political institutions. (27)

One of the initial signs in British Africa of the new policy was the appointment in 1942 of K.A. Busia and A.L. Adu (both of whom were to become well known in later life, Busia as politician and Adu as international civil servant) to the Gold Coast Administrative Service, the first Africans in decades to join it at the European level. (28) In 1944-45 the British Government called upon its colonies to produce development plans, which were to be implemented by groups of technicians under the control of a District Commissioner called District Teams. The advent of the Labour Government in 1945, with all its 1930s Fabian enthusiasm for colonial reform and its Fabian Colonial Secretary, Arthur Creech Jones, speeded the implementation of Lord Hailey's ideas.

Within a year after the end of the War, the results of the new policy were clearly evident in the field. In 1946, for example, the Chief Justice of the Gold Coast, Sir Walter Harragin, chaired a Commission that abolished racial pay scales in the public service of British West Africa. (29) Perhaps the best known of the Labour Government's innovations appeared the next year. Creech Jones' Local Government Dispatch of 1947 called for the immediate revamping of local government in the colonies with two basic aims: effective use of the large amounts of Colonial Development and Welfare funds and acceleration of the moves towards self-government in each colony. Other measures followed, all along the same lines: a gathering of African governors in 1948; a conference of unofficial (that is, nongovernment-in West Africa, African) Legislative Council members; the creation of an African Studies Branch in the Colonial Office to act as a clearing house for African information and problems; the establishment of the Journal of African Administration; and the organization of a series of summer conferences held at Cambridge University, where senior British and African officials, academics, and visiting experts discussed problems of African local administration. Finally, the Colonial Office reorganized the syllabi of its administrative training courses, bringing them more into line with the new emphasis on local government and social development. (30) In a way, Britain's plans here resemble those of France in 1920; that is, she was aiming at an empire-wide policy with central focus and direction. To be sure, the various secretariats in the field were still allowed a wide degree of discretion, because conditions varied so in the different colonies. But they were now supposed to be working towards clearly defined, if rather general developmental goals, and this was new.

Although African nationalists thought the pace of Africanization too slow, genuine advances were made, even in a white-settler colony like Kenya. In 1946 the first Africans joined the Nairobi Municipal Council. The same year Africans were admitted as cadets in the Administrative Service under the cumbersome title of African Assistant Administrative Officers. In 1946 and 1948 more Africans joined the Kenya Legislative Council. In 1954 and again in 1957 the British Government proposed new constitutions, increasing African representation further. (31)

In West Africa the pace was quicker. Ghana

achieved a measure of internal self-government in 1951. In addition, between 1949 and 1954 the number of Ghanaians in senior public service posts there rose from 13.8% to 38%. (32) In Nigeria, Africans began to play increasingly important political and administrative roles, as the British realized that self-government was going to come far sooner than they had expected and that they had not prepared enough Africans for the takeover. (33)

From 1955 to 1960, the watershed year of Independence, Britain speeded up her Africanization programs. It was in this stage of British colonial policy that the counterpart system as we know it today emerged. Certainly Adu, Busia, and other AAAOs in the early and mid-1940s had been apprenticed to British officials, but these were isolated instances. Training--for agricultural, medical, veterinary assistants and the like--was usually done in the classroom. With Ghana's independence less than a year away, Britain belatedly began to admit Africans in her West African territories to the administrative services. In 1956 in Northern Nigeria, for example, able local graduates were nominated for training as future District Officers and assigned as a counterpart to a carefully chosen European district officer for six to twelve months. (34)

Although the British Government had no consistent specific policy about skills transfer, as we have just seen, there was a marked growth of it in English-speaking African colonies after World War II. One must start with the realization that the civil and administrative services (the field officers and those in the Ministries who serviced them) were treated differently. I noted earlier that even before World War I there had been some localization of governance in British East and West Africa. In the interwar period, more and more Africans came into the lower and middle grades of the Civil Service, primarily because European salaries were so much higher than African ones that it became too expensive to import Europeans to fill low-level jobs. But it was different with the Administrative Service. Despite the appointment of a very few Africans during World War II, the Administrative Service was the last to be Africanized. It was not until 1953 in the Gold Coast and 1955 in northern Nigeria, the home of indirect rule, that African cadets began to enter the administrative service. (35) At first glance this sounds as if they were the true local precursors of the post-Independence counterpart system, but, in actual fact, black faces had merely replaced white in a system that went back to Lugard's rule some fifty years earlier. From 1945 to 1955, as noted above, the emphasis had been on general skill transfer, on training in local government, in agriculture, and in community development rather than planning for the still indefinite future. It had been argued that it was senseless to train African District Commissioners, for when Independence finally did arrive, the administrative service would be nothing more than a useless relic of the colonial past. In addition it was widely believed that chiefs would not serve under African District Officers or Commissioners and that the Colonial Service could not successfully transfer African officials from one territory to another--from, say, Nigeria to Tanganyika--as it did European ones. (36)

If the Local Government Dispatch and the other post-War measures related to it signalled a major change of direction, there were still echoes of trusteeship and of scaffolding. In a sense this was inevitable, for 1945-55 were transition years during which a cadre of able Africans had to be chosen, trained and then put in the field. The District Team members who worked to implement the post-War ten-year development plans were more like teachers--of soil conservation, of irrigation techniques, of livestock production, of social work--more animateurs in fact, than actual counterparts. One European, for instance, could be responsible for the soil-conservation techniques of a district of a quarter of a million people. But after 1955 more and more Africans went to technical schools in Britain to be trained first to assist the expatriate offices and then to replace them. It was here that analogues with the 1960s counterpart system can begin to be found.

To sum up, by 1960 the British emphasis on local government training and local technical assistance, on Africanization of the Civil before the Administrative Service, had produced a situation where most of the top Government posts were held not by Africans, but by Europeans. At the time of Nigeria's independence in 1960, for example, 58 of the 73 "superscale" posts were held by Europeans, 8 by Nigerians and 7 were vacant. (37) The same was true in Sierra Leone and in the three East African territories.

Post-1945 France

French colonial policy changed after World War II for a variety of reasons, including de Gaulle's gratitude for African support (the black Governor General of AEF, Felix Eboue, for example, brought the Federation to the Free French side in 1940), the Atlantic Charter, the United Nations' insistence on self-determination, and the hardheaded realization that the costs of maintaining colonies in the post-War era would have to be borne increasingly by the colonies themselves.

The Brazzaville Conference of France's African territories in early 1944, often hailed as the beginning of the post-War African independence movements, actually stated specifically that "...the eventual constitution, even in a far-off future, of self-government in the colonies is out of the question. (38) Yet it did signal a marked change, particularly on the African side, for out of it arose the post-World War II political parties. It also helped set the stage for the two constituent assemblies in 1945 and 1946 that were called to create the constitution of the Fourth Republic. The recommendations of the First Assembly were defeated in referendum, but those of the Second were accepted for the basis of the constitution of October, 1946. This validated the laws passed the previous April establishing the development agency known as <u>Fonds d'Investissements pour le Developpement Economique et Social</u> (FIDES) and made the inhabitants of France's Overseas Territories French citizens, effectively abolishing the old distinctions between <u>sujet</u> and <u>citoyen</u> that went back to 1848. Under the constitution the empire became the French Union.

The post-War political development of French West Africa is well known for there was the formation of the <u>Rassemblement Democratique Africain</u> (RDA), and then the establishment of elected assemblies in each territory. Next, many more African representatives were added to France's parliamentary assemblies. A great increase of African voters in major French elections (from 51,900 in 1946 to 3,305,000 in 1956) occurred; then the <u>loi-cadre</u> of 1956, the "yes" or "no" referendum of 1958, in which only Guinee refused to stay in the French Community; and, finally, independence for the other AOF and AEF territories and Madagascar in 1960. (39)

Compared to the pre-War years, the pace of political advancement was indeed rapid. But administrative reform did not keep up with it. Despite the increased number of Africans in the French National Assembly, the Government still ruled by decree and the colonial administrators stayed where they were. The Commandant de Cercle and his sub-divisional chiefs remained supreme. If the hated forced labor and summary justice systems had gone off the books at the end of the second World War, the threat of them was still there. There was, however, a new element, the technicians, who came to implement the concept of FIDES.

FIDES was analogous to Britain's 1940 Colonial and Development Welfare Act and had much the same purpose: expansion of an economic infrastructure and of the social sector of the African Colonies. The broussard and his British counterpart, the District Commissioner, were not technically trained, so these years saw an influx of agricultural advisers, social workers, engineers, and a new generation of teachers into the colonial system. They were to put the FIDES' funds into use.

Certainly, as Rene Dumont claims, France could have provided more FIDES money. Also, as he says, much of it was unwisely spent, and perhaps there was too much emphasis on the social sector. Perhaps it was unrealistic to expect to bring Africa to the level of France immediately, and perhaps there was not enough thought about the vast difference in the standards of living or of economic development. Most important of all, perhaps the FIDES, because they were controlled from Paris and stressed the provision of French technicians rather than the training of local Africans, did prolong the dependence of French Africa on the Metropole and the "raw material" economy of Africa. (40) But the fact remains that FIDES money was the engine of change in post-World War II French Africa.

As tightly centralized as France's control over her African colonies had been before World War II, the general theory was that they should be self-sustaining. This changed radically after 1945 with the politique of development--within, of course, the embracing arms of the French Union. Both the British and the French emphasized economic and social advancement. But for the French it was advancement towards equality, while, as we have seen, for the British it was towards eventual self-government and independence. Both countries realized that this sort of political progress would be impossible without a firm economic base to support it. For the French, as well as for the British, this was a radical change from the law-and-order, day-by-day rule of the interwar years. Yet in French West Africa prefectorial administration survived into the 1940s and 1950s. The system of reliance on chiefs did not lend itself to closer contact between colonizer and colonized, especially since the chiefs were seen as static, the residue that remained after the elite had joined the upper stratum of French colonial society. It must be re-emphasized that for all France's talk of "association" during the interwar years, it was the earlier policy of assimilation that had the most impact after 1945. Educated French Africans tended to become involved in politics rather than administration. One notes, for instance, that in Senegal in 1956, 15.9% of those employed in the public sector were Europeans, while in Ghana in the same year, the figure was 1%. (41) As late as 1958 Africanization of the local administrations in francophonic Africa had barely begun, mainly, one assumes, because even at this late date the towering figure of de Gaulle made independence seem distant and, for most of the West African elite, not particularly desirable. (42) With regard to skill transfer, then, the French lagged behind the British, both practically and in terms of attitude. In 1950, four years after the Harragin Commission recommended the end of racial salary differences for civil servants, the French followed suit. Almost a decade after Creech Jones' Local Government Dispatch, the loi-cadre increased the powers of the AOF and AEF Territorial Assemblies and established universal suffrage, promoting the end of rule by decree, which had existed since the French set administrative foot in their African territories.

But they were still only thinking of the upper levels of society and there was no real interest in expanding local government. French aid, mainly in the form of FIDES, increased dramatically after World War II (some $84,000,000 at its pre-Independence peak in 1958) and was designed more to bind those who accepted it closer to France than to help them on their way to self-government. (43) The end result of it all was that, while specially qualified Africans had been admitted to the Ecole Coloniale (by now the Ecole Nationale de la France d'outre-mer, ENFOM) before Independence came, after 1960 the fledgling countries had to call on Mother France for large numbers of technical experts, who could then begin the real process of counterpart training.

Without doubt, the basic administrative philosophies of Britain and France were different. I noted earlier the apparent irony of two such dissimilar systems of colonial rule resulting in the same need for the counterpart system of the past eighteen years. As we have seen, the British favored indirect rule and a degree of autonomy for each colony, while the French believed in direct rule, guided by the firm hand of Paris. There was no British equivalent of assimilation; it would have been unthinkable, for example, for an African to have been a member of the British government. Also, for all its post-Sarraut wavering, France's mise en valeur policy pre-dated Britain's interest in organized development of her African Colonies by twenty-five years.

But if we look closer, there are many similarities. Both Britain and France had the same entry into 19th century Africa-apathy, followed by hectic immersion--both had the same extractive aims and both were interested in the same areas, the Niger and the Nile, for instance. If the initial French expansion was more military, both countries had to "pacify" Africans who resisted their intrustion--Samori in what became French West Africa and various peoples in British East and Central Africa. (44)

Both Britain and France tried to use private companies as their agents for rule and development and both attempts failed. In each country there was a pre-1914 pause before the post-war shifts of colonial policy towards "paramountcy" and "trusteeship" in British Africa and towards the French mise en valeur. Concern with domestic affairs in the late 1920s, intensified by the Depression, dulled inter-war interest in Africa and sharply reduced the two countries' support and development of their African holdings.

At the beginning of the post-World War era of colonial development then, there was a lack of skilled manpower in both British and French AFrica. Indirect and direct rule had produced the same result; many clerks, a few secondary school (Achimota, Alliance, Lycee Faidherbe) graduates and far fewer with higher degrees, usually acquired in Britain and France or, occasionally, the United States, for there were no African universities. (45) Had the two countries foreseen that it would only be twelve years before the first sub-Saharan colony became independent, they would have undoubtedly accelerated their manpower training programs, but in 1945 it looked as if there was plenty of time, the end of their empires seemed literally decades away, particularly to the field officers who had to implement the post-war development plans, the most senior of whom had been in the colonies before the war. Very few of Sir Ralph Furse's Oxbridge all-rounders had technical experience and even those who did often found it difficult to shift from the general "status quo" trustee approach of the inter-war period to the emphasis on development of the years after 1945. There was often an accompanying feeling of reluctance to turn over jobs to people many administrators thought were not capable of performing the jobs properly, and who could undo the work of decades to which the administrators had given their professional lives. (46)

In the sense that we use the phrase in this book, technical assistance began with three events: the United Nations General Assembly's December, 1946 charge to the Economic and Social Council to investigate the feasibility of providing economic, social and cultural advice to member countries that asked for it; President Truman's "Point Four" inaugural address in January, 1949; and the meeting of Commonwealth foreign ministers in Ceylon a year later that resulted in the Columbo Plan for Economic Development for South and Southeast Asia. (47) But these programs, with their crowds of experts and their money, passed Africa by. They were designed to help the losers in World War II and the newly independent ex-colonies, not the areas still under colonial rule.

So one returns to the essential point. For a variety of reasons, when the British and the French African colonies and protectorates became independent, they did not have enough trained people to replace the departing Europeans. They needed technical assistance, one form of which was the counterpart system discussed in the following chapters.

NOTES

1. See R. Robinson, J. Gallagher and A. Denny, Africa and the Victorians: The Official Mind of Imperialism, London, 1961. The Robinson-Gallagher thesis about the importance of the Suez Canal in triggering the Scramble set off a lively academic debate. Most of the arguments--pro and con--are discussed in Wm. Roger Louis, ed., Imperialism, the Robinson and Gallagher Controversy, New York, 1976.

2. Lord Lugard, The Dual Mandate in British Tropical Africa, London, 1922 (reprint 1965) p. 96.

3. Ibid. p. 198

4. Lord Hailey, "Some Problems Dealt with in an African Survey", International Affairs, March-April 1939, p. 202.

5. The Secretary of State for the Colonies, the Duke of Devonshire, declared in 1923 that the interests of Africans should be "paramount". This "Devonshire Declaration" arose out of a controversy between Indians and Europeans in Kenya, but it is best remembered as the first interwar British policy statement concerning "trusteeship." It appeared in Indians in Kenya, Cmd. 1922 (1923), p. 9.

6. The phrase is that of Sir Andrew Cohen, Governor of Uganda, Assistant Undersecretary of State for the Colonies, and head of Britain's Ministry for Overseas Development in the 1960s. Sir Andrew Cohen, British Policy in Changing Africa, London, 1959, p. 25.

7. The 1928 Hilton Young Commission appointed to study the possibility of closer union between Britain's three East African Territories decided that it would be a long time before Africans could be admitted to the Kenyan Legislative Council because of their lack of education and also because "it would be impossible to find any single man who could represent, or command the confidence of, more than a section of the people." Quoted in George Bennett, "Imperial Paternalism", in Kenneth Robinson and Frederick Madden, eds., Essays In Imperial Government, Oxford, 1963, p. 149.

8. Actually, in a situation that had been atypical in British colonies, there had been seven African District Commissioners in the Gold Coast in 1883 and in 1907 two of the nine Legislative Council members were Africans. D. Kimble, A Political History of Ghana 1850-1928, London, 1963, pp. 94, 101 (Plate 3), and 107.

9. Guggisberg quoted in A.L. Adu, The Civil Service in New African States, London, 1965, p. 18.

10. Margery Perham, Native Administration in Nigeria, Oxford, 1937 (reprinted 1962) p. 361.

11. Margery Perham coined the "scaffolding" phrase in her book, Native Administration in Nigeria, London, 1937, p. 361.

12. A. L. Adu, The Civil Service in New African States, pp. 19-21.

13. For a description of this process, see John Smith, Colonial Cadet in Nigeria, Durham, 1968.

14. L.H. Gann and P. Duignan, Burden of Empire, New York, 1967, p. 14.

15. Virginia Thompson and Richard Adloff, The Emerging States of French Equatorial Africa, London, 1960, p. 5.

16. John Hargreaves, Prelude to the Partition of West Africa, London, 1963, p. 91.

17. See William B. Cohen, Rulers of Empire, Stanford, 1971, pp. 35-57. There is little doubt that the products of the Ecole were well trained and generally able. But there were not many of them. Too often the members of the French administrators service were of a far lower quality than their British counterparts. One visitor to French West Africa in the 1930s wrote that "... there is no tradition of colonial administration, and the posts are usually filled with hotheads who for some reason cannot be fitted into the home administration, or by poor people who have passed the necessary examinations and hope to make their fortune by work in the colonies... colonial administrators are grossly overworked and ludicrously underpaid...original initiative, at all times subject to the whim of...Paris, was completely quenched." Geoffrey Gorer, Africa Dances, London, 1935 (reprinted New York, 1962) pp. 87-88.

18. Raymond Leslie Buell, The Native Problem in Africa, Cambridge (Mass.) 1928, Vol. I, p. 924 and Vol. II, p. 22).

19. Henri Brunschwig, Myths and Realities of French Colonialism 1870-1914, quoted in Rene Dumont, False Start in Africa, New York, 1966, p. 51.

20. Catherine Coquery-Vidrovitch, "French Colonization in Africa to 1920: Administration and

Economic Development," in L.H. Gann and Peter Duignan, Colonialism in Africa 1870-1960, Vol. II, p. 174.

21. Thompson and Adloff, pp. 13-16. See also Steven H. Roberts, The History of French Colonial Policy 1870-1925, London, 1929 (reprinted 1963) pp. 347-356, and Jean Suret-Canale, French Colonialism in Tropical Africa, New York, 1971, pp. 17-58.

22. Hubert Deschamps, "French Colonial Policy in Tropical Africa Between the Two Wars," in Prosser Gifford and William Roger Louis, France and Britain in Africa, New Haven, 1971, p. 544.

23. L.H. Gann and Peter Duignan, Burden of Empire, New York, 1967, p. 213.

24. Hubert Deschamps, "France and Black Africa in Madagascar Between 1920 and 1945," in L.H.Gann and Peter Duignan, Colonialism in Africa 1870-1960, Vol. II, p. 229.

25. Roberts, French Colonial Policy, p. 134. Hubert Deschamps, "French Colonial Policy in Tropical Africa Between the Two Wars," pp. 552-560.

26. For example, the Kenya Government appointed the first African to the Legislative Council in 1944, but its Executive Council had considered doing so in 1939. George Bennett, "Imperial Paternalism," p. 158.

27. J.M. Lee, Colonial Development and Good Government, Oxford, 1967, pp. 16-17.

28. Creech Jones became the Assistant Secretary of State for the Colonies when the Labour Government took over in 1945. He succeeded the first Colonial Secretary, the ailing Georgo Hall, in 1946. David Goldsworthy, Colonial Issues in British Politics, Oxford, 1971, p. 16.

29. I.F. Nicolson, The Administration of Nigeria 1900-1960: Men, Methods and Myths, Oxford, 1969, pp. 249-250.

30. A.H.M. Kirk-Greene, The Principles of Native

Administration in Nigeria: Selected Documents, 1900-1947, London, 1965, pp. 28-29.

31. See John Spencer, "KAU Becalmed: Some Thoughts on African Nationalist Leadership in Kenya,1944-1950/51," paper presented at African Studies Association Annual Meeting, San Francisco, October, 1975.

32. Dennis Austen, Politics in Ghana, Oxford, 1970, p. 158.

33. In 1949 4 percent of the entire Colonial Service, 12,000 out of 300,000, had been recruited externally. Kenneth Younger, The Public Service in New States, London, 1960, p. 1.

34. A.H.M. Kirk-Greene, "Administrative Training in Africa: The Northern Nigerian Experience and Beyond," International Review of Administrative Sciences, Vol. XXXV, 1961, No. 1 (reprint), p.3.

35. At about this time, in 1954, the British Government published its first policy statement on the staffing effects of self-government, Reorganization of the Colonial Service (Colonial No. 306). It laid out the conditions under which Colonial Service Officers would work if they decided to continue to serve in a self-governing territory. In a situation where there were so few Africans in senior positions, it was an attempt to keep trained administrators on the job by assuring them of HMG's continuing salary and benefit support. Younger, The Public Service in the New States, pp. 3-6.

36. "The Administrative Service in Africa: 1, "West Africa, 8 March, 1976.

37. West Africa, 29 March, 1976.

38. Robert Delavignette, "French Colonial Policy in Black Africa," in L.H. Gann and Peter Duignan, Colonialism in Africa 1870-60, Vol. II. p. 253.

39. See Ibid, pp. 260-261. Michael Crowder, "Independence as a Goal in French West African Politics: 1944-1960", in William H. Lewis, ed., French Speaking Africa, the Search for Identity, New York, 1965, pp. 15-41, and Teresa Hayter, French Aid, London, 1966.

40. R. Dumont, False Start in Africa, pp. 41-51.

41. Hayter, French Aid, p. 40. Administration was conducted largely by Frenchmen, of whom there were 90,000 in West Africa alone in 1958 (compared with about 15,000 Englishmen in Nigeria and about 10,000 in Ghana). Ibid., p. 28.

42. Deschamps, a former member of the Corps of Colonial Administrators, thought that the French lost the initiative in colonial reform because of the rigid centralization of the interwar years. "We fell asleep somewhat from a political point of view...when it would have been wise slowly and resolutely to lead to an evolution." After World War II "...we would do nothing more than follow developments without being able to guide them." Hubert Deschamps, "La France d'outre-mer et la Communaute," quoted in Cohen, Rulers of Empire, p. 108.

43. In 1962, two years after Independence, French aid rose to $977,000,000! Both figures are from Hayter, French Aid, p. 45.

44. For an interesting discussion of France's takeover in West Africa, see A.S. Kanya-Forstner The Conquest of the Western Sudan: A Study in French Military Imperialism, Cambridge (England) 1969.

45. Some institutions in British Africa were affiliated to British Universities before World War II, e.g., students at Fourah Bay College in Sierra Leone could take courses there for degrees granted by Durham University. In 1945 the British Government accepted the recommendations of the Commission on Higher Education in the Colonies (the Asquith Commission) that H.M.G. organize and support a colonial system of University Colleges "in special relation" with the University of London which would insure its academic standards by giving advice and help with syllabuses and examinations. (Lord Hailey, An African Survey, Revised 1956, Oxford 1957, p. 1180.) As a result, three university colleges were founded, two in West Africa, at Ibadan in Nigeria and Achemota and one, Makerere, in Uganda. (See Ibid., pp. 1179-82.)

46. I drew these conclusions from interviews in England and Kenya with former District officials. See J. Spencer "The Kenya African Union: a Party in Search of a Constituency", unpublished Ph.D. dissertation, Columbia University, 1977.

47. F.X. Sutton, "Technical Assistance" in the International Encyclopedia of Social Sciences, Vol.15, New York 1968, p. 566. This article is a helpful account of the evolution of technical assistance up to mid-1960s.

3. Damned If You Do—Damned If You Don't: Counterparts, Neocolonialism, Dependency and the International Balance of Power[1]

Philip G. Altbach

Foreign assistance, of which the counterpart relationship is inevitably a part, is a tricky business in the best of circumstances. (2) It is bound up with the colonial legacy, the interests of the industrialized powers, and with an international balance of power and technology that strongly favors the industrialized powers. There is no doubt that much positive comes from the counterpart relationship -- skills are transferred, technologies learned, and Third World nations helped toward full participation in an international system which is based on technology. Yet, there are many negative results of the counterpart relationship--and of foreign aid generally. (3) Some of these results stem from the policies of the industrialized nations, who seek to use foreign aid as a means of advancing their own national interests. Some are unintentional, and stem from a nexus of relationships such as a history of colonialism, racial factors, linguistic elements, and many others. In short, a seemingly simple one-to-one relationship between an "advisor" and a "trainee" or "junior colleague" may well carry with it the intellectual, economic and political baggage of a long history and of current international realities.

The purpose of this paper is a simple one--to point out some of the structural elements involved with the counterpart relationship and to indicate that some of these elements can work to the distinct disadvantage of the recipient of whatever assistance or expertise is being provided. (4) In short, in most instances much more than bits of technology or expertise are being transferred. It is my contention that the counterpart relationship and foreign assistance generally is part of an international system of dependency and inequality and that those providing "aid" are, in many instances, seeking to perpetuate their influence over the Third World. Even when altruistic motives are involved, the fact that the flow of expertise is essentially one-way, with the industrialized nations providing the assistance and for the most part determining the nature of the relationship, is significant. The "counterpart" situation, like most interaction between the Third World and the industrialized nations, is complex and for the most part weighted against the Third World.

It is not unusual to have relationships of inequality in an educational situation: indeed, the very essence of the teacher-student relationship is in some ways one of inequality. But in most cases teachers are from the same cultural background as their students and similar goals are shared. In educational situations where there is a wide gulf between teacher and students, for example in the typical racial "ghetto" school in the United States, education suffers. The differences in power, expectations, cultural backgrounds and other factors are great and often have a detrimental effect on learning. Typically, the teachers attempt to impose their own "metropolitan" values on the students. While it is not possible in this paper to fully draw the analogy between teacher and student in the American "inner city" and the broader problems of counterparts in the Third World, there seem to be certain relevant similarities.

In the best of all possible worlds, counterpart assistance could be eliminated, as all nations would have an adequate technological base for independent development. Or it could be conducted on a basis of general equality, as for example when European engineers study American technical innovations, or when Western experts study Japanese transistor technology. But this is not the best of worlds, and it is likely that counterparts will continue to function. It is my hope that this paper will provide some insights into the broad implications of counterpart relationships and foreign aid generally. This awareness, when considered seriously by those on both sides of the relationship, may at least ameliorate the situation and make it more balanced in terms of increased benefit to Third World nations.

When a relationship, like that of the counterpart, is bound up in an international economic system, historical traditions of colonialism and racism, and with a modern technological system which has its base in the industrialized world, virtually all of the cards are stacked against the Third World. This paper does not claim that all of the negative elements of the counterpart relationship stem from the avarice or narrow foreign policy goals of the industrialized nations. Many of the results are related to unintended consequences of policies which may be undertaken with the best of intentions on both sides. It is impossible to state in any general way or with any assurance just what should be done to improve the situation. The arguments advanced in this paper point in the direction of encouraging Third World nations to be as self-reliant as possible, perhaps even to the extent of slowing industrial or technological development. But it seems unlikely that many countries will be willing, or able, to forego interacting with the industrialized nations.

The counterpart is a relationship which is common not only in the Third World but also in apprentice situations in the industrialized world. In it, individuals, usually foreigners, with expertise are placed in positions of responsibility with the task of transferring their skills and expertise to local staff. When the skills are transferred, the "counterpart" withdraws and the job is carried on by the local individual who is now in a position to handle its complexity. The need for this kind of skill transfer exists in areas from highly complex technical processes to basic literacy programs. As Irving Spitzberg points out, there is often very little planning put into counterpart relationships, and very little training provided to those responsible for providing the needed expertise. (5) As a result experts may be competent in their speciality, but are often ignorant of the social and political context of their work.

It is this context which is the concern of this paper. There are certain structural and historical elements of the process which must be considered, as they have inevitable consequences for the counterpart relationship as a microcosm of a broader social and political reality. These consequences may be subsumed under the general terms of dependency and neocolonialism. (6) Both of these terms have received considerable attention in recent years, although all too often the debates have been political rather than analytic in nature. For our purposes, dependency includes the various ways in which Third World nations rely on the industrialized nations in the modern era, which are a "natural" consequence of the world's division of resources, education, expertise, military and economic power, and other factors. Europe, North America, and recently Japan have long dominated the world in terms of political and economic power. They also dominate its intellectual resources, educational institutions, research institutions, publishing houses, and the like. The industrialized nations are the "centers" of a world increasingly dependent on technology and the Third World is at the "periphery", dependent for knowledge on the "center." (7)

Neocolonialism differs from dependency in some important ways. While dependency stems from the current division of economic and other resources, neocolonialism results from the conscious policies of industrialized nations to maintain their power and influence over the Third World, and to protect what are seen as vital interests. Neocolonial policies are expressed in many ways, from a web of military and other pacts to the allocation and nature of foreign aid. For the purposes of this paper, two kinds of neocolonial policies are relevant. The first are governmental policies concerning foreign aid in the educational and technical assistance fields. The second are the policies of private firms, often multinational corporations, which engage in counterpart programs in the Third World. The policies of both governments and multinational corporations have a variety of motivations, but primary among them is the desire to maintain influence and to maximize profits either directly in monetary terms or indirectly through the long term maximization of influence. In a sense, neocolonialism and dependency are opposite sides of the same coin, as both assure the continued domination of the industrialized nations over the Third World.

The problem of the transfer of skills and knowledge, of which the counterpart relationship is an element, cannot be isolated from the structural elements which determine many of the relations between industrialized nations and the Third World. Counterparts may contribute to dependency, or they may help the Third World to obtain the skills needed to minimize their dependency. Knowledge has many uses, and cannot be isolated from its societal context. It is this relationship between knowledge, skills and the counterpart and the implications of these elements that is the concern of this paper.

It must be recognized that the counterpart relationship takes place in a situation of multiple inequalities, and that these inequalities will play a role in determining the "micro" relationships between the counterpart and the learner, and also the "macro" relationship of what kinds of information are transferred and the overall effectiveness of this transfer. (8) At the macro level, which is in most respects beyond the control of those planning counterpart relationships, it is clear that the economic, intellectual and political relationships between the parties are unequal, and that Third World countries are dependent on the West and will remain so for the foreseeable future. They must import high level technology, and no amount of skill-transfer will permit the establishment of expensive and high level research capability. Along with this technological gap is the need to import sophisticated technology based products, insofar as these are needed in the Third World. While some, like Ivan Illich, M.K. Gandhi and others have argued that Third World nations should get along with simpler technological tools and thereby gain their independence from the West, these notions have relatively little policy support in the Third World. (9) And while some nations, such as India, Argentina, China, and Mexico have the capability to produce sophisticated industrial goods, in general technology and its by-products will continue to be imported commodities. Even such impressive scientific achievements as the manufacture of nuclear weapons by China and India and the development of fairly simple missile technology in those countries does not obscure the fact that even these most advanced of Third World countries still require considerable external technological inputs.

As has been pointed out, the research capability and technological advantages of the industrialized nations is far superior to that of the Third World, and there is evidence that this superiority will grow rather than diminish. Thus, this inequality will become even more pronounced in the future, and will no doubt affect the nature of relationships between the industrialized and Third World nations. The implications are considerable in terms of foreign educational assistance and the counterpart relationship. It means that Third World nations will have difficulty in catching up in technological terms, and that continuing assistance of some kind will be necessary for a long period of time. While it seems clear that basic skills in terms of functioning of a modern state and educational system can be obtained by Third World nations, the need to keep abreast of the latest technological developments will require continuing dependency on the industrialized nations.

There are psychological implications of the counterpart relationship which are linked, perhaps structurally, to the system. While these implications are complicated and have not been subject to adequate research, it is important to at least mention some of these factors. The colonial heritage leaves a residue on the psychological relations between the former colonizers (European Whites), and the former colonized (non-Whites). (10) This heritage expresses itself in many ways. Racial attitudes persist, even if in an often subconscious manner. It is not uncommon for Europeans working in a Third World context to feel superior to their colleagues, and these feelings cannot but affect the relationship between the counterpart and the individuals engaged in common work. It is often assumed that the only correct way of doing a job is the way that it is done in Europe (or North America), and that adaptation of techniques is not necessary. Again, this assumption may well be linked to psychological feelings of suueriority on the part of the counterparts. Interpersonal relations may well be affected by psychological factors, especially where the Western counterpart personnel are not trained in human relations skills and have little understanding of the culture in which they are working.

The recruitment and training of counterparts often reinforces the psychological implications of the system. Most counterparts are in technical areas and are individuals who have not been selected for their sensitivity to the Third World and its cultures, but rather for their technical skills in the narrowly defined sense of the term. With the exception of certain programs like the U.S. Peace Corps and some academics who function as counterparts in the university context, most Western counterparts are motivated to participate in counterpart programs because of economic advantages to themselves. This combination of circumstances means, in many cases, that the counterparts have little understanding of the cultures in which they are working and little systematic orientation to the adaptation of their work to local conditions. It is not atypical for counterparts to interact in only limited areas with their indigenous colleagues, to live in relatively isolated situations from the indigenous culture, and to learn little if anything of local languages. The living standards of the counterparts, both in their home countries and, more dramatically, on their Third World assignments, is often far higher than that of their local compeers. All of these elements must have considerable, although as yet relatively unexplored, impact on the whole counterpart relationship and the ways in which skills get transferred.

There is a need to carefully select the individuals who are to act as counterparts, to know about the personality characteristics that can maximize effectiveness, and to fully understand the psychological "baggage" of the colonial heritage, racism, and other factors which those on both sides of the counterpart relationship may bring with them. (11) On the indigenous side, the colonial heritage also has implications, and these should be kept in mind. Ready acceptance of Western models and ways of doing things may be a result of the colonial mentality. Disinclination to argue with European "experts" may also enter into the equation. The personal and psychological elements which impinge on the professional aspects of the counterpart relationships are of major importance. The details of these relationships are beyond the scope of this paper and are covered, in part, by Russell Stone's paper. (12) When analyzing these elements, however, it is important to keep in mind that the heritage of colonialism often operates not only at a broad societal level, but in the lives of individuals. (13)

The modern institutions of the Third World, are, for the most part, of Western design, from the ways in which government ministries are organized, to the organization of the school system and of industrial enterprises. The course of colonialism destroyed many of the economic and cultural structures of traditional Asian and African societies. In addition, modern industrialism is of Western origin, and has been exported to other parts of the world. In this situation, Western experts, teachers, and technicians have an immediate advantage over their compeers from the Third World. They are seeking to transfer what are essentially Western skills to the Third World. In many instances, these are not simply technical skills, but involve at least some of the values and attitudes of Western societies.

The very concept of modernity is a Western idea, involving as it does Western technology, Western attitudes toward work, Western institutions such as schools and universities, and other accoutrements of

Western life. All too often it is assumed that the process of "modernization" is somehow value-neutral. It is not, and there are many of the attitudinal elements of Western societies attached to the creation of an industrial system. Concepts of time, the use of commodities, bureaucratic norms rather than ascriptive characteristics, and other elements are all associated with modernity. In this situation, the counterpart relationship is necessarily involved in the transfer not only of skills but also of attitudes.

This process of attitude transfer, and the reaction which it may engender on the other side, is a complicated one which is not usually understood, or even recognized, as part of the counterpart relationship. It may well be possible to adapt certain traditional practices to fit into a modern economic system without major disruption or loss of "efficiency." (14) The point is Western counterparts seldom even recognize the general impact of many of the attitudinal elements of their work. And they seldom attempt to fit their skills into the value system of which they are a part. There is no doubt that many elements of traditional cultures do not fit neatly with a bureaucratic governmental system which most nations accept as necessary. But when skills are being transferred, it should be possible to recognize the implications of these skills and of the possible ideological and attitudinal baggage that often goes along with the skills.

Counterparts do not function in a political vacuum, and they cannot expect to do so. Nevertheless, there should be a recognition especially on the parts of the recipients of counterpart assistance that there are political assumptions and policies behind much counterpart aid. Nations conduct their foreign policies to further their own interests and not out of altruism or as part of an international community. And as Philip Coombs has pointed out, education--and by implication counterpart assistance--is an instrument of foreign policy. (15) Where counterparts are sponsored directly by government agencies like the United States Agency for International Development or the British Ministry for Overseas Development, the link between foreign policy and counterpart projects is clear. The project would not be sponsored by a government of an industrialized nation unless it fit into the overall policy goals of that nation. Where counterparts are sponsored by private industrial firms working in the Third World, the link among the firm, its economic interests and the counterpart's work is clear, and although the direct link between private corporations and government policy is usually indirect, it is at least questionable that such corporations would violate the interests of their governments in any basic way. The link between foundations or educational institutions in the industrialized nations and government policy is less clear, although it can usually be assumed that such agencies would not fundamentally go against the wishes of their government.

The governments of capitalist powers will not usually be interested in supporting public sector projects where private sector efforts are available, and there is no doubt that pressures are placed on Third World governments to accept certain kinds of foreign assistance, including projects involving counterpart aid. By the same token, foreign aid provided by the Soviet Union or China generally goes to public sector enterprises, and to projects that will fit into the broader policy goals of those countries. Multinational corporations do not, of course, provide "assistance" in the usual sense, and their work is aimed at maximizing their own profits and ensuring the success of their enterprises in the Third World. (16) Again, their interests are not necessarily congruent with the interests of the Third World countries themselves. Universities, foundations, and international agencies probably come closest to providing "disinterested" foreign assistance, with the interests of the Third World countries themselves in mind. But even in these cases, the orientations of the countries in which these agencies are located plays an important role. In the case of international agencies, the providers of the major part of their funds have a disproportionate role as well.

Counterpart experts, either as part of a clear plan or as an unintended result of their work, often lock the Third World nation or individual firm or agency into continuing relationships with a specific industrialized nation. Such relations may be illustrated by the example of spare parts for military equipment, which becomes a real problem for Third World nations when supplies are cut off. Similarly, expert counterparts may recommend the use of products or processes which require continuing imports from industrialized countries, or the use of technologies which require continuing contacts. The use of particular school textbooks or audio-visual materials as the result of outside advice might be an indication of this kind of relationship. The problems would be greater with an industrial counterpart who recommends the use of machinery available only in his country.

Counterpart personnel are themselves part of the policies of their sponsoring nations. For the most part, they reflect the dominant views of their countries concerning foreign policy, economic affairs, and the like. Indeed, it is unlikely that individuals strongly opposed to their national "systems" would be chosen to engage in counterpart activities in the Third World. The combination of national interest and the natural propensity of the counterparts themselves to reflect the orientations of their societies means that both the activities undertaken by counterpart personnel and the individuals themselves reflect the systems which they represent.

What, then, is to be done? The foregoing discussion of the structural and cultural elements involved in many counterpart relationships indicates that in many instances these relationships will contribute to continued dependency, and they will have many unintended consequences which are potentially unfavorable to Third World countries. Recipient nations can be much more careful when they contract for counterpart or other foreign assistance. Conditions of such projects can be carefully regulated, elements of control over expatriate staff can be established, care can be taken to make sure that Third World nations are not locked permanently into dependency on spare parts, textbooks or licenses from industrialized nations. In short, an awareness of the long-term and subtle consequences of foreign aid in general and the counterpart relationship in particular will help to provide safeguards to Third World nations.

Third World nations can also minimize their use of counterparts and of foreign aid generally. This is often a difficult process. Even those nations which have most consciously tried to take an independent road to industrialization, such as China and Tanzania, and to a lesser extent Cuba, have had continuing problems of establishing real independence from the industrialized countries. No nation has been willing to forego participation in the process of industrialization which we commonly define as development. Mahatma Gandhi advocated that India turn its back on industrialization and on the West generally and rely on its own resources and on the village system. His advice has been ignored by every Indian leader. Given the nature of the balance of economic, political, and technological power in the world, it is unlikely that any relationship between the Third World and the industrialized nations will be based on equality. If this paper has at least pointed to some potential problems in a small realm of international interaction then it will have served a useful purpose.

NOTES

1. This title is adapted from Remi Clignet's excellent article on the psychological elements of the colonial relationship, "Damned If You Do, Damned If You Don't; The Dilemmas of Colonizer-Colonized Relationships," Comparative Education Review, 15 (October, 1971), pp. 296-312.

2. It is my contention that virtually all counterpart relationships can broadly be considered part of foreign assistance, even when they are carried out by profit-making multinational corporations or international agencies such as UNESCO. All these relationships have similar characteristics and similar aims.

3. For a thoroughgoing critique of foreign aid, see Tibor Mende, From Aid to Recolonization: Lessons of a Failure (New York: Pantheon, 1973), and Teresa Hayter, Aid as Imperialism, (Baltimore: Penguin, 1971).

4. There are, of course, important personal factors involved in the counterpart relationship. These are, for the most part, beyond the scope of this paper and are considered in an accompanying analysis. See Russell Stone, "Interpersonal Relations in the Counterpart System: Some Variations on the Model," (Paper prepared for the meetings of the International Development Association, Amsterdam, November 1976).

5. Irving J. Spitzberg, "The Counterpart System: Some Suggestions for Change," IDR/Focus (no. 3, 1975), pp. 3-9.

6. For elaboration on the theme of neocolonialism and education, see Philip G. Altbach, "Neo-

colonialism and Education," Teachers College Record, 72 (May, 1971), pp. 543-558, and Philip G. Altbach, "Literary Colonialism: Books in the Third World," Harvard Educational Review, 45 (May, 1975), pp. 226-236.

7. There is considerable, although controversial literature on these topics. On center-periphery questions, see Johann Galtung, "A Structural Theory of Imperialism," African Review, 1 (April, 1972), pp. 93-137 and Edward Shils, The Intellectuals and the Powers and Other Essays, (Chicago: University of Chicago Press, 1972). See also S.J. Bodenheimer, The Ideology of Developmentalism: The American Paradigm, (Beverly Hills, Calif.: Sage, 1971), for an elaboration of some of these points. See also Philip G. Altbach and Gail P. Kelly, (eds.), Education and Colonialism, (New York: Longmans, 1978).

8. See Thomas Eisemon, U.S. Educated Engineering Faculty in India, (Bombay: Tata Institute of Social Sciences, 1974) for a discussion of the orientations of an important group of foreign trained individuals.

9. See Ivan Illich, Deschooling Society (New York: Harper and Row, 1970).

10. There is a considerable, although partly polemical, literature concerning the psychological implications of colonialism. See especially Frantz Fanon, The Wretched of the Earth, (New York: Grove, 1968), Albert Memmi, The Colonizer and the Colonized, (Boston: Beacon Press, 1965), O. Mannoni, Prospero and Caliban: The Psychology of Colonization, (New York: Praeger, 1964). See also Chinweizu, The West and the Rest of Us: White Predators, Black Slavers, and the African Elite, (New York: Random House, 1974)

11. See Chinweizu, op. cit.

12. Russell Stone, op. cit.

13. On this point, see Frantz Fanon, Black Skin, White Masks: The Experiences of a Black Man in a White World, (New York: Grove Press, 1967).

14. See Lloyd and Susanne Rudolph, <u>The Modernity of Tradition</u>, (Chicago: University of Chicago Press, 1968), for discussion related to these points.

15. Philip Coombs, <u>The Fourth Dimension of Foreign Policy: Education and Cultural Affairs</u>. (New York: Harper and Row, 1964).

16. See Ali Mazrui, "The African University as a Multinational Corporation: Problems of Penetration and Dependency," <u>Harvard Educational Review</u>, 45 (May, 1975), pp. 191-210.

Part II Disciplinary Perspectives on the Exchange of Expertise in the Counterpart System

4. Rethinking the Change Agent Role in the Technical Assistance Process to Facilitate the New International Order[1]

Graham B. Kerr

"The central problem of our times is the 'two-tier' world, and our central task is to explore paths by which inequalities between and within nations might be reduced." (2)

In this paper I explore one of the paths which may lead to a lessening of the inequalities between nations. It is not a suggestion for a new development program but rather a request that we change the way in which we think about the change agents involved in international technical assistance. Since the "Declaration on the Establishment of the New International Order" was passed by the United Nations in 1974 there has been considerable discussion of ways of reshaping the basic economic and political processes that underlie international relationships. (3) This discussion will become more focussed at the UN Conference of Science and Technology for Development during 1979. The basic objective of this conference calls for "ways of applying ... and using ... science and technology to solve development problems". (4) To meet this objective all of us will need to look very carefully for ways of assisting the transfer of technology between countries.

The demand for increased access to the world's technological resources has become more insistent as the economic power of OPEC dollars has added a new dimension to the voices of the LDCs. (5) Williams, while summarizing the progress of the recent North-South Dialogue, stressed that an area of continuing concern and discussion was technology transfer --

"more effective methods of transferring management skills and technology are essential". (6)

It has recently been noted that the technology transfer may also help to solve a potential problem in developed countries. As their technology becomes more sophisticated their labor forces will require retraining and upgrading. As birth rates in these countries drop to low levels the labor force will cease to increase in size and will steadily age. This means that sectors of the economy will be short of homegrown labor and will be required either to import labor from other countries (probably third world) or to transfer those sectors to other countries. (7) Given the recent experience with "guest workers" from Southern Europe in West Germany and Switzerland, it is likely that transferring major portions of industries to other countries will be the most acceptable solution. Indeed you can already see this transfer taking place to countries such as Taiwan, Hong Kong and Singapore where sizeable portions of many multinationals are located.

There seems to be little doubt that technology transfer will, and must, take place at an increasing rate, and therefore we should take a careful look at the methods used in the transfer so that they may be as efficient as possible. A common method of transferring technology is through the technical assistance process, which has been defined as:

> "a form of international collaboration whose purpose is to secure the transfer of skills by despatching experts in specialized fields from countries when they are available in large numbers to countries where they are less numerous or nonexistant." (8)

In a recent paper on this same subject I note the rapid rise in the number of personnel working in technical assistance, the increasing contributions of OPEC funds to finance the assistance and the new sources of personnel to be technical experts. (9) The traditional view of donor and recipient is becoming outmoded as more money and personnel originate in the third world and there is growing recognition of the Technical Cooperation among Developing Countries (TCDC) movement in international circles. (10) These are additional reasons for a careful assessment of this mode of technology transfer so that it may be made more useful, effective and just.

We, in the social sciences, have as much of an

obligation to help as the technicians who are actually involved in the day-by-day transfer of skills, because we are called upon to study the process -- especially when it breaks down. We make recommendations and shape others' perceptions of the process so we must examine how we do this and how our work affects the process. We observe behavior, build models to describe and explain our perceptions of those behaviors and then use the models to make predictions about future behavior in similar circumstances. Our models are abstract creations of words and symbols, but often we behave as though the models are more real than the actual behavior we are studying. We fail to recognize the difference between the language we use to describe a phenomenon and the phenomenon itself. Also we fail to realize that our symbolic models exert great influence upon the way we perceive behaviors and, therefore, indirectly on the ways those with whom we talk perceive those same behaviors.

Berlo suggests that "the major units of thought are units of language", and that we cannot think about objects or processes for which we have no name or label. (11) Sapir and Whorf, developing the thoughts of Wittgenstein, (12) hypothesize that language will, in part, determine what a person sees, what he thinks about and how he makes decisions.(13) Language limits and defines our view of the world.

In the social sciences our units of language are concepts -- the tools of our trade that we use to organize our perceptions of the world. Human behaviors, which are meaningful to the observer, have some constituency over time, and some probability of being related to other sets of perceptions, are given conceptual labels. (14) The labels or concepts are linked in theoretical models and frameworks from which we derive hypotheses which we test through observation of further human behavior. Building these models into broader based theories enables us to better describe, explain, predict and control the behavior of people.

Our concepts and theories determine, to a great extent, the aspects of the world we study, how we "see" those aspects and how we go about investigating them. The concepts we use will determine how we think about social situations and also how and what we think about other people involved in that situation. The concepts that we use to analyze the technical assistance process will, I am suggesting, go a long way in determining how we will behave when we, ourselves, are studying the process, making recommendations about the process, or personally participating in the process.

In an earlier paper I addressed the problem of the terms that we use to name the participants in the technical assistance process. The variety of terms include technical assistant, expert, advisor, foreign technician, international consultant and so on. Here we will discuss the implications for us of the most commonly used -- expert and advisor.

The name we give to a position in an organization, or a person occupying a position and a role is important because it provides us with the first cues about the person and role. A number of studies have indicated that the first cues are important because they shape much of our subsequent thinking and behavior. (16) In studies of agricultural extension agents in the U.S., a role similar to the one we are discussing in this paper, it has been noted that role expectations differ considerably even when the name is used by all parties to describe the agent's role. (17) In the technical assistance process there are usually several national and international agencies involved in any assistance agreement; and each may choose its own label, with its accompanying expectations, to describe the central actors in the skill transfer. Conflict and frustration may be generated by false expectations engendered by the use of different labels.

The most common label used for technical assistance personnel has been "expert" as you will note from our definition earlier in the paper. This implies a person with a special skill or knowledge which is required in a technical assistance project. An implication of using the label is that the persons selected have the highest technical qualifications and are ranked near the top of the field of interest. This may be because the early publications and international conferences concerning technical assistance were written by and staffed by those who were leaders in their fields or became so because of their high visibility on the international conference circuit. (18)

There has always been considerable debate about the degree of technical expertise (vs. other necessary qualifications, such as "ability to adapt") required in the skill transfer process, and recently there has been increasing doubt about the "expertness" of many of the personnel in aid programs.(19) Jesse and Smith, later in this book, mention the dislike of a group of technical assistants in Thailand for the term "experts". "They disliked the term 'expert', partly because the term was vague, carried false implications and raised false hopes, but mostly because they felt so inexpert". (20)

It has been my experience that many experts (especially consultants) feel constrained to suggest solutions to problems, based on their experiences in other countries, without appropriate study of the new situation, to establish their credentials with their hosts. Unfortunately, this often has the opposite effect; that of casting doubt on their credibility with local nationals who may be polite but ignore their suggestions. (21)

The role connoted by the word 'expert', in my mind, is very close to that described as performance technical assistance,

> "which involves actual performance in another country by an (American) technician of a task which the local people lack the skills to perform." (23)

Here the primary emphasis is on the task being performed and, probably, the 'expert' fulfilling this role expectation will be perpetuating the dependence of the developing country upon further 'experts'. For technical assistance to be successful a second component is essential -- only if skills are communicated to the recipient countries can they develop their institutional capabilities and hope to become independent of assistance in that particular skill in the future. This second aspect is well described by Ohly as communication technical assistance:

> "which is designed to communicate information, skills, values, attitudes or patterns of behavior to the people of another society and which, if successfully carried out, will result in the improvement of the individual and institutionalized capabilities of the recipients." (23)

It is this role that corresponds much more closely to that indicated by the term 'advisor'. The implication of communication is strong when we use 'advisor', but is missing when we use 'expert'. The advisor role as described above is very close to the change agent model developed in studies of planned change. In its simplest form the change agent is cast in a "knowledge linking role" between a knowledge source (researcher) and a knowledge user (practitioner). The technical assistance process can also be represented in this format; the advisor performing the linking function between technology source and user as follows:

Technology (knowledge) source	⟶	Change Agent (linking) role Advisor	⟶	Technology (knowledge) user

Figure 1: Filling the Technology Gap (24)

A review of the technical assistance literature, both professional and academic, written in English since the 1940s, shows that "advisor" is increasingly replacing "expert." A cursory review of material in French and German, however, indicates that the term "expert" is still frequently used, but it must be remembered that the connotations of the word in these two languages may not be the same as those that I have suggested pertain in English.

Simply dropping 'expert' from our vocabulary, however, and replacing it with 'advisor' will not automatically lead to any change in the skill transfer system; it may just confuse people. Along with the change in labels must go an education program that informs all the parties concerned of the reasons for the label change and its implications for their subsequent behavior. My recent experience in Afghanistan made me very aware of this problem.

In the languages of recipient countries there may be only one word for 'advisor' and 'expert' that is currently in use and it may require some careful work by translators to find suitable alternatives. All the project documents of Afghan Demographic Studies, where I was an advisor, were produced in English and Dari. We were always very careful to use the word advisor when writing in English. These materials were then translated into Dari and distributed to the staff. At some later date some of these materials would be translated back into English and we always found that where we had originally used 'advisor,' 'foreign expert' showed up. It made us realize that we had to explain the difference between the terms and the precise implications of using one rather than the other.

It is most important that all technical assistance personnel make sure that appropriate terminology for his position is applied in both donor and recipient languages. If he is expecting to fulfill the role of an 'advisor' then it is essential that the recipients also expect him to be an 'advisor' and provide him with a counterpart, rather than expecting him to be an 'expert' and fill an executive position where no counterpart is supplied. These role expectations that can be generated by labels we attach to people and positions must be clear to avoid later confusion, frustration and an unsuccessful project.

When we think of the technical assistance process we perceive the advisors as occupying the central change agent role. Our research has concentrated upon the advisor (25), and our agencies concerned with the practicalities of technical assistance have refined details of his qualifications, election and training.(26) We have gone to considerable lengths to explore and refine the advisory role, and technical assistance agreements often have very detailed specifications concerning aspects of the advisors work. It appears that the advisor, usually very closely related to, or even a part of the technology producers (often First World), is closely identified with the success or failure of the skill transfer. This conception ignores an important part of the skill transfer, and tends to bias the way in which we think about the change agent role. It leads us to neglect the considerable contribution and responsibility of the technology users (Third World).

The advisor is usually, though not always, asked to work in close cooperation with a national from the recipient country -- a counterpart. If he is not assigned a counterpart then he will probably find himself working in an executive capacity (27), which is closer to performance technical assistance mentioned earlier in this paper than to the advisory role. Ideally the counterpart is a part of the technology users system and will learn the skills brought by the advisor so that he can use them or teach them to others after the advisor has left his country.

The counterpart, as a major focus of interest, has, in the past, been missing from our research studies. A select bibliography concerning "Advisors and Counterparts", compiled in 1973, contains references to about 80 articles. (28) Most of them discuss only the role of the advisors, six talk about advisors and counterparts, and only one reports a study of counterparts by themselves. The bias of our writing is quite clear. This might be different if we could unearth all the agency reports about advisors and counterparts. There are many studies which have not been published because of the sensitive nature of the subject, and the feeling that persons may be identified from the results. An example is contained in this collection; Jesse and Smith's study was completed in 1957-59, and first appeared in 1970. (29)

We have not, until recently, done much to explore the counterpart's role, his selection, necessary qualifications and training. We have, perhaps understandably, spent most of our effort helping "our" advisors in their role, and have expended very little energy helping "their" counterparts to be more effective participants in the change process. During the past year or two this situation has been redressed somewhat with the publication of a higher proportion of articles dealing with the counterpart (30), and an entire session at the 15th Society for International Development World Conference devoted to "The Counterpart System." We have to beware, however, of biasing our conceptual framework in the other direction. The most egalitarian conceptualization is to consider the change agent role as comprising the advisor and the counterpart, working as a dyadic unit to bring about the transfer of technology.

The advisor-counterpart dyad is illustrated below:

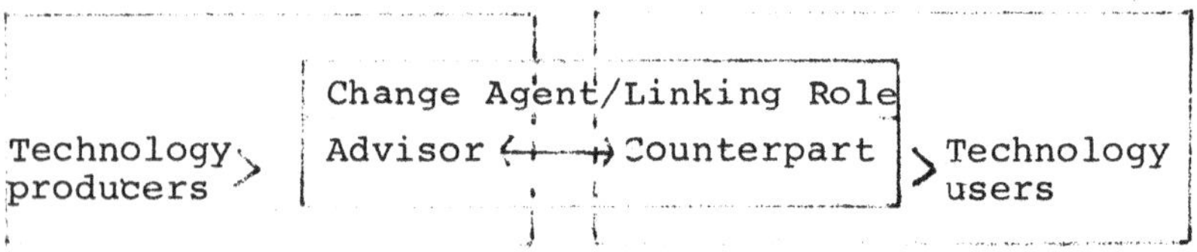

Figure 2: <u>The Advisor-Counterpart Dyad as Change Agent</u>.

The dyadic nature of the change agent role is receiving some support in more recent literature with strong suggestions that it is important to study both advisors and counterparts if we are to fully understand this system of skill transfer. (31) Some studies have collected information from both advisors and counterparts (32), but only a few have studied dyads <u>in situ</u> as they worked together on their development projects. (33)

Viewing the role in this way suggests several practical and theoretical possibilities.

First, the counterpart is as important as the advisor in the process of skill transfer. Both are integral parts of the change agent role. Spitzberg has noted that counterparts are often not provided for projects, even when clearly called for by the project agreements.(34) This has the effect of immediately turning advisors into executives with few advising functions. (35) I personally know of an advisor who was not given a counterpart. During his two year assignment he did an excellent job of operating some useful and very expensive equipment for the host country. As no counterpart had been assigned to his project, the donor agency withdrew the advisor after one tour and the expensive equipment was not used again. In spite of considerable investment of time, money, and advisor's time, no new skills were transferred in that project. It was a failure.

The second implication of our dyadic model is that we should consider the contribution of each participant to the total change agent role. At the planning stage of a technical assistance project a complete description of the role should be developed. This would allow us to assess which aspects can be optimally performed by the advisor and which by the counterpart.

Third, we need to take as much care in selecting and training counterparts as in selecting and training advisors.

Fourth, that communication between advisor and counterpart plays an important part in the functioning, and probably the ultimate success, of the dyad and therefore the transfer of technology (36).

To assess more specifically the heuristic value of considering the change agent as a dyad I will use Lippitt's model of planned change. (37) The model comprises a number of phases and we will note the potential contribution of the counterpart and advisor during each phase of the change process. Remember that the phases represent an abstract model developed while studying social change as it takes place. It is a general model and may not fit any specific set of real events, but it has value in that it enables us to talk about and analyze the process.

The phases in Lippitt's model are as follows:

1. Develops need for change
2. Establishes a change relationship
3. Diagnoses the problem
4. Creates intent to change in the client
5. Translates intent into action
6. Stabilizes change and prevents discontinuances

7. Achieves a terminal relationship

Phase 1. Develops a need for change

"The change agent is usually involved in the identification of clients' needs." (38)

"The most common way for a change process to begin is for the potential client system to become aware of its own difficulty and itself seeks help from an outside agency." (39)

The counterpart, being a part of the client system from the beginning, is in an optimum position to help to articulate the need for change. This assumes, of course, that the counterpart, who will join the advisor in the change agent dyad, can be identified at the beginning of the change program.

A recent experience of my own illustrates this phase of the process. During the development of a proposal for a project in another country, a colleague and I traveled on a planning visit to the country. We were accompanied by a member of the agency who was going to finance the project. As we visited the officials of the host government, it became obvious to us that there had been little discussion between the donor agency and these officials. Our visits were being used as opportunities to sell the project to the host government. There was no one in the country at that time who was appointed to work on the project and might be a counterpart in the future. In fact, the project had been conceived by the donors to provide themselves with data which they needed for their planning of technical assistance programs.

The host country cooperated nicely and signed the documents required for program initiation. We were selected as the contractor. We finalized the budget and began to establish an operational base in the donor country. The lack of counterparts and host country participation in planning soon became evident, however. Shortly before we were about to leave for the host country we were summoned to appear immediately in the capital and explain more fully the purpose and scope of the project.

It appeared that another group of consultants were planning a related project and the host country wished to make sure that the projects did not overlap and were complementary. Had our project been developed in the host country and counterparts appointed at the beginning, this second emergency visit would, probably, not have been necessary, because they would have been familiar with the objectives of the project.

Phase 2. Establishes a change relationship.

> "Often the clients' system seems to be seeking assurance that the potential change agent is different enough from the client system to be a real expert and yet enough like it to be thoroughly understandable and approachable. What the client system really wants is two change agents in one."(40)

The dyad provides two change agents in one -- the counterpart, "who will identify with the clients system's problems and sympathize with the system's needs and values," -- the advisor, "who will at the same time be neutral enough to take a genuinely objective and different view of the system's predicament" (41)

Phase 3. Diagnoses the problem.

Further information needed to clarify the problem statement may be collected and analyzed to produce alternative solutions to the problem during this phase. The counterpart should be able to locate and collect the local information (if it is available in the country) required by the change agent while the advisor plays a major role in analysis and production of solutions. (42) The advisor will also be responsible for providing additional data from outside the client system if it is required -- this knowledge is presumably part of his expertise. "To arrive at his own diagnostic conclusions, the change agent must view the situation from his clients' perspective."(43) The counterpart should be able to provide the client's perspective.

Phase 4. Creates intent to change in the client.

This phase is one of motivating the technology users to use the new ideas. In many international programs this presents few problems because the goals of the project have been clearly specified in the program agreement between the donor and the recipient. This is not always the case, however, the goals, and particularly the methods of reaching the goals, may need clarification at this point. "The change must be client-centered, rather than change for change's sake". (44) Once again we find a place for the counterpart in ensuring that change is client-centered.

Phase 5. Translates intent into action.

"The active work of changing is the keystone of the whole change process". (45) The sympathetic support of other parts of the client system may be critical and it is essential to obtain adequate feedback on the consequences of the change program. Here the program goes beyond agreement and intent; it requires action and behavioral change in a culturally appropriate manner. It is unrealistic to expect an advisor who moves frequently from one assignment to another to be aware of the cultural differences of each of his assignments. This is an aspect of change which can be handled by the counterpart.

Phase 6. Stabilizes change and prevents discontinuances.

Will the change remain a stable and permanent characteristic of the user's system? All too often development projects collapse or regress when the advisor leaves the user's system. This is not always because the changes were bad for the system; sometimes programs collapse because they have not had sufficient time (or money) to become institutionalized in the system. Leaving the counterpart within the user's system should help to keep discontinuances to a minimum and assist with institutionalizing the change.

Phase 7. Achieves a terminal relationship.

It has been suggested that by this phase the client's system should have developed self-renewing behavior and have institutionalized the new technology. (46) The fact that the counterpart is a part of the client system should facilitate the transition from dependency to independence of the change agent role (especially the advisor component).

In the international context, however, I think we should reconsider the terminal relationship phase of Lippitt's model. No technology is static, it is constantly being refined and changed. Most of this refinement takes place in developed countries and ways of transferring new developments to LDCs on a continuing basis should be explored. A development program that successfully transfers a unit to technology which then slowly becomes an antiquated relic is not serving the long term goals of reshaping the international order. The linkage between the producer and user systems should be maintained to ensure that improvements are rapidly incorporated into the previously transferred unit. Here again is a potential role for the counterpart. If he has been participating fully in the change agent role then he should be aware of the linkages established by the advisor during the technology transfer. When the advisor leaves it should not be too difficult for the counterpart to maintain the contacts and, to a certain extent, permanently assume the total role of change agent.

Conclusion

The change agent role in the technical assistance process should be redesigned to include both the advisor and the counterpart in a dyadic relationship. This will allow a more equal participation in and responsibility for the change process by people from the LDCs. This, in itself, will help to reshape the international order. But, also, as a preliminary assessment of the new concept using Lippitt's model of planned change indicates, the change agent role will be enhanced. This will lead to a more rapid reshaping of the international order.

NOTES

1. An earlier version of this paper was presented at the Annual Meeting of the International Studies Association, St. Louis, Missouri, March, 1977.

2. Freeman, C., Quote from article by Adamson, "Consensus on Crisis," New Internationalist, No. 32, 1975, p. 3.

3. For a summary of thinking on this topic see Tinbergen, RIO: Reshaping the International Order. (New York, Dutton, 1976).

4. Development Forum, November-December, 1977, p. 6.

5. Abelson, P.H. and Tinker, I., "Technology Transfer," Science, Vol. 195, 1977, p. 4276.

6. Williams, M.J., "Emerging New Realism in North-South Development Cooperation," Presented at the 15th World Conference of the Society for International Development, Amsterdam, Holland, December 1976, p. 8.

7. Khane, A.R., Address to the 15th World Conference of the Society for International Development, Amsterdam, Holland, December, 1976, p. 6.

8. Harari, D., The Role of the Technical Assistance

Expert. (Paris; OECD, Development Research Center, 1974) p. 11.

9. Kerr, G.B., "Communication and the Advisor-Counterpart Relationship in the Technical Assistance Process," presented at the 15th World Conference of the Society for International Development, Amsterdam, Holland, December 1976, p. 2.

10. Hanley, M.L., "Developing Countries--A New Source of Expertise," *Development Forum*, Vol. 3, No. 6, 1975, *Action*, UNDP Supplement, p. 11. Jayaraman, K.S., "Third World Self-Help," *Development Forum*, Vol. 4, 1976, pp. 1-2. Albertal, E. and Duncan, R.L., "Technical Cooperation Among Developing Countries," *International Development Review/Focus*, No. 4, 1974, pp. 308.

11. Berlo, D.K., *The Process of Communication*. (New York, Holt, Rinehart, and Winston, 1960), p. 44.

12. Wittgenstein, L., *Philosophische Unterschungen* (Anscombe, G. translator), (Oxford, Blackwells, 1953).

13. Worf, B.L., *Language, Thought and Reality*. (Cambridge, Massachusetts, MIT Press, 1956), pp. 134-159.

14. Berlo, D.K., "The Process of Social Research." Mimeo., East Lansing, Michigan, Department of Communication, Michigan State University, 1967.

15. Kerr, G.B. (1976), pp. 3-7.

16. Asch, S.E. (1946), "Forming Impressions of Personality," *Journal of Abnormal and Social Psychology*, Vol. 41, 1946, pp. 258-290.

17. Rogers, E.M., *Diffusion of Innovations*. (New York, Free Press, 1962), p. 265.

18. A report of such a conference is Opler, M.E., *Social Aspects of Technical Assistance in Operation*. (Paris, UNESCO, 1954).

19. Myrdal, G., *Asian Drama*. (New York, Pantheon, 1968). Gibbons, D.S., "Utopias without Expatriates," *International Development Review*, Vol. 1, 1971, p. 37.

20. Jesse, M. and Smith, D., "Experts and Counterparts: A Professional Problem," in Spitzberg, I. (ed.), The Exchange of Expertise: Counterparts and the New International Order. (Boulder, Colorado: Westview Press, 1978).

21. Ascroft, J., "A Conspiracy of Courtesy," International Development Review/Focus, Vol. 1, 1974, pp. 8-11.

22. Ohly, J., "Planning Future Joint Programs," Human Organization, Vol. 21, No. 2, 1962, pp. 137-53.

23. Ibid., p. 137.

24. After Havelock, R.G., Planning for Innovation through Dissemination and Utilization of Knowledge. (Ann Arbor, Michigan, CRUSK, ISR, University of Michigan, 1969).

25. Amuzegar, J., Technical Assistance in Theory and Pracitce: The Case of Iran. (New York; Praeger, 1966). Bass, B.M., "The American Advisor Abroad," Journal of Applied Behavioral Science, Vol. 7, No. 3, pp. 285-308. Benveniste, G. and Ilchman, W.F. (eds.), Agents of Change: Professionals in Developing Countries. (New York: Praeger, 1969). Byrnes, F.C., Americans in Technical Assistance: A Study of Attitudes and Responses to their Role Abroad. (New York: Praeger, 1965). Jun, J.S., "Ambiguity in the Professional Role: Perceptual Differences among AID Advisors." Ph.D. dissertation. Los Angeles, California, University of Southern California, 1969. Reining, H., "The Role of the Technical Advisor Overseas," in Symposium on Research Needs Regarding the Development of Administration Capabilities in Developing Countries. (Washington, D.C. Agency for International Development, 1965). Useem, J.D. and Useem R.H., "Men in the Middle of the Third Culture: The Roles of Americans and Non-Western People in Cross-Cultural Administration," Human Organization, Vol. 22, No. 3, 1963, 1969-179.

26. Institute for International Cooperation, The International Advisor: His Role, His Selection, and His Training. (Ottawa, Canada: University of Ottawa Press, 1970). Schwarz, P., A Study

of Selection Requirements for the Chief-of-Party Position. (Washington, D.C., AID, 1972). Trager, F.N. and Trager, H.G., "Exporting and Training Experts," The Review of Politics, Vol. 21, No.1, 1962, pp. 88-108. Winslow, A., "The Technical Assistance Expert," International Development Review, Vol. 4, No. 3, 1962, pp. 19-24.

27. Kerr, 1976, p. 8.

28. AID, Advisors and Counterparts: Relationships between Foreign Technical Assistance Experts and Host Country Colleagues. (Washington, D.C.: AID Bibliography Series. Technical Assistance Methodology, No. 1, 1972).

29. Jesse and Smith, 1978. Also see Smith, D. and Jesse, M. "Barriers between Expert and Counterparts," International Development Review, Vol.12, No. 1, 1970, pp. 22-25.

30. Kerr, G.B., "Counterparts and Advisors--A Bibliography," in Spitzberg, I. (ed.) The Exchange of Expertise: Counterparts and the New International Order. (Boulder, Colorado: Westview Press, 1978).

31. Spitzberg, I., "The Counterpart System: Some Suggestions for Change," International Development Review/Focus, No. 3, 1975, pp. 3-9.

32. Johnston, M.B., "Training Needs of Overseas Americans as Seen by Their National Co-Workers in Asia," International Development Review/Focus, No. 4, 1974, pp. 21-25.

33. Winter, D.K., American Professors in West Pakistan: A Study of Cross-Cultural Relations. East Lansing, Michigan. Unpublished Ph.D. dissertation, 1968. Glaser, W., "Some Preliminary Conclusions about Social Roles in Technical Assistance," in Kumar, K. (ed.) (in press), Experts and Counterparts in Technical Assistance. (Honolulu, Hawaii: East-West Center Press, 1974). Glaser, W., "The Performance of Expert-Counterpart Dyads in Technical Assistance," mimeo. (New York: Bureau of Applied Research, Columbia University, 1974). Glaser, W., "Improving Communication in the Technical Cooperation Relationship," International Development Review/Focus, No. 3, 1975, pp. 10-14. Glaser,W.

Making Better Use of Technical Assistance Experts," International Development Review/Focus, No. 4, 1975, pp. 21-25.

34. Spitzberg, 1975.

35. Kerr, 1976, p. 8.

36. Ibid.

37. Lippitt, R., Watson, J. and Westley, B., The Dynamics of Planned Change. (New York: Harcourt, Brace and World, 1958), pp. 129-143.

38. Rogers, E.M., with Svenning, L., Modernization among Peasants: The Impact of Communication. (New York: Holt, Rinehart and Winston, 1969), p. 171.

39. Lippitt and others, 1958, p. 133.

40. Ibid., p. 134.

41. Ibid., p. 134.

42. For a detailed description of the potential role of counterparts in the search for local resources see Kerr, G.B., "Regionalism in Afghanistan: Strategies of Identifying and Collecting Data," presented at Rural Life in Afghanistan: The Prospects for Development, (Omaha, Nebraska: Center for Afghanistan Studies, University of Nebraska, September, 1977).

43. Rogers with Svenning, p. 172.

44. Rogers with Svenning, p. 230. Tinbergen, p.109.

45. Lippitt and others, p. 139.

46. Rogers, E.M. and Shoemaker, F., Communication of Innovations: A Cross-Cultural Approach. (New York: Free Press, 1971).

5. Interpersonal Relations in the Counterpart System: Some Variations on the Model

Russell A. Stone

Background

The expert-counterpart system for technical training and skill transfer from developed to developing nations has evolved through a process of trial and error, apparently with little evaluation of the implications of the method. It is used by both the public and private sectors, by non-profit governmental and voluntary organizations, as well as by multi-national corporations for training personnel in Third World countries. The few available evaluative studies of the process focus on the governmental or voluntary organization sector. The largest study of which I am aware was sponsored by USAID in three developing nations and has resulted in publications in Focus, on technical cooperation as well as internal reports to USAID from Columbia University's Bureau of Applied Social Research (1) and from the OECD Development Center. (2) Most other studies (3) have been based on limited samples or single-case observations of training or knowledge transfer relationships. This chapter is an attempt to study the expert-counterpart relationship in a more general, if somewhat abstracted manner, in an effort to generate an understanding of the nature of the relationship and to point to more systematic and comprehensive research needed to improve effectiveness of this system of training.

Introduction

A key feature of the counterpart-expert system is that it is based on two-person groups, highly individualized interpersonal relationships, no two examples of which will be the same. The unique characteristics of the two-person group have been the subject of considerable sociological analysis (see for example, the classic work by Simmel) yet our understanding of the dynamics of this relationship leaves room for considerable additional research. Particularly, the two-person group as an apprenticeship relationship (a model which Spitzberg suggests we assume in analyzing the counterpart-expert system) has not been the subject of much analysis. An anomaly emerges when this group is viewed in its social context. Expert-counterpart groups are intended to function within very large-scale organizations. The two people are supposed to form a personal bond enabling the transfer of knowledge and/or skills against the background of a large government ministry, an aid agency with hundreds or thousands of employees and a score of different divisions, or a large multi-national corporation operating under the constant pressures of international business competition. Despite their differences, all such organizations have in common large size, bureaucratic structure, the pressures, and the depersonalization which accompany large scale. It is truly anomalous that a pattern of dyadic relationships which is antithetical to the patterns imposed by the larger organizational context, has emerged in many different settings as the preferred pattern for skill and knowledge transfer.

This paper examines three dimensions of the relationship, in an attempt to highlight those aspects which cause variation and affect the success of knowledge transfer, and to suggest what research is necessary to further our understanding of the efficacy of the system. We will begin with the organizational setting within which the dyad functions, then analyze the social structural influences and constraints on each member of the dyad plus how this affects the functioning of the small group, and finally, look at personal characteristics and interpersonal relationships between the two people involved.

The Organizational Setting

The dyad emerges as an island in a sea of bureaucracy or, quite often, in the confluence of two seas of bureaucracy; one the organization for which the counterpart works, a government ministry or government-owned and sponsored organization, sometimes with a mixture of government and private control; the other a bilateral aid agency (USAID, SIDA, etc.) or multilateral international assistance agency (or a private voluntary organization, often with religious or other ideological overtones) which employs the expert on a regular basis, or has been responsible for recruiting him for the specific assignment. In private industry, expert and counterpart often work for the same multinational corporation, although the expert is likely to work primarily in the "home country" division of the corporation and the counterpart in the "international" division. The differences between these two branches of the same corporation can be almost as great as differences between the two employing organizations in the public sector. This paper focuses on those instances when the dyad functions in the organizational context of the Third World bureaucracy. Thus the counterpart will be more familiar with, and more linked into the bureaucracy than will the expert. This has implications to be discussed in the next section of this paper.

The well-known "negative" attributes of bureaucracies such as inefficiency, excessive "red-tape" and multiple steps in performing any operation, centralization of power, unwillingness of subordinates to make decisions, redundant jobs and excess number of employees, irrational procedures, etc. seem to characterize developing nations' bureaucracies even more than in more developed countries. Likewise, standards of maintenance and operation of support services (cleaning, office supplies, etc.) seem to vary more or less directly with a level of development. Delays in supply and operations, unanticipated technical difficulties, and other logistics problems are more likely to occur in the training setting than in the expert's "home" working environment.

While such an organizational setting can create serious problems of adjustment for the expert, and considerable anxiety for the counterpart who must tolerate and facilitate the expert's adjustment process, it can also strengthen the informal and unique interpersonal aspects of the relationship. The more the "island" is buffeted by the surrounding "seas", the more it must strengthen and solidify in order to withstand the onslaught. The alternative, of course, is that the island breaks up from an inability to withstand the pressures.

Working out ways of dealing with the bureaucratic setting, and sharing the experiences involved in the process can form a basis for an effective interpersonal relationship in terms of which training can take place effectively. Frequently the expert or teacher in the relationship must become the student as the counterpart helps his adjustment to the new organizational setting and interprets or explains the bureaucratic anomalies which are experienced.

In addition to supplying the experiences which can cement (or break up) a viable interpersonal relationship, and which establish the informal ties of liking and respect between the two, bureaucratic delays create the time necessary for the expert to provide on-the-job instruction within the work setting. Work rules frequently require the counterpart (and the expert, if he is conforming to the host country's work patterns) to be on the job between set hours regardless of whether work can be accomplished during that time. Thus administrative delays provide time gaps, albeit unpredictable and irregular, in which instruction, discussions, explanation etc. can take place in a seemingly spontaneous context. Furthermore, this setting enables the expert to adjust the training to fit these specific contexts in which the counterpart will continue working, just as it enables the counterpart to ask questions, pose problems, and shape his own training to the realities he inevitably knows better than the expert.

Organization Structure and the Counterpart Relationship

The fact that training takes place in the developing nation usually means that the expert is removed from his "home" work setting, or else his job is defined entirely in terms of his role as visiting expert. In either case the expert is expected to devote all or most of his time to the training relationship. (Welch has indicated, in an accompanying chapter, that in the military setting "experts" frequently have other duties in terms of relaying information or evaluating use of resources. I doubt that this duty, even if it does exist, would take up a great deal of time outside the military setting.)

The counterpart, on the other hand, typically remains fully engaged in his own work setting. He might be expected to continue fulfilling all of his previous duties in addition to participating in the counterpart relationship, or he may be moving into a newly-defined job which he is expected to learn.

In any case, the counterpart is very likely to have other duties, and many other distractions outside the training relationship, arising from continuing participation in the employing organizations. Issues of promotion and/or pay raise, relationships with superiors in the bureaucracy, political alliances, ties, and duties, and sometimes even another job or family business interests are potential sources of distraction to the counterpart and disruption in the relationship. Undoubtedly these other duties filled the gaps in the work load mentioned in the previous section. Thus the counterpart is often faced with conflicting duties and obligations which distract him from devoting his full attention to the relationship with his mentor. As the mentor doesn't have these distractions, he in turn may become annoyed or disillusioned about the earnestness of his trainee. These distractions, rather than individual ineptitude or lack of motivation are likely the most frequent cause for an oft-observed phenomenon: The experts carrying out the functional responsibilities of the role rather than teaching the counterpart what to do and/or carrying out the duties jointly.

It often appears that the host organization structures the counterpart relationship in such a way that this outcome is inevitable. The training duties may be added to an already-full work load, or if the person is released from other duties, the visibility of this status may make him vulnerable to cooptation for special short term duties, tasks which superiors delegate to the counterpart on a short term basis, but which takes him away from the relationship with the expert. The magnitude of this latter problem is related to the degree to which the host organization is convinced of the value of the counterpart system.

In some cases the donor organization, or the parent company may be more convinced of the value of the counterpart system than is the host agency or subsidiary. In such cases counterparts may be included in the program plans, but the work situation is structured so that it is impossible for the counterpart to devote his time to learning from the expert, or it may be impossible for the expert to devote his efforts to training the counterpart.

Another situation is one where high level officials desire and are convinced of the value of the counterpart system, but the immediate supervisors of the counterpart and expert, or the counterpart and/ or expert himself might not be interested in the training relationship. In such a case the usual avoidance mechanism is for the counterpart or expert to be "unavailable" because of other pressing duties. Yet another situation, as illustrated by the example in Spitzberg (4) involves the expert being saddled with too much direct functional responsibility to enable him to devote time and attention to the training aspect of his duties. Education and training is always a luxury when there is "a job to be done," and in such circumstances devoting time and effort to training involves a positive commitment on the part of everyone involved, and a willingness to defer short term goals to reap the longer range benefits of improved skills.

A phenomenon which can disrupt the counterpart relationship is political or organizational unrest in the host agency or the government itself. The rationale of a stable, relatively permanent civil service in the case of government agencies, or a permanent labor force in the case of private companies, often yields to the exigencies of nepotism and patronage. Tribal loyalties, extended family ties, or obligations incurred in the battle for power often mean that a change in political leadership, or a change in the occupancy of a high-level position in a company, results in an initial period of uncertainty and insecurity for people lower in the organization. This in itself can disrupt the counterpart relationship by distracting the counterpart from his training duties and delaying the training program. Worse yet, from the point of view of the training process, is the possibility that counterparts will lose their jobs as a result of the power shuffle. Even if the power shift works to the advantage of the individual counterpart (by virtue of his supporting the new incumbents to power, or being a member of the correct group), a promotion or change in job duties can wipe out the accomplishments of the training relationship. If the counterpart moves to a higher job in the middle of his training, he is not only very unlikely to utilize the knowledge he has gained, but the expert will have to start all over again retraining a new counterpart. Disruptions of this magnitude can also mean that the program itself must be renegotiated, causing extensive delays in the transfer of technology. Even if former programs are continued, delays in appointing new counterparts to the training positions set back the timetable significantly.

Interviews with experts indicate that their own relationships with their employing or sponsoring organizations are also the source of considerable distraction. Anxieties over the length of appointments, subsequent jobs, evaluation and recognition of competence as well as opportunities for professional advancement are some of the problems which have been indicated (5). An expert with any degree of professionalism as an instructor or trainer should be able to isolate these problems, removing them from the training context. However, other dimensions of the expert's relationship with his sponsoring organization are more difficult to isolate.

The gap in income and standard of living between expert and counterpart has been mentioned by several observers (6). This may be a source of guilt or embarrassment on the part of the expert, or jealously on the part of the counterpart, and possibly a serious impediment to the relationship. Experts should be sensitive to these problems and willing to minimize them as much as possible, without destroying their own motivation.

Another fringe benefit of many "expert" jobs is frequent and/or lengthy vacations and home leave. The training program must be carefully planned so these do not result in untimely disruptions in the transfer of knowledge. Accounting for such generous fringe benefits remains problematic to the relationship, but is apparently considered a necessary inducement to attract good-quality experts to positions in the Third World.

A final source of interplay between organizational structure and the counterpart dyad has to do with the relative positions of the expert and the counterpart in their own organizations. Three patterns are possible. The expert and counterpart may occupy similar-level positions in their respective organizations. In this case they will view themselves as occupational equals, with the expert simply having some measure of specialized knowledge which the counterpart lacks, but is attempting to gain through their relationship. In such a situation both parties will feel free about treating each other as "colleagues" from the outset. A second situation is one where the expert occupies a higher status than the counterpart. This will frequently be the case in multi-national corporations where the expert has more technical training or occupies a more senior administrative position than the person he is training. A third situation involves a counterpart of a higher status than the expert. This situation arises when experts are hired, either directly by the host company organization or by a donor agency, to train the counterpart in some specialized skill. High level counterparts can have three or four different experts working with them providing specific skills in such a situation. Often recent university graduates or trainees, who will be both younger and more highly skilled than their Third World counterparts, serve as experts in such positions.

In each of these settings a very different relationship between counterpart and expert is likely to emerge. The more extreme the status difference, in either direction, the more likely the relationship is to remain functionally specific and business-like. Status equality is more likely to occur when the counterpart system is part of a more formal technical assistance protocol, either between governments in a bilateral structure, or between a host country and a multilateral agency, such as a branch of the United Nations. These cases can result in perfunctory relationships, as neither party may view the training role as primary, or the counterpart may feel he has little to learn, or little time to devote to the training aspects of the relationship. It is in these equal status settings that the more intangible and highly personal dimensions of the relationship, including the personalities of the two parties, determine whether the relationship will be at all successful.

Interpersonal Relationships in the Dyad

The quality of interaction in any given counterpart-expert dyad will be unique. The wide range of variation this implies, plus the fact that it is extremely difficult to identify the factors which make for successful or unsuccessful relationships, makes this aspect of the counterpart system extremely difficult to analyze. However, because it is also the aspect which is probably most crucial to the success of the counterpart system, we must at least attempt to identify some of the variables involved.

The issue of equality or inequality between expert and counterpart has been raised in a number of accompanying chapters. Altbach and Spitzberg both recognize that the counterpart system is an outgrowth of relationships between colonial agents and "natives". This in turn was modeled on an earlier form of apprenticeship training. Spitzberg has advocated a form of the apprenticeship model as suitable for the counterpart system. (7) In the present collection he alters his opinion in line with the principle of justice which requires a more equal relationship. In essence he feels both expert and counterpart should be in a position of learning from each other, in a relationship that is symbiotic, if not completely equal. Altbach feels that the very nature of the counterpart system perpetuates the relationships of colonialism which are essentially unequal, and therefore, he feels "abnormal". If relationships between two people are abnormal merely because they are unequal, then we could assert that the vast majority of all known interpersonal relationships are "abnormal". Even if we focus more narrowly on teaching or learning relationships, we would be hard pressed to identify situations of equality between the parties involved.

Almost every article written on the topic of technical assistance and the counterpart system reminds us that the expert must take into account the culture and societal norms in which the counterparts must operate, both in order to establish a meaningful relationship with the counterpart, and to tailor the training and advice so it is suitable to conditions where it will be applied. Social scientists invariably find that in most "traditional" societies, which applies to most developing nations, social structure is extremely hierarchical, relative status is always clearly understood by interacting parties, and knowledge and power are almost always closely associated. Thus the very notion of a "foreign expert" implies a person who will have a claim to authority over the counterpart. Of course, the extent and manner in which the expert exercises his implied authority can vary widely. However, if the relationship in the dyad is to be a relatively equal one, it will usually be up to the expert to set the tone of equality, and in many situations it will not lead to a viable relationship, as too many other expectations of the counterpart are violated in the process. Justice or fairness in a counterpart relationship, to say nothing of effectiveness in transferring knowledge, might not necessarily be achieved through maximizing equality.

The question of equality or inequality is further complicated by the many dimensions of the relationship involved. Each party develops a perception of the other in which his own status relative to that of his partner in the dyad is evaluated. Status inconsistencies <u>within</u> the perceived role set of a partner, or <u>between</u> the two members of the dyad are almost inevitable, and lead to a wide degree of ambiguity in the nature of the relationship. For instance, within a given role set the expert may be both younger than his counterpart and of a lower rank in his organization or on his career ladder, while at the same time he has a higher income and standard of living, and much better training than his counterpart, not only in the specific area in which he is supposed to be transferring technical knowledge, but in more general terms as well. On some criteria the counterpart is justified in treating the expert as his inferior,and on other criteria the expert has claim to superior status respect. How this problem is resolved in the mind of the counterpart determines the ease with which he can enter into a relationship with the expert. Systematic study is necessary to determine how such inconsistencies are dealt with. It is obvious however that they can be crucial to the success of technology transfer in the counterpart system.

The expert, in turn, will receive conflicting signals regarding the status of his counterpart relative to himself. Spitzberg has cited an example, in an accompanying chapter, of how high status in Kenyan society was not understood by foreign experts working in the education system. Both members of the dyad have the obligation to emphathise with the position of their partner within his own society, and to work out a relationship which is mutually comfortable. To use the guideline that anomalies be resolved in the direction of equality is a solution consistent with liberal tenets of education, and therefore can be advocated in the spirit of technology transfer leading to greater equality between nations in standards of living and ways of life.

In addition to the social structural dimensions of equality or inequality, some subjective aspects are involved. Given the colonial legacy of the system, and the history of most developing nations in their relations with people from the Western world, there might be a natural tendency for the counterpart to exhibit deference and respect toward the expert. This might be a genuine feeling, or it might be dissimulation in an attempt to reconcile perceived public expectations with the private attitudes of the counterpart. Many experts have found that counterparts who have been coopted into the relationship without consent or enthusiasm display outward deference, while at the same time ignoring or circumventing the expert when carrying out the duties of their job. This may be a matter of convenience, or it may mask feelings of resentment, national pride, or superiority over the expert, depending upon the position and attitudes of the particular counterpart.

A catalogue of the possible structural and subjective criteria for real or perceived inequality between the two parties in the counterpart system would be a huge document, with only a small number of items actually relevant to any given counterpart relationship. Therefore, rather than execute this task, let it suffice to say that any analyst, as well as the expert and counterpart themselves, must be aware of this potential problem.

There is not even consensus on whether maximized status consistency or equality between counterpart and expert is a "desirable" condition. Rogers (8) refers to this problem in terms of "homophily" and "heterophily" between communicator or change agent, and the client system. In some cases he found that maximum homophily (similarity between the parties) is most effective for transfer of knowledge. In other cases he found that heterophily (dissimilarity), usually with the change agent (or expert, in our terms) having a higher status, lends more authority to the message and therefore results in a higher probability that it will be accepted and followed. Authority based on superior status made for more effective communication and learning in many situations, contrary to the implicit expectations of the researchers.

Numerous additional dimensions such as mutual trust and respect, effective patterns of communication and mutual understanding (which may be a problem of language, or communication problems on a more subtle level), as well as the confidence and self-evaluation of each individual in the relationship are all variables which can affect the success of the counterpart system.

It is debatable whether the success of a given relationship should be judged in terms of the degree of trust, collaboration, and mutual good feelings which are expressed or manifested by the counterpart and expert, or whether some more objective criterion of productivity should be the measure of success. If the latter is taken as the dimension to be evaluated, the problem of how knowledge can be measured and the extent to which it can be attributed to the efforts of a teacher continue to challenge educational researchers. In some cases the productivity of the relationship can be measured in objective terms, such as specific demonstrable skills, increased output, or the counterpart's ability to take on new duties and responsibilities. These criteria can be judged directly, or in terms of satisfaction expressed by the counterpart's employer or supervisor. The extent to which they reflect the elusive notion of "quality" of an interpersonal relationship remains problematic. We can assume, however, that if the characteristics of a viable interpersonal relationship are not established between expert and counterpart, other positive outcomes from the relation are unlikely to ensue.

Conclusions

Many research strategies which can be applied to expanding our knowledge and understanding of the counterpart relationship have been outlined in an unpublished paper by Glaser (9), in which he reports on an interview-based field study conducted in three countries. In addition to the interview techniques already employed in separate in-depth sessions with expert and counterpart, it might be fruitful to conduct a joint interview in which the two parties are encouraged to discuss their relationship with each other. This might be the first time they have formally discussed their relationship, and their interaction might shed new light on their perceptions and understandings, not only for the researcher but but for themselves as well. Obviously this should only take place after the separate individual interviews.

Observations of interaction between expert and counterpart, plus analysis of project documents are two other methods suggested by Glaser. Whether suitable documents have been produced by previous projects, either written by the counterpart and/or expert, or by their supervisors or evaluators, is questionable. It is clear that little outright evaluation of the counterpart system has been carried out to date. It will be necessary to interpret documents and reports essentially written for other purposes, if any already-existing material is to be of value.

A further research method which would be of considerable value, but would involve on-going or newly established examples of the counterpart system in action, is participant observation. In this case either the expert, or the counterpart, or both would have defined as part of their task the observation and reporting of perceptions and events as the relationship proceeds. They would also evaluate their relationship at various stages in its progression. This would involve training the expert and/or counterpart to the research task, as they will be primarily involved in the specifically defined activity of technology transfer, which will be closer to their fields of professional expertise than is social science research. With a large enough sample it will be possible to establish some dyads in which only the expert is involved in research observation and evaluation, other dyads in which only the counterpart is involved in the research, and still others where both people are involved, possibly without the knowledge of the other or possibly with this knowledge and the opportunity to discuss their relationship in social science terms as it evolves. Such a research program is unlikely to yield results which directly determine how best to establish and conduct relationships in the counterpart system. However, it should serve to isolate and highlight the crucial variables which lead to relative failure or success of the counterpart system, as well as indications of which kinds of tasks, or which occupations, or which sectors pose specific problems, or are most viable for successful technology tranfer.

It is likely that clear differences will emerge between the public sector (bilateral agreements between governments or programs involving multilateral agencies such as the United Nations) and private (multi-national companies) programs for technology transfer. Most of the writings to date have been based on experiences in the public sector and it would be of considerable interest to know if private sector parties have conducted evaluative research on their own use of the counterpart system.

NOTES

1. Glaser, William (1974) "The Performance of Expert-Counterpart Dyads in Technical Assistance," mimeo, Bureau of Applied Social Research, Columbia University, New York; Glaser, William (1975a) "Improving Communication in the Technical Cooperation Relationship," International Development Review/Focus, 3:10-14; and Glaser, William (1975b) "Making Better Use of Technical Assistance Experts," International Development Review/Focus, 4:21-25.

2. Harari, Denyse (1974) *The Role of the Technical Assistance Expert: An Inquiry into the Expert's Identity, Motivations, and Attitudes* (Paris: OECD Development Center).

3. Lindholm, Stig (1973) "The Expert's Ghetto," CERES, Sept.-Oct.:30-33; Lindholm, Stig (1974) *Appointment with the Third World: Experts and Volunteers in the Field: Their Work, Life, and Thoughts*, Stockholm: Dag Hammarskjold Institute; Spitzberg, Irving (1975) "The Counterpart System: Some Suggestions for Change," *International Development Review/Focus* 3:309.

4. Spitzberg, p. 5.

5. Glaser (1975b) *op. cit.*

6. Glaser (1974, 1975a, 1975b) *op. cit.* Lindholm (1973, 1974) *op. cit.*

7. Spitzberg, *op. cit.*

8. Rogers, Everett (1969) *Modernization Among Peasants* (New York: Holt, Rinehart, and Winston).

9. Glaser (1974) *op. cit.*

6. The Contribution of Learning Principles to the Counterpart Relationship

James A. Draper

Introduction

The intent of counterpart contracts is that adult learning should occur, regardless of the political and economic motives that brought about the contract. Therefore, it seems essential that a knowledge of learning principles be applied when conceptualizing the counterpart relationship since, by definition, it is a learning transaction.

In this article, the term "counterpart relationship" implies both the traditional functions of 'expert-advisor' and 'recipient-learner' or 'counterpart'. The counterpart relationship refers to the human interaction of these two categories of people. Both parties are part of an organizational and cultural context within which they work, learn and interact.

As in most learning transactions, one can identify three major categories of learning, the learning of skills (manual, communicative and other skills); cognitive or knowledge/content learning; and affective learning which includes the learning of attitudes and changes in feelings. Too often, the counterpart relationship, when conceptualized, fails to stress the inter-relationship of these dimensions. Frequently, the acquisition of skills focuses on the teaching and learning of manual skills, forgetting that in the counterpart relationship the conscious desire to learn communication skills is also essential. Furthermore, the feeling dimension of learning is frequently minimized. All three dimensions of learning are highly interrelated and must be planned and accounted for if one is serious about facilitating effective counterpart relationships. When applying principles of learning, both the "expert" and the "recipient-learner" perform teaching and learning roles as part of their relationship. Both must listen to and be open to learning from each other.

What follows in this article are discussions about selected current terminologies and principles relevant to teaching and learning, as these relate to the counterpart relationship in the New International Order. It is not understanding of learning principles per se that is important but that these and other theories help to plan for and bring about human interaction. It is the understanding and resultant application of the principles which is important. It is not enough to know, for instance, those factors which facilitate learning and teaching such as conducive 'learning environments', trust, openess, cultural sensitivity, and so on, but how these are to be applied.

A definition of terms and the implications for counterpart relationships

Educational terms are frequently among the most difficult to define because they often refer to subjective concepts. The International Standard Classification of Education (1) defines the following terms:

Learning: Any change in behaviour, information, knowledge, understanding, attitudes, skills, or capabilities which can be retained and cannot be ascribed to physical growth or to the development of inherited behaviour patterns.

Education: Organized and sustained communication designed to bring about learning; not as an instructional package provided to children and young persons, but (as) a continuing process providing opportunities for enlarging experiences, understanding and skill throughout the life of an individual.

The counterpart relationship is characterized by both the components of learning and education, the former being the process of receiving, coding and storing stimuli from one's environment, and the latter being a conscious and organized attempt to bring about behaviour change towards pre-determined goals. Frequently, the focus of the counterpart relationship is on the educational component whereby skills and knowledge are acquired, to the neglect of the wider institutional and cultural environment which profoundly affects not only what is learned but how it is used. That the 'advisor' and 'advisee' will learn is unavoidable. What is important is the evaluative and other mechanisms which are developed in order to allow all parties to reflect, interpret and test out what is learned. Such a process is obviously more than agreeing on the definition of terms. It involves an application of these within the specific cultural milieu within which they are used.

Other terms further help to clarify the distinction. It is realized that most of what is known about learning has been derived from studies of learning in children. Furthermore, adult education has frequently been thought of as an extension of child education or pedagogy. In terms of teaching and research relating to adults, this association has been distracting. Hence, the term andragogy (2) is increasingly being used, meaning the art and science of helping adults to learn, in contrast to pedagogy which focuses on the teaching of children. Furthermore:

> the development, organization and administration of programs in applied andragogy involves a continuous circular application of the following seven steps:
>
> - setting a climate for learning,
> - establishing a structure for mutual planning,
> - assessing interests, needs and values,
> - formulating objectives,
> - designing learning activities,
> - implementing learning activities,
> - evaluating results (reassessing needs, interests and values).

If the term andragogy was used only to describe the role functions within the counterpart relationship, then this function would be limited to the act of teaching, which of course does not present the overall picture. New theories of learning highlight the principle of continuity and the importance of needs and motivations, of choice of content, of the hierarchal nature of learning, and the interrelationship between educational content and environment. Whereas the act of teaching is noted by the term andragogy, the act of learning is described as mathetics (3), which is the science of behavior of people learning. The mathetic processes and their study are assuming increasing importance and are highly significant when conceptualizing the teaching-learning dialogue which forms the very foundation of the counterpart relationship.

The above concepts are supportive of two trends which are emerging internationally. One is that education is now being seen as a continuing, not a terminal, process. Second, the concept of "studentship" is being revised, or may even be replaced by the term "learner". Many of the stereotypes of "student" are being re-examined, such as the connotation of "immaturity" and "inferiority". The trend is to a term which implies responsibility, self-directiveness, enquiry, exploration and self-discipline. Paralleling this, one expects drastic changes in the relationship of student and teacher. In many ways, the relationship is increasingly becoming that of learner to learner. In any event, the freedom to learn will become inextricably linked to the freedom to teach.

Traditionally, the counterpart realtionship was characterized by a teacher-pupil relationship, posing such dichotomies as expert/non-expert, knowledgeable/unknowledgeable, superior/inferior and so on. The terms frequently lead to defining a subject-object relationship, or at least one in which inequality was implied. Developing and using new terms is the first step to nurturing different attitudes which in turn re-defines human relationships, wherein the members of the counterpart relationship see others as well as themselves as teachers and learners and as such, as equals.

Learning: Principles and Applications

Learning theory is not exclusively the domain of any particular discipline but stems and is applied by both the social sciences and humanities, as well as the natural sciences. More is known about how learning happens than about what it is per se. Learning means change; it is active, not passive. Learning theory is an applied science and it is interdisciplinary in nature, which adds to its complexity.

According to Kidd, (4) much of what has been learned about learning in adults can be summarized by referring to what he calls "the Three R's of adult education - relevancy, relationship or relatedness, and responsibility," that is:

Relevancy - No adult will deeply absorb himself in study unless he sees, unless he feels, that the subject is part of his life and destiny ... without relevance there will not be the engagement that constitutes genuine learning.

Relationship - No knowledge or skill or attitude is discrete; the adult wants to understand how it relates to his experience, to what he is, to what he knows.

Responsibility - Requires that one act upon what is learned.

Kidd goes on to point out that:

> The constellation of feelings associated with love (respect, admiration, generosity, sympathy, friendliness, encouragement) are of constant influence on learning. They are much more powerful than constellations associated with rage and fear. The first leads to calm, serenity, hope, joyousness, confidence. To the second and third response is anxiety, withdrawal, despair, greed, hate.

Kidd identifies several examples of formulation which are applicable to learners, especially to older ones. These are summarized briefly below.

1. An aesthetic perspective is one way of becoming sensitive to another person's culture. (To know something about the mythologies and art forms of a culture is important since these frequently give clues to thinking processes or the way in which information is processed.)
2. A formulation based on humanistic psychology makes the point that "learning should be experimental, that it should help people confront problems and that the primary goal is the discovery of personal meaning."
3. Information processing includes the selection and coding of information, that is, "the learner becomes aware of selected features of a learning situation." He cannot attend to all the information in the situation. The information is stored selectively and is coded and transformed for later retrieval. New information may be linked to concepts already known without changing them, or refinements in the established concept may occur. Frequently, one of

the goals of the counterpart relationship is the learning of new concepts. This learning will be influenced by the concepts one already knows as well as the learning styles of the individuals within their cultures.

4. Finally, motivation and expectancy theory is based on the assumption that performance in learning is affected by choices made by the learner. Kidd's writings on learning also refer to "teachable moments", that is, times in an adult's life when he is more ready to learn. He points out that one of these points in time is when there is an impressive achievement or shift in technology, such as that which might be reflected during counterpart relationships.

Applied to the counterpart relationship, Kidd reminds us that all parties must want to be associated with it. They must see the relevancy of it to their own growth, that what is learned will in fact be used and that there will be some assurance of this. Such an assurance must be clearly stated in a 'counterpart contract'. Kidd's work suggests a learning style that focuses on individuals discovering their own meaning. A teaching style is also implied, requiring skills that facilitate the learning of others, helping others to discover and learn. Finally, learning should be based on feelings of trust, respect and friendliness.

Focus on adult learning

In his paper on "Fundamentals of Adult Learning", Jerold W. Apps (5) mentions seven guidelines for effective learning:

1. The focus of the adult educator must be on the individual.
2. The focus of the adult educator must be on the entire person, minimizing the segmentation of people into discrete roles, realizing that the role of worker is not in isolation from the emotional roles of, say, parent and spouse.
3. The learner must be involved in decisions about what he will learn and how he will learn it.
4. The instructor must be willing to take risks.
5. The instructor must cease being the sole knowledge authority and become one of several resources to the learner.
6. A climate of trust between the learner and the instructor must exist.
7. The process of learning must be considered as

important as the content. Helping people learn how to learn should be as important to educators as imparting content.

When applying the above points to the expert/counterpart, one can insert the terms 'adult educator' 'educators' and 'instructors' for "members in the counterpart relationship".

Apps examines three learning models. The first of these is a model which focuses on learning as the acquisition of content. The second is on learning as problem-solving, where the function of the content is a means for solving the problem the learner brings to the learning situation. Finally, there is the learning as inquiry model, which is a kind of cross between the previous two models. The content has some value inherent in it, but the value of the content will vary from person to person. The starting place is the content, but the focus is on the relationship of the content to the individual learner and the sense that this makes to the learner, as in the counterpart relationship.

One of the problems for those in the counterpart relationship is to know which of these learning models is most important. Furthermore, how does the adult learner know when he should be focusing on learning as acquiring content, learning as problem solving, or learning as inquiry? In answering these questions, one must come back to the basic question of what is the purpose of this learning, with this adult, in this situation?

Many relevant ideas for the counterpart relationship come out of the work of Apps. The perception of each person in the relationship must not be restricted to the 'work role'. The point made by Apps is that persons must be viewed as 'whole', encompassing roles other than that of worker. The evaluation done by Smith and Jesse, included as a chapter in this book, makes reference to the importance of social contacts among the counterparts.

The extensive study done by Smith and Jesse illustrates many of the points discussed in this chapter on learning principles, for instance, the need for formative or on-going evaluation in a counterpart relationship; the concept of time which must be accounted for in the relationship; the importance of the process for selecting both nationals and internationals; the fact that nationals do feel that they have something to teach and are resentful when this is ignored; and the need to specify the respective role of each party, such as in a counterpart contract

It is obvious that feelings can either get in the way of learning, or they can enhance it, depending on the ease with which feelings can be expressed, how they are expressed, and the sensitivity or listening skills of the 'recipient' member. It is important to remember that both members in the counterpart relationship must make the effort to learn the culture of the other. During the times of meeting to reflect and evaluate, some analysis of cultures should be thought of as a continuing agenda item. This phenomenological approach to learning requires focusing on experience by describing it, seeing what an experience is for another person, and not just looking at what causes it, but why it exists.

Another point, relevant to the topic is that a knowledge of a culture and a philosophy of a people is not synonomous with skills in working with them. One of the points stressed in this chapter is that special skills in communication are required. DeCrow (6) endorses this and makes other relevant points in his publication "Cross Cultural Interaction Skills: A Digest of Recent Training Literature".

Cultural courtesies can be misinterpreted. For instance, in the case study by Smith and Jesse, reference is made to the "culture of silence" shown by the nationals. In his article, "A Conspiracy of Courtesy", Joseph Ashcroft (7) talks about the silent treatment of the host country and the verbal wizardry of the 'expert', both of which grow from the cultural values of each.

Regarding particular learning theory models, in the evaluation by Smith and Jesse, the role of the expert was seen as passing to his counterpart the special skills or knowledge he has, like pouring knowledge from one container to another. This misleading model completely ignores the process of discovery, dialogue, critical thinking and personal grwoth which is one of the essential points stressed in this chapter on learning theory.

In his book, Teaching and Learning in Adult Education, Harry Miller (8) identifies six conditions for learning.

1. The student must be adequately motivated to change behavior.
2. The student must be aware of the inadequacy of his present behavior.
3. The student must have a clear picture of the behavior which he is required to adopt.
4. The student must have opportunities to

practice the appropriate behavior.

5. The student must get reinforcement of the correct behavior.

6. The student must have available a sequence of appropriate materials.

Exchanging the word "counterpart" for "student", it is important that members in the relationship must openly admit that they want to continue to learn. Each is involved in reinforcing the learning behaviour of the other.

In their discussion of internal conditions prerequisite to learning, Verner and Davidson (9) point out that in order for learning to occur successfully, the learner must be motivated to learn; must establish an 'attentional set'; be in a state of developmental readiness to learn; and the learning environment must be conducive to learning in ways acceptable to the learner. To elaborate further, "...motivation arising from within the individual is far more important than that which is external to him. This internal motivation springs from an adult's need and desire to achieve or succeed and it is derived initially from curiosity and related dispositions to explore, manipulate, and cope with the environment". That is, there must be some measure of freedom, not cooptation, for persons to associate themselves voluntarily with the counterpart relationship. Motivation must derive from one's learning goals, professional aspirations and personal growth.

"Attentional sets" enable the adult to concentrate upon crucial elements in a learning task rather than being distracted by irrelevant features or events within a learning situation. Other contributors to this book notably Stone, point out the organizational structures within which counterparts work and point out the dangers of distracting elements which frequently exist such as the "host-counterpart" being required to undertake tasks in the organization that are unrelated to the primary goals of the counterpart relationship.

"Readiness" is a developmental state that results from physiological growth, from psychological conditioning, and from experience in living and learning. "Learning cannot occur unless there is a sufficient degree of maturation....(and)...will be hindered when an adult lacks the previously learned abilities that are prerequisite to the new learning". Part of the procedure for selecting counterparts should be to assess maturity and abilities, in light of what is to be learned in the relationship.

Finally, learning may not occur because of conditions in the immediate learning situation. That is, adults are influenced by the environment in which they attempt to learn; this environment consists of the physical setting as well as the emotional atmosphere.

To further understand the importance of relevancy and motivation, one might look to some of the literature on action research and the role of the consultant. McGill (10) points out that training and development needs lie with those to be trained but that this is greatly determined by the levels at which the needs are felt. There is a relationship between convergence of interest and 'consultant' entry. He elaborates on two alternative models:

1. The consultant makes the organization aware of its needs for his services and procures an invitation to enter;
2. The organization becomes aware of the need for outside assistance and invites the consultant in.

In #1, the consultant creates convergence of interest, by drawing attention of top level officials, and seldom goes beyond this level. In #2, interest converges, often at levels distant from the top. Here, individuals seeking information and action on their own problems converge with other individuals with similar needs. McGill goes on to say that the consultant who engineers an invitation to enter may create an artificial commitment to information and action that will adversely affect training and development. The pitfalls of false commitment are not as prevalent where consultant entry follows rather than precedes convergence of interest. Within the context of learning theory, motivation, commitment, and a supportive environment for learning are likely to be greatest if the convergence is indigenous.

Learning environments

Since numerous references have been made in this section to "learning environments", it is useful to expand on the meaning of this, especially since it is one of the first steps in the teaching-learning process. A discussion of the "climate for learning" can be pursued from three perspectives:(11) the physical (or biological), the human (or interpersonal) and the organizational (or interactive). In discussing the climate for learning, Ingalls points out that:

> Certain environmental factors seem...to either facilitate or be disruptive of adult learning activities. All kinds of messages are constantly being communicated from the physical, human and organizational environments in which we live and work, and most of us have become quite adept at picking up and decoding messages that may be expressed either verbally or nonverbally. A name that has been used to describe this web or network of messages and meanings is "climate".... Organizational climates can vary considerably from being warm, informal and stimulating to being stuffy, formal and dull. While it is difficult to pick up and identify all of the elements or messages that contribute to how we feel about the climate in a particular environment, we cannot deny our feelings; they are real to us and they affect our behavior.
>
> It is quite obvious that learning can be stimulated or blocked by climate factors. Physical discomfort, frustration, anxiety, apathy, and indifference all have a negative effect on the learning process while excitement, joy, enthusiasm, humor and comfort etc., all seem to facilitate it. In any event, climate exists and must be recognized.
>
> The key issue for climate setting, ...lies in recognizing the value of persons in an organization or social situation. If adults are not recognized as self-directing and autonomous persons and if they are not allowed to function as adults, the resultant frustration will most likely have a negative effect on the learning or working climate.

The physical surrounding, then, refers to anything from the kind of arrangement of furniture, to the geographical relationship of home to place of work, to temperature or sound level. The inadequacies of any one of these can lead to frustrations, and hence interfere with learning within the counterpart relationship.

Human and interpersonal relations essentially refers to the "psychological" environment, and in dealing with this, in order to enhance learning, one attempts to reduce anxieties, fear, threat, and other factors relating to feelings and the concept one has of oneself.

Finally, the organizational setting includes the organizational structure within which one works as well as all those ways in which the organization communicates, which are indicators that express the values and priorities of the organization.

Learning with a time frame

Learning, that is, personal change, occurs within a time frame. It is important that all those persons associated with the counterpart relationship understand the concept of social time and its role in development. For instance,

> Timing, i.e. the way in which activities are arranged in relation to each other, the way in which social agents who have to work together or in relays establish contact, and the way in which the various time-sequences which mark the pulsation of social life fit in with each other.
>
> The handling of time, i.e. the way in which individuals and groups space out their activities, arrange their actions in series, and when faced with one or more immediate tasks, break them into a succession of steps to be taken....
>
> Forecasting, i.e. the ability to imagine occurrances in the future, to set oneself more distant objectives and to model one's activity on future events....
>
> Time as a value, i.e. the way in which people evaluate and use the time available to them.... (12)

Understanding the concept of time is only one part of understanding another person's culture. Those in the counterpart relationship will need to work out realistically the time components in the planning and learning process.

The breadth and depth of learning

There are many different approaches to learning and obviously great differences in individual learning styles. Furthermore, there are differences in one's self-concept, in experience, in readiness to learn and in orientation to learning. Learning must serve the needs of individuals as well as the organizations with which they are associated. It makes sense that learning is more meaningful when the learner is working on problems important to him but learners must go through a learning process to learn what their objectives are. That is, learning can be perceived as an evolutionary process within which goals frequently change. What is essential, prior to entering a counterpart relationship, is determining the kind of learning model which will guide the relationship - that is: does one assume that the learner is responsible for his own learning, that the teacher-facilitator has trust in the learner's ability to learn, and to become self-directing? Furthermore, is it assumed that learning builds on the emotional and intellectual component of the individual, that the emotional climate of the learning situation is crucial, that learning is enhanced if the physical environment reinforces the desired emotional climate? Does one facilitate the atmosphere for learning by encouraging people to be active, promoting discovery, recognizing people's right to make mistakes, tolerating ambiguity, or does one have contrasting assumptions and methodologies relating to the learning process?

Learning styles and creativity are individually and culturally based. In expressing his ideas on thinking, Edward de Bono (13) says that "vertical thinking, logical sequential thinking, is for using ideas, whereas lateral thinking is for changing them". Regarding creativity, "Vertical thinking is like digging the same hole deeper; lateral thinking is moving sideways to dig a new hole in a different place". Learning and thinking in the counterpart relationship has depth and breadth, and feeling.

Principles of Learning and the New International Economic Order

Understanding some of the basic principles of learning is intended to 'humanize' communication between people. An educational theorist who perhaps more than any other has bridged the relationship between learning theory and change is Paualo Freire. (14) His philosophy encompasses particular views of the nature of man, the essence of culture and a historical perspective. At the risk of oversimplifying the complexity of his work, one might say that his line of reasoning begins with a realization that man is constantly in the state of transforming his environment. Liberation is the process of recovering ones 'world'. To do this is to raise the consciousness of man and the importance of language. The consciousness of the oppressed is a culture of silence, and this is a dehumanizing situation. People can be helped towards a greater critical consciousness through a dialectic process of reflection and action.

Through education, one can be helped to rename one's world, and an essential component of this re-naming is to change the 'subject' and 'object' relationship between people. 'Subjects' are knowing and active human beings. 'Objects' are human beings viewed passively or as being acted upon by others. In order to bring about communication, it is necessary to bring about equality between persons, that is, to bring about a 'subject' to 'subject' relationship. The absence of this, in extreme terms, is to perpetuate 'oppressor'-'oppressed' relationships, the opposite of intended counterpart relationships. Another way to put this is to say that dialogue cannot occur if one person or group of persons want to name the world for others or deny others the right to speak. Both factors historically, have been characteristic of the 'expert' role in development, whereby the foreigner, through language, forced a description of the world upon the recipient. UNESCO, an organization that has greatly influenced development programs, has continuously used the term "expert". It seems advisable to change this in favor of one that stresses 'subject' to 'subject' interaction in the counterpart relationship.

Oppressors, according to Freire, are individuals who do not allow other people to realize their humanity. Often the oppressed learn to internalize the very assumptions which are the shackles of their oppression and in doing so experience feelings of inferiority, powerlessness, perhaps apathy and other such forms of behavior.

Education is a way of increasing the critical consciousness of man, the result of which is to change the relationships between men, to enhance communication and dialogue, and to involve all persons in setting goals and determining strategies for changing the environment, that is, of renaming one's 'world'. All this is to bring about greater justice, self-determination, a re-orientation of power, and a decrease in dependency. These, among others, are the goals of the NIO at the 'macro' world level. The theory of learning and communication helps to conceptualize these goals as well as give some guidance in how to bring them about. The counterpart relationship can be thought of as the micro level of the NIO, helping to bring about change, dialogue, and interdependency.

Learning and Other Perspectives on Counterparts

The reader will note that other chapters in this book reinforce and compliment many of the topics discussed in this chapter, for example, learning, communication, role definitions, language, organizational structure and motivation. In their article, "Focus on Increasing Skills and Technical Independence", Harwitz and Haspel point out that one way to improve manpower potential in a given country is to increase the efficiency and effectiveness of the formal educational system. An additional approach is to improve the effecitveness of the 'informal' system, such as through the counterpart relationship as well as by on-the-job training. One way to bring about this effectiveness is to understand and apply what is known about learning and teaching.

Kerr discusses language and concepts and their effect upon our behavior, many of which are closely related to some of the basic ideas of Paulo Freire. For instance, Kerr points out that language will in part determine what the person sees, what he thinks about and the methods he uses to think and arrive at decisions. In quoting Wittgenstein, "...the limits of my language are the limits of my world", he complements Freire. Furthermore, the name we give to a position or a role in an organization is important because it provides us with the first cues about the person and the role. The concepts we use will determine how we think about social situations and also how and what we think about other people involved in the situation.

These ideas also are expressed by Jesse and Smith in their case study from Thailand. In this present article on learning and teaching, it is emphasized that the terms that are used help to define the relationships one has with others. The terms 'learner' and 'expert' imply quite different things. The latter implies something that has terminated in reference to an acquisition of knowledge or skills. An alternative word would be one implying a process of evolving, "I have more to learn". All parties can learn within the counterpart relationship. All parties are change agents.

Kerr refers to the dyadic nature of the change agent role. In an earlier section of this article on learning, reference is also made to the advantages of a tryadic relationship. Kerr underlines the importance of equality and cooperation as a basis for these relationships.

Stone also refers to the dyadic, two person group. He points out the influence organizational structures have on the counterpart relationships and that these reflect the 'cultures' of each part. The argument in this present chapter is that the structures also form the extent to which support for learning will come. The question is, to what extent is the organizational setting conducive to a 'learning environment'?

The careful selection of counterpart members is very important. This point is made by Stone and Jesse and Smith. However, there is a danger that one or both of the counterpart members will have been coerced into the positions, and this can result in disinterest and low motivation. Stone does point out that little evaluation between expert and counterpart has taken place. The Thailand case would be one example of where such evaluation was carried out, using, as Stone suggests, joint interviews to discuss the relationships counterpart members have with each other. Participant observation is one approach for collecting information and reflecting on the relationship. We need to develop many more innovative methods of monitoring and reflecting on the process. What is important is that the evaluation is open to identifying the unintended outcomes as well.

In his article, Altbach makes the point that the very essence of the teacher-student relationship is one of inequality. No doubt the terms learning and teaching also have their limitations, but less so it seems when the terms are inter-linked and applied to each member of the counterpart relationship. Each has something to teach and something to learn. Altbach supports my view that there are psychological implications of the counterpart relationship which are linked to the system: most counterparts have technical backgrounds and are individuals who have not been selected for their sensitivity to the cultures of others. There is a need to select carefully the individuals who are to act as counterparts; to know about the personality characteristics of each in order to maximize effectiveness.

Finally, Spitzberg makes a number of points

which support much of what is being said in this present article. He points out that there is often very little planning put into the counterpart relationships, and very little training provided to those responsible for providing the needed expertise. Furthermore, he feels that both 'expert' and 'counterpart' should be in a position of learning from each other, in a relationship that is symbotic, if not completely equal. One way to analyze the relationship is to view learning and teaching as one. He supports my view that not only is the quality of learning important but that it is not a one-way process. The expert is not just the provider but also the receiver of knowledge. He also points out the need for institutional support, the importance of clarifying and describing the roles of counterpart members, and the importance of understanding the learning styles of a particular culture. In essence then, all counterpart relationships must be educational.

Variation on the theme

Invariably, the counterpart relationship is thought of as dyadic. In fact, an argument might be made that it be a tryadic one, especially in attempting to strengthen the supporting environment of the counterpart relationship. It is fully realized that the success of the relationship is very much dependent on the organization and political support that is given to it. If the immediate supervisor of the host-counterpart is not informed and supportive of the relationship, he may, knowingly or otherwise, thwart the attempts for learning and change. One important role of the supervisor is to 'protect' the counterpart from being distracted from the learning involved in the counterpart relationship. One way to gain the support of the supervisor is to involve him as a third member in the relationship, although not necessarily to the same extent as the core counterpart group.

Another way to involve a third member in the relationship, illustrated in the case study by Jesse and Smith, is to involve a 'national' or an 'international' who will assist in facilitating the learning and communication of the principle parties. The facilitator might meet separately with each. Then all counterparts might meet together with the facilitator to evaluate programs, and problems as well as help in planning. All this would be undertaken in light of the learning principles discussed previously.

An example of a tri-partite arrangement is the POSTD (program of staff training and development) at the Ontario Institute for Studies in Education. All student members in the program are sponsored by an organization, usually one in business or industry. All members are also involved in some post-graduate program at OISE (University of Toronto). A working triad consists of the employee-learner, his organization supervisor and an academic member from OISE. All members are involved as planners, learners and evaluators in the program. Involvement of the supervisor and the academic-'expert' greatly reinforces the goals of the program.

Whatever the number of persons involved in the counterpart relationship, it seems that some continuity should be built into the relationship, either formally as through a contract, or informally. After the formal presence of the expatriate, it is assumed that the counterpart has acquired the skills to undertake certain tasks, without the need for outside assistance. On the other hand, one of the skills associated with the relationship is learning how to continue and extend the skills, so that they do not become obsolete. The foreign member of the counterpart relationship, and his agency, might informally continue the ties by drawing attention to new research and techniques, that are developed and related to the work of the patriate counterpart. Another way to build in a continuing education approach is to assume that at sometime in the future, the local counterpart may himself become a foreign advisor within some other developing country. Keeping up with the content literature in his work, and retaining the skills of communication are important to the change agent role and in keeping with the basic principle of adult learning.

Conclusions

The counterpart relationship is characterized by political, ethical and educational relationships. In one sense, the macro relationship of culture to culture, of "giver" country to "recipient" country is exemplified in the micro relationship of those that most closely interact in the counterpart relationship. The macro description has a direct effect at the interpersonal level and is most effective when both levels perceive themselves as givers and receivers, as teachers and learners.

However else interpreted, the counterpart contract implies a learning-teaching contract and hence is a form of non-formal education, aimed at decreasing dependency of one party on another. In conceptualizing this relationship, it is important to be aware of and practice the fundamental principles of learning and teaching theory and the learning context within which change is intended to occur. Encompassed within this context is cognitive and affective learning which takes place as a result of the counterpart relationship. Perceiving the relationship in terms of learning principles helps to identify indicators for assessing behavior change and the achievement of educational goals. Assessing the outcomes must be in human terms, quite apart from monitoring economic and political outcomes.

The application of learning principles helps to understand and deal with such things as planning what is to be learned, the motivational commitment to learning and creating optimal physical and psychological learning environments. That is, a support system which enhances learning, which goes beyond the typical two-person counterpart relationship and involves, as learners and as teachers, many others who are likely to influence the climate for learning on the one hand, and on the other, the effective application of what is learned. Learning theory also gives guidance to the kind of evaluation and reflective system which directs the formative evaluation of the learning act. The counterpart relationship is more than an act of transferring knowledge. Skills and attitudes are inseparable from the acquisition of content. Furthermore, as part of the relationship, one is continuously developing one's skills of learning how to learn. The learning-teaching orientation one selects will determine the kind of human relationships that develop, the way in which materials are organized, and the interpretation one will give to assessing the experience. There should be nothing secretive about one's preferred styles of working and relating. It is essential to communicate appropriately these preferences prior to contracting and especially with those directly involved in the counterpart relationship. It is important to decrease ambiguity in the nature of the relationship and to enter the relationship requires a degree of humbleness and personal security.

What is required is a particular socio-cultural sensitivity, where those in the counterpart relationship understand the values and behaviors of their respective cultures, as a first step to understanding the cultures of others. It is especially important to understand the effect that culture has upon learning and teaching styles, and the processes of thinking. Many skills are required in order to make the counterpart relationship work, including the writing of learning contracts. A basic understanding of learning and teaching principles can contribute greatly to the effectiveness and humaness of sharing, which is the intent of the counterpart system.

NOTES

1. The International Standard Classification of Education, Paris, UNESCO, March, 1976. pp.18 and 19.

2. Ingalls, John D., A Trainers Guide to Andragogy, Washington, D.C.: U.S. Department of Health, Education and Welfare, 1973, 242 pp (pp. 10-11).

3. Faure, Edgar, et al., Learning to Be (the world of education today and tomorrow), Paris: UNESCO, 1972, 313 pp. (see p. 130).

4. Kidd, J.R., "Adult Learning in the 1970's", Adult Learning: Issues and Innovations, edited by Robert M. Smith, Information Series No. 8, DeKalb, Ill.: Northern Illinois University, July, 1976, 122 pp.

5. Apps, Jerold W., "Fundamentals of Adult Learning", Adult Learning and Instruction, by Stanley M. Grabowski, (ed) a joint publication of the ERIC Clearinghouse on adult education and the American Association for Adult Education, 1970, 121 pp (see pp. 101-3).

6. DeCrow, Roger, Cross Cultural Interaction Skills: A Digest of Recent Training, Syracuse, N.Y.: ERIC Clearinghouse on Adult Education, 1969.

7. Ascroft, Joseph. "A Conspiracy of Courtesy", in Going Abroad with CIDA, Ottawa: Canadian International Development Agency, Kit 2.

8. Miller, Harry L., Teaching and Learning in Adult Education, New York: The MacMillan Company, 1964 (pp. 37-51).

9. Verner, Coolie and Catherine V. Davidson, Psychological Factors in Adult Learning and Instruction, Tallahassee, Florida: Research Information Processing Center, Department of Adult Education.

10. McGill, Michael E. & Melvin E. Horton, Jr., Action Research Designs for Training and Development, Washington, D.C.: National Training and Development Service Press, 5028 Wisconsin Ave. N.W., 1973, 93 pp.

11. Ingalls, pp. 12-15.

12. Rezsohazy, Rudolf, "The Concept of Social Time: Its Role in Development". International Social Science Journal, Vol. XXIV, No. 1, 1972.

13. de Bono, Edward, About Think, London, Jonathan Cape, 1972, 46 pp. (p. 10).

14. Freire, Paulo, Pedagogy of the Oppressed, New York: The Seabury Press, 1970.

7. Increasing Skills and Technical Independence: An Economic Analysis

Mitchell Harwitz and Abraham E. Haspel

I. Introduction

Third world nations that seek economic growth often experience a shortage of skilled manpower in both the private and public sectors. The problem may be more acute in the public sector (e.g., government ministries) in that the private sector may successfully bid away the available skilled manpower by offering higher rewards. Consequently, government agencies are often unable to accomplish necessary tasks. In order to avoid failure in doing their jobs, ministries must resort to a number of alternative personnel policies. One of the most frequent is the importation of manpower possessing the necessary skill levels. This remedy, however, increases the dependence of the developing nations upon the industrialized world. Another solution is to augment the exising skills of the indigenous population. This can be accomplished through the use of formal institutions of learning or through the use of less formal on-the-job training techniques. The purpose of this paper is to analyze the efficient use of these alternatives.

A planning theory of this kind requires detailed specification of the costs incurred by each training option.[1] Formal education implies total absence from the labor force of the person being trained. Hence, in addition to direct costs for tuition, room and board, books and other relevant expenditures, a social cost in the form of a loss of government service is also incurred. On-the-job training implies that the skill to be transferred is already possessed by someone. In many cases this must be an imported technical expert. Since the imported expert spends some time teaching a counterpart, he cannot do as much work as he would have otherwise. Such a loss may be larger in hierarchical counterpart relations then in those which expert and counterpart are exchanging specialized knowledge in which the counterpart already possesses skills and knowledge complementary to those of the expert.

The history of Third World economic development policies from 1950 to 1970 was mainly a history of effort dedicated to the attainment of quantitative goals of economic growth that are now widely regarded as unsatisfactory.[2] Had we done our research in this period, we would have applied our effort to achieving the most rapid possible increase in the labor skills and qualifications available to the governments of these countries over the relevant planning period. In other words, we would undoubtedly have taken an expansionist view of the goal of our program, and we would have seen our task as the organization of the largest possible complement of skilled labor, both foreign and indigenous. We have chosen instead to organize the planning of skill transfer around a combination of both of the goals mentioned in the preceding paragraph: 1) training, and 2) the achievement of the lowest possible level of foreign "presence" in the government bureaucracy, a philosophy in keeping with the New International Economic Order.[3]

In section II we present the rationale and explicit equations of an optimization model which can be used to study the above goals. Section III contains an illustrative example. Concluding remarks and directions for future research are found in the last section, section IV.

II. An Optimization Model

A. Rationale

Many economic models are designed to maximize or minimize some goal subject to a variety of constraints. One good reason is that such a logical organization is exceedingly convenient computationally, and is rich in implications for policy and testing. In the context of a Third World country that accepts the orientation of the New International Economic Order, we must ask ourselves, "What are the appropriate goals to be considered?". Since skilled or highly trained personnel are a scarce resource in many of these countries, it seems to us that one goal might reasonably be to maximize the total educational level of the labor force. Since many of the necessary skills can be obtained only through instruction provided by imported foreigners, the above goal seems contrary to the NIEO philosophy. It appears necessary, therefore, to modify the original goal so that we are maximizing the goal of increasing skills while, at the same time, minimizing another, the number of foreign experts (a measure of technical independence) needed to accomplish the training. It would seem, then, that an economic theory of counterpart training and its alternatives that makes "technical independence" and "maximum education" dual goals would fit the situation of developing countries quite well. Unfortunately, the real world of government decisions is not this simple. We believe that, while the scarcity of expertise is a major element in planning educational goals, it need not be thought to dominate every decision in this area.

Our claim is more subtle than simple dominance. First, scarcity and importance do entail, at the least, that some rationality in the decision process is thought to be highly desirable by the relevant governments. Second, the use of a formal model of optimization has the remarkable feature that all the factors that constrain the optimization can be given explicit costs as part of the calculation.[4] Thus, any limitation on simple optimization imposed by social, political, or organizational factors can be given a specific cost in terms of the stated goal. Finally, the use of a theory that emphasizes the long-term and interdependent character of educational planning helps to remind the user constantly that what is being analyzed is not an accidental grouping of individual decisions but the movement of a whole system of government and/or administration toward a long-term goal.

B. The Basic Model

The basic framework of a maximization model contains a criterion function and a set of elementary activities. The criterion is a combination of these elementary activities which the user of such a model may manipulate to reach an optimum. In our model we have three such elementary activities: three alternative ways for a government to increase the skills of its labor force, or to produce its demand level of services, or both. For purposes of exposition, we shall develop the model concentrating primarily on the goal of "Technical Independence" and indicating only briefly the impact of the maximum training goal.

There are two well-known training methods to consider. The traditional method of increasing skills is to use a formal educational setting (e.g., 4 year college, postgraduate degree work). An alternative method is to use learning-by-doing or on-the-job training. Skilled foreigners can be imported to provide this kind of training. The two techniques are mutually exclusive for an individual once he/she enters a particular program for a particular period of time. For a nation seeking to augment its skill reserve, however, the two techniques can be used in any combination feasible under scheduling constraints.

Making use of these two training techniques a ministry, taking into account its required workload, will attempt, under the goal of self-reliance, to reduce its dependence upon foreign personnel. That is, a ministry has as its goal in this simplified form of our model the minimization of foreign "experts" (Z). We must introduce the "time" concept at this point, in order to know at what time foreign personnel are to be a minimum. Various answers or goals may be offered here (e.g., immediately, continuously, after some stated time

We assume that some equivalence in productivity can be drawn between the three groups. For example, we will assume that two counterpart training periods each of six months duration are equivalent to one year of formal educational training and that a national who obtains a "Ph.D." (the highest level of skill) is equivalent to a foreigner. We need not further distinguish the sources of skills. Each training level has associated with it a particular productivity level in terms of the measured workload of the ministry (denoted by the symbol a(K) for the kth category of indigenous personnel, and by the symbol a(k) for foreign advisors who are at the highest level, k = K).[5] For this particular exercise, we assume that two counterpart levels (i.e., two short courses) are equivalent to one formal education training level (a year's schooling), while six counterpart or three formal education training levels are the same (in terms of productivity) as a Ph.D. (foreign or domestic).[6]

Given a productivity measure for each class of training we describe the output of the ministry by summing the products of class productivity and the number of members in each class as follows: Output = output of foreigners + output of local personnel. The measurement problem is more complex than this equation would indicate. First, we must realize that, if any training is occurring during the tth period, the productivity of both the indigenous and foreign personnel will be affected. In the case of formal training, anyone in school will be unavailable for work, while in the case of counterpart training some production losses will occur because of time spent by both the "expert" and the "counterpart" teaching and learning, respectively. Consequently, we have to take careful account of the facts that: (i) training takes time; (ii) the effects of training on productivity are felt after training is completed; and (iii) training at any level presupposes that the student or participant is already trained up to the necessary prior level.

We take account of all these complexities as follows. First, we date the level of training. For example, $F(t,k)$ means the number of indigenous personnel trained up to the equivalent of k counterpart courses as of the end of the tth period. Second, we assume that output productivity during the tth period is determined by the level of training achieved by the end of the prior period. Hence, the productivity in period t of those who achieved k-level training as of the end of $t-1$ is measured by $a(k)$. The sum of their contributions to the workload of period t over all training levels is $\sum_k a(k)F(t,k)$.[7] Third, we denote by $u_t(k-1,k)$ the number of people the ministry decides to train in period t up through the kth level by the end of that time. Thus $u_3(2,3)$ is the number of people who have completed the equivalent of two counterpart courses by the end of period 2, and are ready to be trained to the third level during period 3. (Don't confuse time periods with training levels. They do differ!) People who work but do not train have the general symbol $u_t(k,k)$. Now, those who do not train do work full time. Those who train on-the-job do work, but only at a fraction $1-b$ of their level, the fraction b

being devoted to learning. Those who are being trained full-time do no work in the ministry, so they aren't counted for "output".

Let us sum up all this glorified counting in a formula for the possible level of work, $Q(t)$:

$$Q(t) = \sum_{k=0}^{K} a(k)u_t(k,k) + (1-b)\sum_{k=0}^{K-1} a(k)u_t(k,k+1)$$
$$+ a(K)Z(t) - da(K)\sum_{k=0}^{K-1} u_t(k,k+1) \qquad (2)$$

The work that can be done is determined by the capabilities of those available (the $F(t,k)$'s and Z) less the losses. The letter d indicates the percentage of a foreign person's productivity lost due to his/her assuming teaching responsibility for one trainee. Therefore $-da(k)\sum_{k=0}^{5} u_t(k,k+1)$ is the total loss to foreign productivity arising from the counterpart program.

For purposes of optimization, we note that a symbol such as $F(t,k)$ is not computed directly. Supposing that k is even for illustration, we know that everyone who reached level 4, say, at the end of $t-1$, got there by: (i) already being there at the end of $t-2$ and taking no training; (ii) going through a counterpart course via $u_{t-1}(3,4)$; and (iii) completing the university year via $v_{(t-1)2}(2,4)$. Here $v_{(t-1)2}$ refers to the number of trainees finishing the <u>second</u> part of the university course during period $t-1$, and parenthetical (2,4) says that the course moves the trainee from the second to the fourth level. Thus, $F(t-1,4)$ would be $u_{t-1}(4,4) + u_{t-1}(3,4) + v_{(t-1)2}(2,4)$.

period). Consequently, the goal of the ministry is not simply the reduction of foreign personnel but that foreign personnel should be reduced by some specified time and according to some path. Hence, "minimize Z" becomes "minimize Z(t) for some value(s) of t". The simplist example is to put t = T, where T is the end of the period over which the ministry's program is drawn up. We can therefore represent the minimand of our optimization model as

$$Z(T) \tag{1}$$

The "instruments" or "choice variables" which influence the optimization problem are actually rather simple, despite the formidable complexity of the algebra required for the computer model: the ministry has to decide which of its personnel to send into what type of training, and when, and it has to know how many foreigners to hire. In order not to lose track of anyone, we must interpret these options as including "no training this time".

As we have already pointed out in the previous section, optimization occurs within stated constraints. We note that in the case of a ministry the workload of the ministry must still be accomplished in face of its foreign personnel goal. We shall represent the workload or output of a ministry during a period of time as Q(t). The work of the ministry is performed by its personnel. These can be of three different types. First, there are foreign personnel; second, there are indigenous personnel who have received formal education; and third, there are indigenous personnel who have received on-the-job training or counterpart education.

To summarize the argument up to this point, we have constructed an approach to the maximum replacement of foreign personnel at the end of a certain time (the end of the planning period) by considering the options of training people on the job (counterpart work) or in formal courses, taking into account that the ministry has jobs that must be done and that any form of training takes up the time of someone who can be doing something else. The constraint that "certain jobs must be done" we characterize in this model by stipulating that the work capacity of the ministry cannot fall below a specified level, $Q^*(t)$, or $Q(t) \geq Q^*(t)$ for any periods in the planning horizon. Using equation (2) and the algebraic fact that our stipulation is the same as $-Q^*(t) + Q(t) \geq 0$, we can write our constraint in terms of F(t,k)'s, Z's, u's, and v's. Further, we can substitute u's and v's for the F(t,k)'s, thus putting the constraint in the form of a long but well-defined inequality in the decision variables (u's, v's, and Z's).

There are two further constraints that we shall consider explicitly. The first is that foreign personnel cost money (usually foreign exchange) and therefore have to be covered by a special budget. Algebraically, we stipulate

$$p_z Z(t) \leq X(t) \qquad (3)$$

where p_z is the average foreign exchange cost of foreign personnel, Z(t) is the number of foreigners present in period t, and X(t) is the budget limit for that period. The second constraint is that formal education also may have special costs, so that the cost of university courses ought to be recognized explicitly. We recognize this by counting the total number in university courses in the tth period and attaching to that number a price, p_f, the average cost of one person in one university course. Therefore,

$$\sum_k p_f v_{(t-1)s}^{(k,k+s)} \leq B(t)$$

where B(t) is the formal education budget in period t.

The values of both these budgets are determined outside of this analysis. They come from the political and social process by which the resources of the country's government are distributed among alternative needs. Obviously, the ministry we are considering is only one such need and must therefore vie with all other ministries for shares of the limited total budget. We begin our analysis after the political mechanism has divided the total budget among ministries. As a matter of historical observation, foreign aid policies have made foreign exchange available to cover the cost of bringing in foreign experts and sending university students abroad. These resources are often more easily available than domestic funds for training purposes.

So, in this simplest version (covering, in our numerical example, a 3-year calculation with up to six counterpart programs in sequence), the ministry minimizes Z(6) subject to the constraint that "output" cannot fall below a specified level, or $Q(t) \geq Q^*(t)$, and to constraints (3) and (4), by manipulating the variables u, v, and Z, all of which are to remain non-negative. This model is the one on which we shall make an illustrative calculation in the next section.

We should return for a further discussion of

the criterion to see how the goal of maximizing overall training fits in. A minimization is simply the maximization of a negative argument (e.g., $\min Z(6) = \max [-Z(6)]$). The training goal involves maximizing the number of people who pass through each portion of the training programs. The statement "maximize total increase in the levels of training" translates into $\max \sum_t \sum_k u_t(k,k+1)$ in the notation of our model. It is possible to linearly combine the two maximands. The resulting criterion becomes $\max [\sum_t \sum_k u_t(k,k+1) - Z(6)]$.

There remain, in this subsection, two points to make, both of them concerned with variations on this basic model. The first is, in our view, quite important. Each course of training pursued by each individual may fail to give him the desired skills, for a variety of reasons. These may be connected to his personality or that of the training officer or institution. They may be connected to the general characteristics and difficulties of counterpart learning as distinct from learning at school. In addition, they may be related to problems inherent in the level of training (for instance, that the failure rate in Ph.D.-level programs is higher than that in M.A.-level programs). Whatever the reason the decision to put a particular member of the ministry staff into a particular training program at a particular time does not actually guarantee that he will move from level k to level k+1 after the training period. He will do so with a certain probability, π, less than one, that depends on the cited variables so far as we can observe them: the individual, his initial training level, and the type of training are the minimal list of causal factors determining π. The notation and the mathematics of such choice are more complex than we are able to expound at the moment. Let it suffice to say for now that there have been proposals to solve the theoretical problem, and that we are reasonably confident that rational policy is still well defined. We would expect that the main consequences of probability instead of certainty about outcomes of training would be the need for more people in training, and more resources allotted to maintaining the activities of the ministry during the planning period.

The second point is that the parameters of the basic model of this section, without any uncertainty, can be varied a great deal once the problem is solved in simple form. It is quite easy to assign a real value to particular training activities, or to vary the objective function by assigning a positive set of values to activities of the ministry in each year, rather than simply constraining the ministry to keep up its workload. These variations in parameter value indicate the sensitivity of the basic model to each of the parameters.

III. An Example

One may get some feeling for the complexities of this optimization problem by considering a policy that is feasible so far as budgets are concerned under each of the maximands reported in the last section. Given the prices, productivity and time constraints, and budgets shown as data in Table 1, a "partially feasible" policy for the five choice points before the horizon ($t = 1,2,3,4$, or 5) is to set $Z(t) = 5$, the most allowed by the foreign ex-

TABLE 1

Data for Illustrative Problem

Productivity Constants	Time Costs	Prices	Constraint
a(0) = 20	d=.10	p_z= 20	X = 100
a(1) = 35	b=.20	p_f= 10	B = 20
a(2) = 50			Q*= 625
a(3) = 60			
a(4) = 70			
a(5) = 80			
a(6) =100			

Initial Conditions

F(0,0) = 8 F(0,2) = 4 Z(0) = 3

F(0,1) = F(0,3) = F(0,4) = F(0,5) = F(0,6) = 0

change constraint ($p_z Z(t) \leq$ (t) or $20Z \leq 100$). If we wished to maximize training with little or no concern about technical independence, this would enable the ministry to put every member of the local work force (12 persons) into on-the-job training. At the end of six periods, all of the local personnel have been trained up to Ph.D. level. This is depicted by the heavy lines in Figure 1.[8] Thus one could have Q(7), even with Z(6) = 0 , equal to 1200 units. In the preceding period, one could, in fact, have had Q(6) = 1040 from local personnel without using any foreigners (Z(5)=0) or doing any training. Alternatively, one could work from the conditions at t=5 to define a solution that finishes the training. That is, one could have 8 people at the 80 level (a(5)), devoting 80 percent of time to work and 20 percent to training. These 8 trainees use .8 of the time (8 times d) of one top-level person. Adding the available net output for Q(6) we have (4) (100)+ (.8)(80)+[1-8(.1)](100) = 932. As it happens, this policy would be feasible even though it represents a loss in activity from the previous Q(5) level with Z(5) = 5.

By using the revised simplex method for solving linear programs we find that the optimal solution is not the same when technical independence dominates the criterion. In this case the training sequence is one in which the four MA members are trained in periods 1, 2, 3, and 4 to the Ph.D. level and the eight BA members are trained to the MA + 1 year level during the same periods. No training occurs during the fifth and sixth periods. The ultimate output level under these conditions is 960 as opposed to 1200 under the former criterion. Tech-

Figure One

Solutions with d = .1

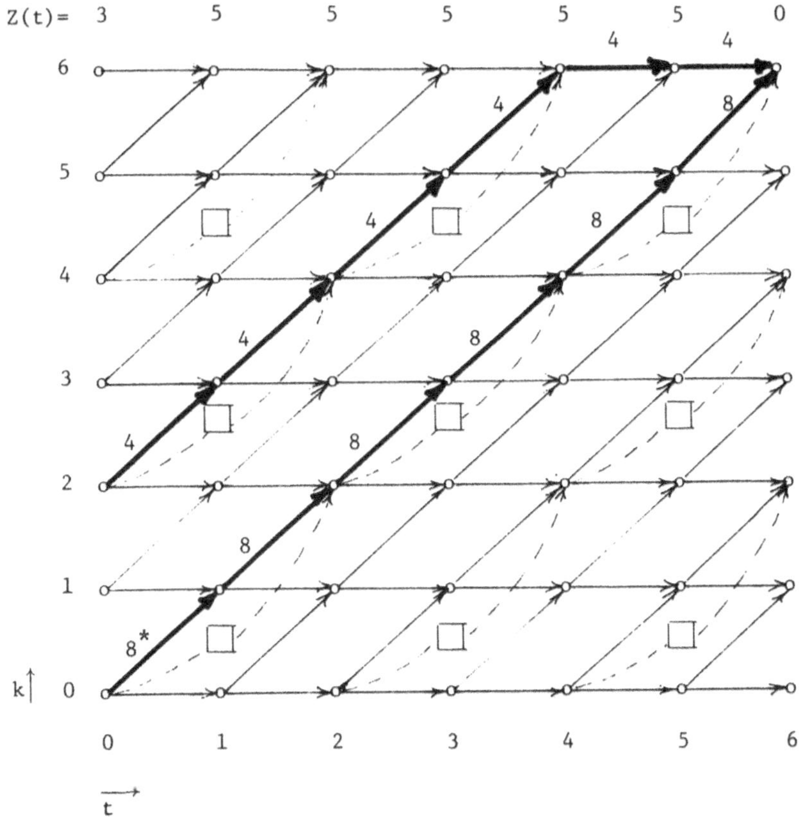

Note:

o = on the job training node

□ = university training node

* = number of persons on this path

nical independence can therefore be attained in either case, but the lack of weight on training in the latter case means that the technique does not look for added output once independence is achieved.

Another insight can be gained by considering the output costs and the benefits of training one person on the job. If teachers are foreign, and one student ("counterpart") uses up 10 percent of the teacher's time and 20 percent of his own in training, one can compute: to train one person from $a(0)$ to $a(1)$ gains 35-20=15 in productivity, and costs 10 in teacher work plus 4 in lost "student" work. There is a bare net gain of 1. The same effort to train from $a(2) = 50$ to $a(3) = 60$ is a marginal loss is output of 10. But the goal of the model is not output. It is independence. Such a step might be taken if it did not violate the production constraint.

If we change the data in this example so that $d = .5$ we find both on-the-job and university training being employed. In this case the solutions paths dictate that by the sixth period 1 Ph.D., 1 MA and 1/2 year, and 10 MA's will have been produced. See Figure 2 for the actual paths. As the time spent by the foreign "trainer" becomes relatively more expensive in terms of lost output ($d = .5$ vs $d = .1$) we observe a shifting to the relatively cheaper university method. We note that only 2 persons can attend the university because of the limiting educational budget constant, $10v \leq 20$, and that the university budget is, in fact, used to this limit.

IV. Concluding Remarks

The parameters of the optimization system

Figure Two

Solutions when d = .5

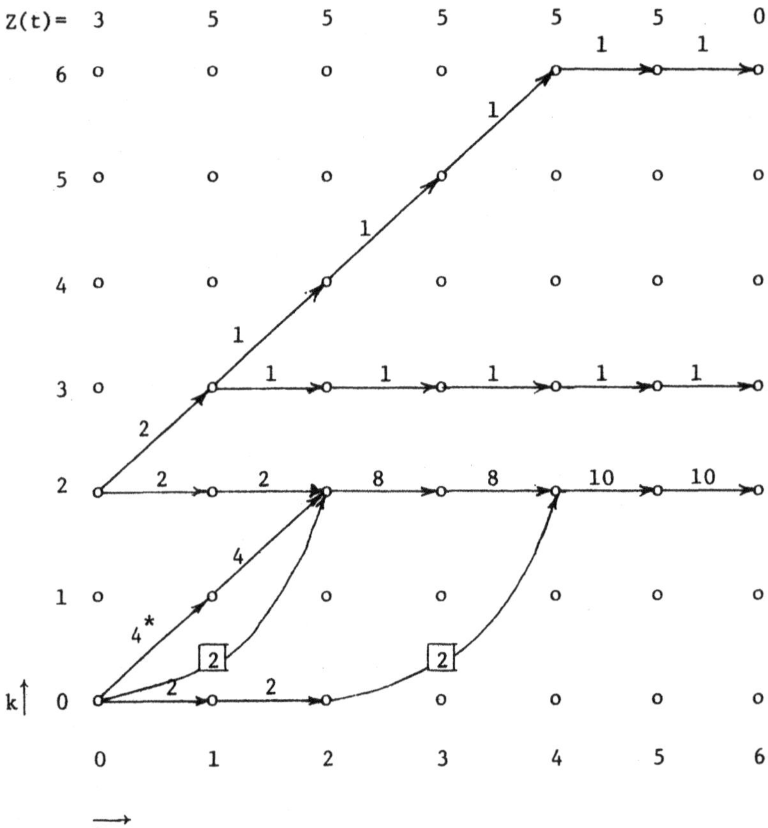

Note:

o = on the job training node
□ = university training node
* = number of persons on this path

include a(k), b, d, p_f, p_z, s, X, B and Q*. We must examine the impact of changes in these parameters on the solutions. One approach, which would not rely much on collecting data from actual practice, would be to simulate the system under a large number of variations in each of the parameters. For example, the set of productivity measures, {a(0),... a(K)} might vary from a sequence which portrays increasing marginal returns to one which portrays decreasing marginal returns.

An alternative method would be to gather actual empirical data and obtain estimates of these crucial parameters and observe the outcome solutions. To devise these estimates, two problems must be solved. First, an acceptable workload or output index must be constructed for any agency to be studied. Second, a measure of "worker capacity" or productivity will be needed, probably in a form that can be estimated from historical data. These two methods need not be mutually exclusive. The simulation procedure can help to show which parameters have the greatest (least) effect on outcomes, and thus require the greatest (least) effort at measurement.

An important assumption that needs real world examination is the ratio of the number of training levels covered by a year of university training to the number covered by a year of counterpart training. We have assumed that two counterpart training courses each of one-half year duration equals one formal university course of a one-year duration. Would it be more realistic to assume, for example, that three counterpart training courses, each of one-half year duration, equal one formal university course of a one-year duration? To answer this question, we must locate situations in which multiple training options have been taken by government agencies, so that comparisons of effectiveness are at least conceivable.

A larger consideration, which links our research to a pervasive problem of educational policy of Third World countries, is that the most highly-trained members of ministry staffs become part of a world market for high-level personnel.[9] We have not included in our calculations, the possibility that people leave, taking with them their skills and their abilities to accomplish ministry tasks. These losses do reduce the benefits of training efforts, and limit the freedom of Third World governments to establish their own incentive and income policies.

We expect that the simulations and real world testing of this model will be able to offer realistic guidelines to Third World governments, indicating the information they should seek in order to choose possible combinations of alternative training techniques in light of a two-goal objective.

NOTES

1. In all our models, every option is assumed to lead to the same kind to benefit. The options can therefore be compared by comparing the cost of achieving a "unit of benefit" by each means.

2. Haq, M.U., "Employment in the 1970's: A New Perspective," International Development Review, December 1971.

   Helleiner, G.K., "Beyond Growth Rates and Plan Volumes--Planning for Africa in the 1970's," Journal of Modern African Studies, 1975.

3. United Nations, "Declaration and Action Programme on the Establishment of a New International Economic Order," General Assembly Resolutions 3201 and 3202, May 1, 1974.

NOTES (cont'd)

4. This is the dual solution of a linear program. See: Hadley, G., Linear Programming. Mass: Addison-Wesley Publishing Company 1962.

5. The supposition that a(K) is the same for foreign and local personnel is a potentially testable hypothesis, given enough interest and data.

6. For concreteness, the reader might think of level k = 0 as "B.A.", level k = 2 as "M.A.", and level k = 6 as "Ph.D.", the highest state of accomplishment.

7. Σ = symbol for summation (e.g., $t_1 + t_2 + t_3 = \sum_{i=1}^{3} t_i$)

8. Figure One shows all possible paths of training (or not training) for any initial distribution of skills.

9. Eisemon, T., "Counterpart Training: The Applications for Scientific and Education Policy in Emergent Scientific Communities," this volume, 1978.

REFERENCES

1. Eisemon, T. "Counterpart Training: The Applications for Scientific and Education Policy in Emergent Scientific Communities," this volume, 1978.

2. Hadley, G., Linear Programming, Mass: Addison-Wesley Publishing Company 1962.

3. Haq, M.U., "Employment in the 1970's: A New Perspective," International Development Review, December 1971.

4. Helleiner, G.K., "Beyond Growth Rates and Plan Volumes--Planning for Africa in the 1970's," Journal of Modern African Studies, 1975.

5. United Nations, "Declaration and Action Programme on the Establishment of a New International Economic Order," General Assembly Resolutions 3201 and 3202, May 1, 1974.

Part III Cases and the Context

8. Interaction Between Foreign Assistance Personnel and Local Counterparts

Arye Globerson

In constant search for progress, the Third World becomes party to many developmental cooperation schemes which hold a great deal of promise; it is therefore a source of consternation to one or both of the partners when the development opportunities are not fully explored or totally misfire.

The present article is based on research conducted by the author in six African French-speaking countries in the years 1962-1975, (1) and focuses on two major aspects: (a) typical deficiencies in the administrative system of developing countries which retard the process of development, (b) the attitudes expressed by foreign assistance personnel and their local counterparts on the nature of their work and mutual interrelations. These two aspects were examined in personal interviews with foreign experts and local counterparts and also through questionnaires which members of these two groups filled in. All in all, 399 questionnaires were returned: 248 by foreign assistance personnel and 151 by their local counterparts.

The foreign experts were categorized according to the type of aid they were associated with; thus, 42% of the experts were members of former mother-country assistance programs (in our case France or Belgium); 24% were employed by other bilateral assistance agencies and the remaining 34% were affiliated with multilateral assistance organizations, usually the U.N. specialized agencies. This classification was made since it was assumed that certain important characteristics and attitudes differentiate these three types of aid, and that the attitudes of the local counterparts vary greatly along this demarcation line.

Research revealed a close connection between the two aspects examined: the experts' attitudes were adversely affected by the drawbacks in the administrative system, and the local people's attitudes were determined, inter-alia, by the type of aid. Though the research population was not a representative sample of developing countries, these findings and others affirmed similar data in studies with a larger and more comprehensive research population.

Administrative Drawbacks

The following is a brief review of the major weaknesses in the administrative system of the developing countries included in this study.

Policy and planning deficiencies are at the bottom of numerous problems and in fact, cripple the whole system. Planning outputs suffer from poor inputs and throughputs such as vague decisions and inaccurate or incomplete data on needs, priorities and resources. Insufficient data on cooperation opportunities create a situation where decisions on foreign aid are made at random, and result from the donor's interest rather than the recipients' priorities.

Over-centralization in the political and administrative system of most developing countries is another obstacle to development. Decisions and implementation are encumbered by the absence of delegated authority and by the exaggerated dependence on a small number of power centers. Although a certain degree of centralization is desirable in developing countries, particularly where unity of concepts and resources allocation are concerned, over-centralization has negative repercussions not only on outputs but also on group motivation and human growth. More often than not, minor decisions are made at the top and the rest of the population, including most officials, are confined to obedience and passive cooperation.

The governmental administrative machinery in the developing countries acts as the chief agent of development and consequently public administration plays a crucial role in the process of development. Although low bureaucratic efficiency is not a feature of developing countries alone, in the Third World it gains more importance since the less developed a country the greater the dependence on the public administration. (2) Delays in the daily performance of the administrative machinery caused by over-centralization on one hand, and operational weaknesses on the other, are pointed out by many foreign experts as the reason for their frustrated and pessimistic outlook.

Participation in development activities of the population is an essential factor in the process of growth and may reach reasonable proportions only when accompanied by a decentralized approach. (3) The existent over-centralization is one of the reasons which causes a relatively low level of participation when compared to industrialized democracies. Active political participation on a nation-wide scale is still rare in these countries (4) though some socio-economic participation schemes already exist, usually in the form of rural development associations where central and local authorities share responsibilities with farmers in local development projects. (5)

Human resources are considered by most of the foreign experts as the major vehicle in the development process. The experts spoke of variables such as lack of motivation, or the apathy of the counterparts more often than of the absence of a formal education or insufficient technical capabilities. One cause for friction between the experts and the counterparts is that the former keep pressing for an accelerated change process, the necessity for which the latter do not always understand. This should not come as a total surprise, since it is easier to introduce new techniques and train the counterparts than it is to change their attitudes or values. Despite the limited capability to change socio-cultural ecology, sometimes a false hope exists that increased material inputs may do instead. This has been shown to be untrue by many prominent researchers who have long held that the pace of economic development is set by the human mediator. In the words of Lester Pearson: "Inadequacies in human resources are more of a limitation in development than shortages of financial resources. This situation puts a premium on technical assistance". (6)

The human mediator figures largely in the throughput process of development and his importance is nowadays acknowledged by both donor and recipient countries.

Foreign Assistance Personnel

Although the population included in this research was relatively small (248) and comprised only six African countries, their opinions and attitudes resembled those of their colleagues in other countries and continents. On some issues experts' attitudes were found to accord with the source of aid; other attitudes correlated with the personal profile of the experts, e.g. age and seniority on assistance programs.

Age, Seniority and Source of Aid

Mother country aid accounts for a large proportion of the sponsorship of young experts (Table 1). These donors have developed intensive assistance schemes for their ex-colonies. Moreover, most of these countries have offered their draftees a choice between regular military service and educational assistance in developing countries. This explains the relatively high number of young assistants who are engaged in various educational functions.

Table 1: Experts by age and source of aid.

Source of aid	Age: 35 and less	Age: 36-50	Age: 51 and more	Total
Mother country	42%	40%	18%	100%
Other bilateral	27%	64%	9%	100%
Multilateral	11%	57%	32%	100%

It is interesting to note that the rate of experts engaged in educational activities varies significantly according to the source of aid: 58% of ex-colonial experts have educational occupations as compared to 22% of other bilateral experts and 31% of multilateral assistance personnel. On a world-wide basis it is estimated that 70% of French assistance personnel and 56% of all Belgian assistance staff are engaged in educational assistance as compared to 40% of the entire assistance corps from all sources of aid presently active in the Third World.

A close relation emerged between experts' attitudes and the length of service. The highest rate of veteran experts was found among those from France and Belgium; in other words, mother country experts, 30% of them had served 11 years and more in developing countries as compared to 13% of other bilateral experts and 11% of the multilateral experts. This variable when added to that of the source of aid produced an interesting dissimilarity in experts' attitudes; senior ex-colonial experts showed an inclination to advocate an "execution" type of assistance, other bilateral experts seemed to be in favor of a "joint venture" type of assistance, and the multilateral experts (mainly the U.N. specialized agencies) concentrate on training and institution building. The trends and objectives of multilateral aid are well expressed in the following passage from a UNDP document: (7)

> "Develop human resources through the transfer of skills and know-how, and through training.
> Prepare development plans, strategies and feasibility studies, together with the acquisition of basic data and information required.
> Transfer, adapt, develop and diffuse technology in such areas as agriculture, industry, health, education and other fields.
> Develop an institutional infrastructure for the support of self-sustained development efforts.
> Develop services - governmental, co-operative and private - toward the same end.
> Build and carry out pioneering programmes and experimental models using innovative and interdisciplinary approaches to development goals."

Still, in some cases the U.N. sends out execution personnel for predetermined periods and projects. (8)

The typical execution expert seems to hold views which are often opposed to the philosophy of cooperation. A senior assistance officer with 25 years of experience in developing countries expressed a view shared by many execution experts: "I prefer not to waste too much of my time on training counterparts, the way young experts do, because if I am not going to do the work myself nobody else will do it."

Such an attitude may block increased inputs into counterparts training and human resources development and may also perpetuate the dependence of the developing countries on foreign assistance personnel.

Selection and Upgrading of Experts

The key to success of assistance personnel in the Third World may be described as a balanced synthesis among professional know-how, understanding of the socio-cultural environment plus adequate motivation and personal abilities. This requires extensive inputs in the selection, training and periodic updating of the experts. Most of the experts were of the opinion that these conditions are non-existent. The selection procedures for assistance personnel are often unreliable, and at times the standards applied by the organization are irrevelant since advanced professional elites have emerged in the developing countries. (9)

Strangely enough, although all assistance agencies keep emphasizing the need for greater inputs in training, and recommendations for training appear in numerous international and national reports, most of the organizations do not run systematic training programs. 71% of the experts in the present research said that their respective agencies do nothing for their professional growth and upgrading.

In a comprehensive study on French assistance personnel, 60% of the experts complained that they lack professional information. (10) UNESCO has acknowledged that training of their experts is one of their primary obligations, "If only considering the organization's own interests." (11) Yet, in spite of these positive declarations, nothing of significance has been done.

Professional Career and Employment Security

Most foreign experts have expressed anxiety about their future professional career and job security. Utmost preoccupations were voiced by engineers, technicians, physicians and paramedical staff. The professionals acquire vast experience in developmental work but feel that in a certain sense they are jeopardizing their future career. This was most marked in the medium aged group (36-50). Most of the experts spoke of a lack of professional cross-fertilization in the developing countries where they have no professional community to update them and prevent stagnation. The experts often work in very small teams or on their own and this makes cooperation with their organization and colleagues a strongly felt need. This has been aptly expressed by Lester Pearson: "Individual technical assistance experts cannot usually be effective without strong institutional support... National and international corps of technical assistance personnel should be given adequate career opportunities...". (12)

The resulting outcome is that although experts gain greater experience they lose their professional confidence and feel that they might not find adequate employment in their own industrialized country. This worry becomes more pressing in the multilateral type of aid, where most experts serve on the basis of renewable short term contracts.

Experts who envisage reintegration difficulties in their home country have recommended a service of 5-6 years as optimal for an expert in one developing country, compared to an optimal period of 2-3 years recommended by those experts who enjoy job security in their home country. This suggests that lack of job security has an influence on the experts' tendency to prolong their missions and that they are motivated by personal fears of reemployment difficulties rather than by objective considerations.

Alienation between Field and Headquarters

The criticism voiced by field experts concerning their headquarters was quite astonishing and unamimous; it did not stop at the lines of the type of cooperation. (13) Criticism generally centered on three major areas:

a) Headquarters deficiences in planning, evaluation and supervision of projects. "At headquarters good professionals often become bad bureaucrats", commented a senior field expert. Experts feel that their important cumulative experience is not drawn upon by others: "A reservoir of meaningful knowledge and experience is being wasted", said one project manager. (14)

b) Headquarters is accused of over-centralization and too tight an interference in details, which results in heavy red-tape.

c) Headquarters manifests little concern over the individual problems of its field staff. The experts referred in particular to family problems and the renewal of contracts. A close connection was found between experts' anxiety and two variables: the age of experts and source of aid. Multilateral experts were more concerned over the future than bilateral experts (Table 2).

Table 2: Experts' Anxiety by Type of Aid

Type of aid	Anxiety		
	Anxious	Not Anxious	Total
Bilateral	42%	58%	100%
Multilateral	78%	22%	100%

A supporting explanation for the significant difference between the two groups of experts may be found in the following finding: about two-thirds of the multilateral experts envisage difficulties in finding a proper job once the present contract is terminated, versus only one-third of the bilateral experts who foresee such difficulties.

Another marked connection exists between experts' age and their anxiety over the future: among the three age groups,the medium group (36-50) is most preoccupied by future prospects (Table 3 and Fig.1).

Table 3: Experts' Anxiety over the Future and Age

Anxiety	Age		
	35 or less	36 - 50	51 or more
Anxious	12%	84%	42%
Not Anxious	88%	16%	58%
Total	100%	100%	100%

This finding is most significant since the medium aged group constitutes more than half of the entire assistance corps. They are neither beginners nor close to retirement and their socio-economic considerations are more acute.

Local Counterparts

The local counterparts are the link between assistance inputs (human or technical) and the absorption of aid. It is practically impossible to ensure constructive throughputs without them. This is now

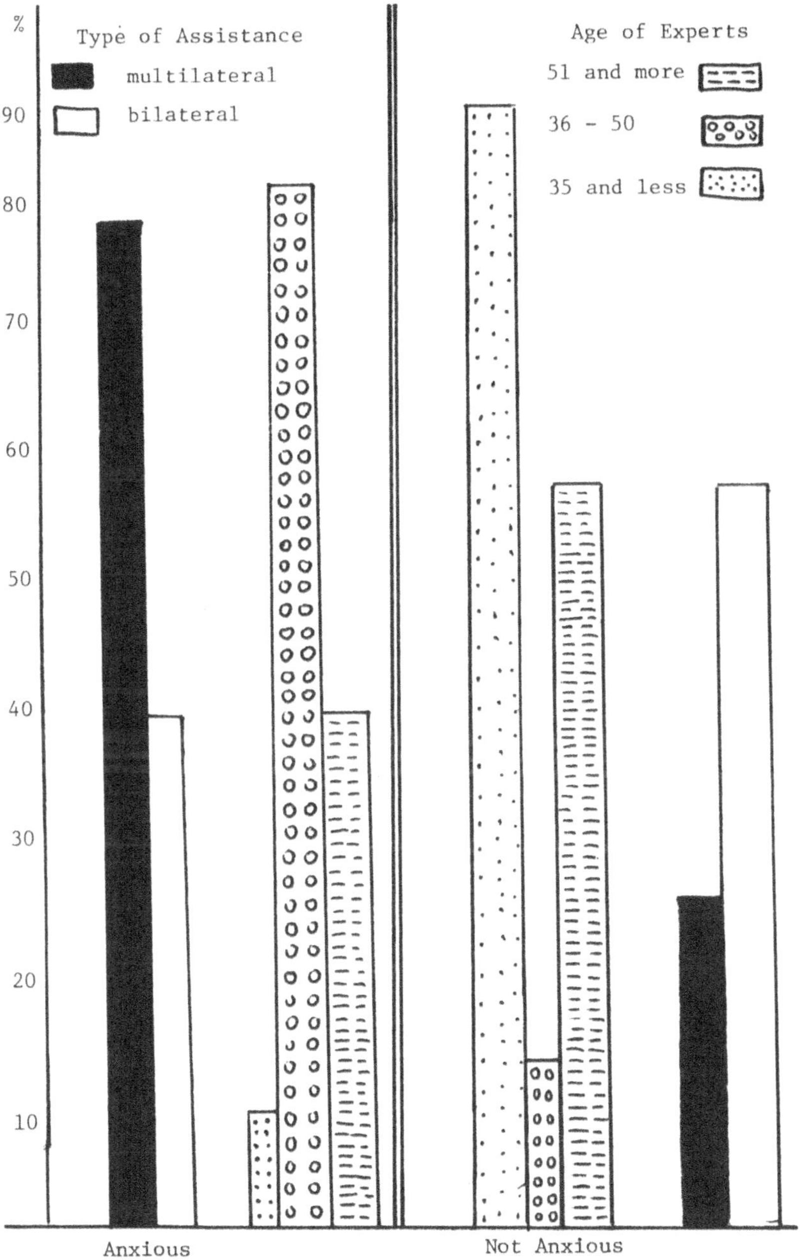

Figure 1: Anxiety of Experts by Age and Type of Assistance

widely accepted and has been learned at the cost of many assistant projects which fell through shortly after they were implemented.

Training and Adequacy of Counterparts

Experts claim that in spite of the fact that authorities in the developing countries fully share the concept of the counterparts' importance, no priority is being given to their adequate selection and training. Many experts doubt whether significant change in the near future is feasible. As a result, too many senior experts devote relatively little attention to training of counterparts. Our research revealed that the longer an expert is engaged in technical assistance, the less his inclination to invest in counterpart training: 89% of the experts with four years seniority or less were of the opinion that training of counterparts is essential, as compared to 70% of experts with 5-8 years of seniority and 58% of experts with at least nine years of seniority. In fact, the counterpart's ability to take over the functions of foreign assistance personnel makes the lasting effect of certain projects most doubtful. (15)

A major difficulty that 50% of the experts mentioned is that during most of their missions they functioned without local counterparts. Experts who did collaborate with local counterparts - whether government officials, managers, or technicians - generally criticized their qualities. The major problem pointed out by 72% of the experts was lack of interest and motivation of the counterparts. Relevant formal education of the counterparts no longer constitutes a problem in most developing countries and in fact, in certain occupational fields the supply of University graduates has already surpassed the local labor market's eventual absorption capacity. (16)

232 experts who were asked about the "major shortcomings of local counterparts" replied in the following manner:

72% - lack of interest and motivation
13% - lack of general education
10% - lack of vocational training
5% - other weaknesses

These findings show that the problem is most complicated since it is relatively easier to define and improve educational or vocational standards than it is to change attitudes, motivations or values. All these play an important part in the relations with the experts and are fertile ground for tension and misunderstandings.

A representative international study on management in developing countries (17) which based its findings on 187 ILO and FAO consultants in 45 countries, indicated that 64% of the experts were of the opinion that managers in developing countries are motivated by personal interest. A marked majority of the consultants (82%) thought that managers show no concern and take no care to ensure appropriate growth of the enterprises they manage. 62% of the consultants said that local management refrains from delegating authority to subordinates. 84% of them stated that managers do not use available information nor do they conduct any consultations with their subordinates.

It seems that in the Third World a serious gap has been evolving between modern technology and relatively backward management. Inputs in local counterparts have not yet attained the desired standards.

Preference for Technical Cooperation

Local counterparts attribute great importance to technical cooperation and to the contribution of foreign assistance personnel; in fact they esteem the experts' contribution more than do the experts. However, there were dissimilarities in their attitudes towards the types of aid. They expressed a preference for multilateral assistance. The distribution of 146 counterparts by their preference for one of the three types of aid was as follows:

Multilateral	-	54%
Bilateral	-	34%
Mother Country	-	12%

The preference for multilateral assistance should be seen as a desire for technical cooperation with a donor who is politically neutral, thus avoiding assumed political identification. This is particularly true of politically controversial donor countries. Politization of assistance has been spreading ever since World War II, or more precisely since the fifties and the sixties. The reluctance or preference of many developing countries to foster steady technical cooperation has in fact very little to do with the substance or quality of the aid; it is being primarily subordinated to local, regional or global political considerations. Thus, the growing preference for multilateral cooperation should be seen as part of this process, since it is chosen in spite of the fact that it entails a lengthy and tiresome process, beginning with the submission of a formal request and followed by a lapse of 3-4 years before the project is implemented.

The tendency to minimize cooperation with the mother country was generally expressed by counterparts as suspicion of "neo-colonialism". This attitude is strongly supported by certain ideologies widely spread in both developing and industrialized countries. Counterparts who were in favor of this type of cooperation (12%) pointed out that this source of aid is more practicable than the other two, due to better knowledge of the local economic and cultural set-up.

Analysis of preference over a length of time revealed that the further the recipient country from Independence Day, the less is it inclined to cooperate with the mother country. This finding is interesting since our hypothesis was the inverse: it may result from the fact that since independence, cooperation alternatives have increased and the developing countries can afford to be more selective. In this sense it may be said that the international cooperation market has gradually shifted from a donor's market to a recipients' market.

However, the various preferences and criticism concerning the source of assistance have little impact on the counterparts' attitudes and evaluations regarding individual experts; these are highly respected regardless of their institutional affiliation.

Attitudes to Identical Issues

The foreign experts and their counterparts were presented with identical questions in an attempt to acquire better understanding of the relations between the two groups. Our comparative analysis concentrated on three major areas: the prospects and obstacles of development and the contribution of technical aid. The major objective was to locate differences, if any, between experts and counterparts, rather than to gain an objective answer.

Prospects of Development

Both groups were asked about the "expected period required to overcome present socio-economic underdevelopment". Foreign assistance personnel appear to be less optimistic than their counterparts. (Table 4)

Table 4: Development Prospects as seen by Experts and Counterparts

Progress envisaged	Foreign experts	Local counterparts
Within 10 years	0%	26%
11 to 20 years	6%	53%
21 to 50 years	36%	16%
More than 51 years	58%	5%
Total	100%	100%
N =	204	115

The majority (79%) of the local counterparts foresaw a substantial breakthrough for their country within 20 years as compared to 6% only of the foreign experts. More than half of the experts (58%) estimated that it would take fifty years or more to overcome underdevelopment versus 5% of the local counterparts.

It is hazardous to suggest reasons for this significant discrepancy but presumably it is caused by the following factors: (a) experts are more aware of the tremendous inputs and meager outputs of foreign aid and are also conscious of the amount of work that has to be accomplished until a level resembling that of the industrialized countries is reached; (b) the counterparts' frame of reference is different from that of the foreign experts; development compares favorably with the state of their country in the past, and particularly with their own past situation, which has improved significantly.

A close relation was found between the experts' predicted pace of progress and their seniority on technical assistance. The longer an expert has been on assistance assignments, the less optimistic he is about growth prospects, and vice versa. (Table 5).

Table 5: Progress Envisaged and Seniority of Experts

	Seniority		
Progress envisaged	4 years and less	5 to 8 years	9 years and above
Within 10 years	0%	0%	0%
11 to 20 years	12	3	2
21 to 50 years	49	27	24
51 and above	39	70	74
Total	100%	100%	100%

The majority of younger experts think that within 50 years the developing country will have progressed substantially. On the other hand, most senior experts (5 or more years of seniority) believe that substantial progress will take longer than 50 years. It became evident that the local counterparts are more confident than the foreign assistance personnel. The latters' confidence is in turn affected by their seniority: the more senior they are, the less their confidence in quick progress (Figure 2).

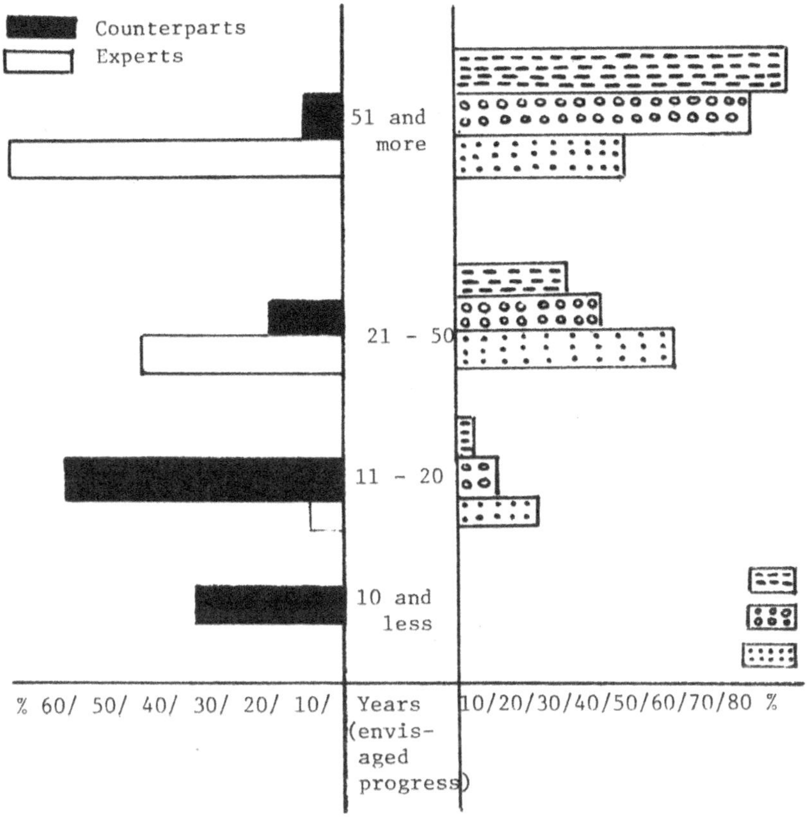

Fig. 2: Substantial Progress Foreseen by Experts and Counterparts

Barriers to Development

The intention was to find out from the involved partners what in their opinion are the major obstacles to development. It was assumed that the two groups would assign different values to the same obstacles. The relative importance attached to major obstacles varied significantly (table 6 and figure 3):

Table 6: Major Obstacles to Development

Major Obstacles	Counterparts	Experts
1. Practically no obstacles	2%	1%
2. Lack of adequate equipment	16%	7%
3. Lack of capital	60%	11%
4. Administrative difficulties	8%	23%
5. Human resources obstacles	7%	56%
6. Other	7%	2%
	100%	100%

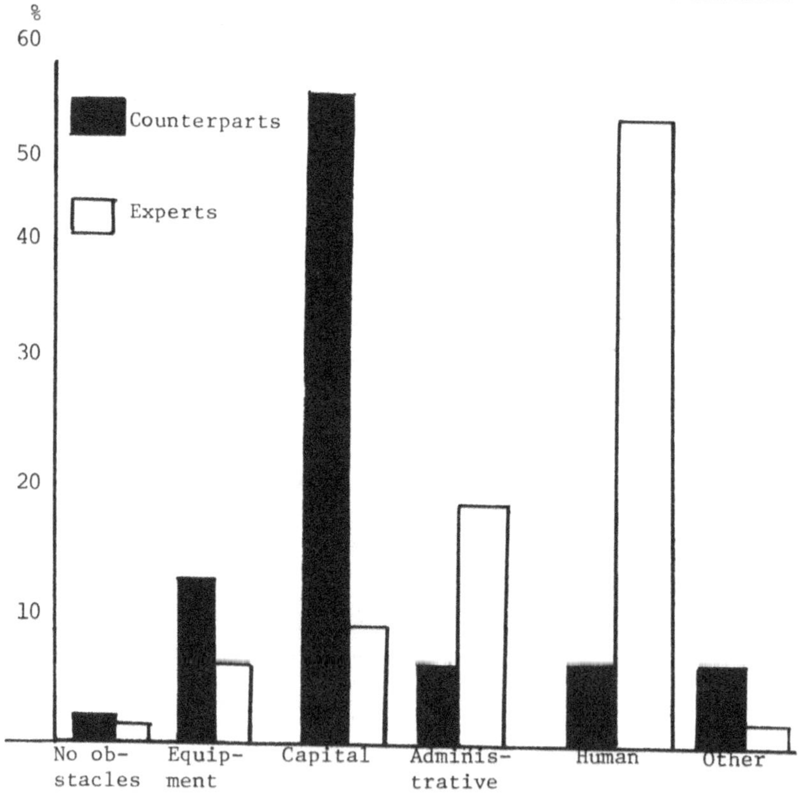

Fig. 3: Principal obstacles to development as seen by the experts and their counterparts

The gap between the two groups is remarkable: only 15% of the local counterparts pointed to human and administrative drawbacks as major obstacles to development, as compared to 79% of foreign experts. 76% of the local counterparts believed that lack of capital and equipment is the worst obstacle to development, versus only 18% of the foreign experts.

These dissimilarities, which reveal a fundamental conceptual gap between the two groups, are ample ground for misunderstanding between the parties. Beneficiaries usually orientate their requests towards increased material inputs while donors claim that the major barriers to development are in the administrative system and in the human factor.

The contribution of technical assistance to development

Experts and counterparts do not see eye to eye on certain phenomena of technical cooperation but both groups agree that motivations for technical cooperation may be of a political, military, economic or humanitarian nature. Thus the establishment or break-up of technical cooperation may be decided upon regardless of the quality of the assistance. When the donor's political leanings and intentions are well known, his chances of establishing or being rejected as a technical cooperation partner are more definite. These chances may fluctuate according to changes in political orientation on the part of the recipient as well as the donor, due to national, regional or global changes.

When experts and counterparts were asked to attribute motives for bilateral and multilateral aid, significant differences between the two groups were evident (Table 7).

Table 7: Principal Motives for Cooperation by Local Counterparts* and Foreign Experts

Type of aid	Motives: Humanitarian		Political		Economic		Guilt	
	CP*	Expert	CP	Expert	CP	Expert	CP	Expert
Bilateral (including mother country)	11	23	19	30	39	39	31	8
Multilateral	83	68	4	20	4	9	9	3

Evidently the majority in both groups (68% and 83%) agreed that multilateral assistance is motivated by humanitarian objectives. As for bilateral assistance, only 11% of the counterparts believed that donors' motives were humanitarian while 58% named political or economic motives. An interesting finding is that nearly a third of the counterparts (31%) claimed that guilt was the major motive behind bilateral aid to the Third World.

The political attitudes towards the types of aid are not extended to assistance personnel: they are evaluated by the counterparts according to their achievements.

Still, many experts expressed a reluctance to serve in their country's ex-colonies. As one senior expert said: "I prefer not to be called a neo-colonialist."

The contribution of assistance personnel to development is generally highly praised by the local counterparts, more so than by the experts (Table 8).

Table 8: Experts' Contribution to Development

Contribution	Experts' Opinion	Counterparts' Opinion
Essential	10%	41%
Necessary	24%	46%
Helpful	43%	12%
Insignificant	16%	1%
Unnecessary	7%	0%
Total	100%	100%
N =	205	121

87% of the counterparts saw the experts' contribution as essential or necessary while only 34% of the experts were of the same opinion. The evaluation gap probably has its root in the different expectations of the two groups. A similar finding was revealed in an international study comprised of a sample of 445 local and foreign cooperation personnel engaged in social promotion programs in 13 developing countries in Africa, Latin-America, Asia and the Middle East. (18) Local counterparts described projects as "successful" more often than did foreign staff: 26% of the foreign experts estimated projects as "very successful" as compared to 46% of the counterparts.

* * *

This research reveals several important findings concerning foreign experts and local counterparts.

a) Politization of international technical co-operation has introduced variables which are irrelevant to the quality of assistance. This is one of the reasons for the preference in the Third World for multilateral aid or bilateral aid from politically neutral donors.

b) Many experts experience anxiety concerning their professional and occupational career, and most donors and assistance agencies have not developed promotion programs for their personnel which may attract new and higher level manpower.

c) Since the level of manpower in the developing countries is rising, it is necessary that multilateral and bilateral aid recruit higher level experts through improved selection procedures and that they increase inputs in the training of their personnel.

d) The availability of capable counterparts still remains a difficult and unresolved problem in most developing countries and results in the dependence of projects on employment of foreign experts. Though in principle the importance of this aspect is recognized by the recipient countries, it remains an acute problem.

e) The attitudes and evaluations of both the experts and counterparts vary significantly; counterparts vary significantly; counterparts are much more satisfied than experts with growth prospects as well as with the contribution of the foreign experts and of technical assistance in general.

It seems that in the foreseeable future there will be no significant substitute for technical co-operation, and it is therefore imperative that both donors and recipients change and streamline some elements of the cooperation system.

NOTES

1. Benin (from Dahomey), Burundi, Ivory Coast, Niger, Ruanda, Togo in the years 1962-65, 1968, 1970, 1971-72 and 1975.

2. On Absorption Capacity of foreign assistance in

the Developing Countries, see: Boserup Ester, Sachs Ignacy: Foreign aid to newly independent countries (Paris, The Hague, Mouton, 1971).

3. On the relationship between development and participation, see: Globerson, Arye: "Participation et Developpement", Cultures et Developpement, Vol V, No. 4, 1973, pp. 795-809.

4. Huntington, Samuel Philips: Non easy choice; political participation in developing countries (Harvard University Press, 1976).

5. In this respect particular reference should be made to the important and successful experience of FRAR (Fonds Regional d'Amenagement Rural) and OPEI (Office National de Promotion de l'Enterprise Ivoirienne), Ministry of Planning, Ivory Coast.

6. Pearson, Lester B., Partners in Development; Report of the Commission on International Development (N.Y., Praeger, 1969) p. 274.

7. United Nations Development Programme, 1975 Annual Report: N.Y. UNDP 1976, p. 7.

8. This is in line with the U.N. General Assembly Resolution on the OPEX program, adopted in 1958, No. 1256 (XIII).

9. Official authorities in the developing countries no longer refrain from expressing their criticism of the quality of foreign assistance personnel. As early as in 1971, during President Pompidou's visit to Senegal, the Senegalese authorities expressed the desire that French experts show more competence. (Le Monde, 5.1. 1971).

10. Cooperation et Developpement No. 40, 1972, pp. 39-47.

11. UNESCO, Draft Program and Budget, 1971/72; pp. XXXVII.

12. Lester Pearson, ibid, p. 20.

13. In this respect see for example: "Meeting of Public Adminisration Project Managers in Latin America - Summary of Report" in Public Adminis-

tration News Letter, UNO Public Administration Division, No. 48, 1972, pp. 15-22

14. This important aspect has been systematically pointed out by Sir Robert Jackson but since then there have been but meager improvements. See: The Jackson Report, A Study of the Capacity of the United Nations Development System, (Geneva, UNO, 1969) Volume II, ch. VIII, paras, 24-26.

15. The importance of training adequate counterparts has been stressed in Jackson's report, ibid, Vol. I, para. 122, and Vol. II para. 157.

16. The availability, and often surplus of university graduates in most developing countries has been shown in numerous studies, see e.g.: Rapport d'une enquete d'evolution de l'offre et de la demande de main-d'oeuvre du niveau universitaire dans quelques pays africains; Commission Economique pour l'Afrique (CEA) -ONU no. E/CN 14/WP. 6/32, 1971. On South East Asia, particularly Laos, see: Globerson, Arye, Formation des Cadres Administratifs UNDP, LAO/72/001, 1974.

17. Ross H., Boummesters, J. et al: Management in the developing countries (Geneva, United Nations Research Institute for Social Development, 1972).

18. Hyment, Herbert H., Levine, Gene N.; Wright, Charles R.: Inducing Social Change in developing countries, an international survey of expert advice (Geneva, United Nations Research Institute for Social Development 1967).

9. Experts and Counterparts: A Professional Problem

Mabel Jesse and David Smith

This essay is a shortened version of an unpublished study of the expert/counterpart relationship made by the authors when they were stationed in UBOL, Thailand, 1957-59.

The material is organized in four sections. The first two deal briefly with the setting and the interviews which constituted a major portion of the study. The third section is an edited and shortened version of one chapter in the study. The fourth section contains three suggestions for improving the effectiveness of expert/counterpart working relations.

The Setting

A small group of experts came regularly to the 'Riviera' in Chachoengsao, 70 miles east of Bangkok, to watch the boats and barges go up and down the river, along with the occasional dead pig, to marvel at the balance and power of the ferryman's oar as he shot his sampan across the current, to drink their beer and talk of their work. They were members of UNESCO's oldest technical assistance (TA) mission, the Educational Pilot Project, and they came to the 'Riviera' because it overlooked the river and so caught a cool breeze, and because it was reasonably clean and the food was good.

Usually their talk revolved about their work - being a TA expert. They disliked the term 'expert', partly because the term was vague, carried false implications and raised false hopes, but mostly because they felt so inexpert. The frustrations were extensive, the successes small. The country had asked for their help, the UN agency had recruited them to provide help, their colleagues at home were jealous of their opportunity to give help, and they thought they could help - but the results seemed so incommensurate with the effort, with the desire - from either side. Ninety percent of their talk was about this problem in one way or another.

But not only in Chachoengsao, wherever 'experts' met - in Bangkok, in Ubol, in Chiengmai - the talk was the same. Sometimes the talk was about counterparts, sometimes about government, or the UN agency, or the conditions of work, but regardless of the talk, the problem that was actually being aired was how can an 'expert' be an expert.

These experts were living and working in Thailand in the years from 1954 to 1959. They came from every major UN agency, AID, the British Council and JUSMAG.

Two of us decided to try to do something about the problem we were always talking about. We were attached to the Thailand-UNESCO Rural Teacher Education Project (TURTEP) and the Thailand-UNESCO Fundamental Education Center (TUFEC) located in Ubol. TURTEP was engaged in training teachers to both teach in rural schools and work with the villagers on community development projects. TUFEC was set up to train village workers in community development. TUFEC had been set up in 1953 and TURTEP was established on an adjoining campus in 1956 because it was thought this would provide some training advantages. The experts attached to these institutions were recruited by several UN agencies plus one from the British Council.

As in most expert/counterpart situations the experts were expected to do two things. They were expected to direct and assist their Thai counterparts in teaching students and at the same time train their counterparts in the work. The experts were keenly aware of the difficulties of their dual role and argued strongly that directive functions should be played by Thai members of staff. The Thai government rejected this suggestion.

To explore the expert/counterpart relation we conducted interviews with 18 of the Thai staff, our counterparts, and with 10 of our expert colleagues. Copies of the results were circulated among all staff members of the two institutions. This created some discussion but modified practice to no appreciable extent.

The interviews revolved around two points, the objectives and work of the institutions and the way in which national and international staff perceived each other.

What the Interviews Revealed

The interviews revealed that national and international staff were agreed on the objectives of TURTEP and TUFEC as these might be stated in general terms. However, given the lack of experience of community development on the part of most of both the national and international staff, and their differences in cultural background, the agreement on general purposes was more apparent than real. Difficulties grew out of our ignorance of the Thai language and our cultural ignorance, expert and counterpart, each of the other. We also discovered that lack of clarity about the role of the expert or his/her failure to perform in that role, or both, created problems. In addition, difficulties grew out of the inappropriateness, in Thai eyes, of some of the suggestions made by the international staff.

Language and problems of cultural difference were accentuated by the fact that English, the language used by experts, was not the mother tongue for a number of them. As a result the cultural mix, rich in variety, contributed to mis-communication. The Thai staff complained that, for a variety of reasons, they didn't know what was being said, especially in staff meetings, and the international staff complained that they didn't know what was being heard, or when the conversation was in Thai what was being said, even when they knew by facial expression or tone what the message was. Both national and international staff complained that the lectures to students, in which lectures delivered by the international staff were translated into Thai by the national staff, not only wasted time but created inter-personal problems between the staffs.

Lack of knowledge of one another's culture was a source of trouble both with respect to the appropriateness of the international staff's suggestions in the work and in their inter-personal relations where even good manners, on both sides, were affected.

The problem of status was viewed differently by the two staffs. For the national staff the problem was their own lower status with respect to the international staff. For the international staff the problem of status was that, over their protests and against their better judgement, they had been fitted into an administrative hierarchy in which they couldn't function adequately. The international staff also felt that the Thai staff attached too much importance to status differences. Of course, the international staff enjoyed their better living conditions, their much higher salaries and the various favors they received as international experts, although some of them tried in their personal lives to minimize the impact of these differences.

An important problem in the expert/counterpart relationship was that the Thai staff often considered that the proposed work assignments were inappropriate and represented ignorance of the conditions of life and work in the villages as well as ignorance of Thai culture. The suggestions for improvement by the national and international staff included suggestions for required preliminary training for both staff groups, for more understanding of the respective cultural backgrounds, a clearer definition of the respective roles of national and international staff, a firmer structure for working relationships, plus greater social contact and a more coordinated approach on the part of the international staff.

On Being an Expert

General Considerations

The most generally accepted notion of the role of the expert is that the expert passes over to the counterpart the special skills or knowledge which constitute expertise. Although this would be generally agreed to, it was not what occurred on the two projects on which we worked. Instead of training the counterpart staff, a high percentage of the expert's time was spent in doing the work themselves, not in training the counterpart to do it.

Some members of the international staff perceived this problem, but others apparently did not. The national staff appeared to be more acutely aware of the problem than the international staff. This was partly due to the fact that the shadow of the approaching departure of the expert was always over them.

It is not difficult to see how this failure occurred. The burden of work at both TUFEC and TURTEP was tremendous and the training program was begun before the Thai staff was ready for it. In both institutions there were too few staff for the work which was being attempted. At the same time failure should be recognized as failure, and firmer and clearer definitions of the role of the expert should be set out and adhered to.

Knowledge of Thai History and Culture

As was stated by both the national and international staff, a great deal of the success of the expert's work depends on his/her knowledge of Thai history and culture. We think this is an obvious truth, but one of the most common failures of the international staff, according to the national staff, was a lack of this essential ingredient. It was also a fact that apart from private reading or conversation no provision whatever was made by anyone, either in the international agencies or the Thai government, to provide this knowledge. It should also be noted that only one member of the international staff made any specific proposal concerning the provision of this knowledge.

The Expert as Consultant

Almost all the experts and many of the national staff stated that the expert should be a consultant. However, as many of the national staff interviews indicated, this was not the role which the international staff played. At TUFEC the international staff member was head of the section to which he was attached. This was done at the insistence of the national director of the institution, over the protests of the international staff. Moreover, the chief of the international staff was the deputy director, and when the national director was not on campus, which was about 90% of the time, the deputy director was the head of the institution.

We consider that for the international experts to have played anything other than a consultant role was a mistake. As a number of the national staff stated, the responsibility for the actual work should have been borne by the national staff with the international staff supplying ideas, suggestions and on-the-job supervision.

Two kinds of pressures create the situation where the international staff member takes responsibility for work as well as advice. One is the pressure to get work done. Administrators want tangible things to show visitors and to put before higher officials, and the apparently slower methods of training staff to produce these things does not appeal to them. In addition, the experts also want to have "something to show" for their work and they also often think in terms of work completed rather than training given.

Another pressure derives from the necessity to

establish an activity within which training can be given. As a result of this pressure and in spite of their knowledge that they should be consultants, the international staff often finds itself in a directive role. Then, because the consultant role is not clearly established the international expert continues in a directive role, eventually producing resistance and resentment. The need to be directive in some training situations could be met if the international staff were sufficiently skilled as consultants to know when to be directive and when not.

As the interviews showed the experts had many fine attitudes but relatively few techniques for carrying these attitudes or ideas into practice. How to be an expert is a professional problem. In the interviews with international staff, we did not distinguish between training required for work and training required for working with the Thai staff. We did this because we wanted to see if the international staff would make this distinction in their answers. We felt that if the distinction was made it would indicate that the international staff had some perception of the professional problem involved. As a further check on this matter we asked the international staff to mention the most and least valuable methods of work that they had used.

From the answers it was clear that most experts had some perception of the difference between their technical knowledge and the knowledge or skill needed to transmit the technical knowledge, but when it came to listing methods of work and the techniques for imparting technical knowledge the experts had little to offer. It was assumed that the technical knowledge would be transmitted through conversation, translation of lectures and written work, and by some joint planning of programs, but consideration of the problems and techniques of the consultant scarcely ever went beyond the conversational level.

The experts interviewed mentioned fourteen techniques:

One expert listed the following techniques -

1 - Sitting down for long planning sessions.
2 - Suggesting ideas in private conversation.
3 - Keeping a written record of discussions and decisions from planning sessions.
4 - Spelling out specifically and in detail plans and decisions
5 - Asking questions rather than telling.

Another expert listed the following techniques -

6 - Use of staff meetings.
7 - Providing each person on the section staff with a definite job.
8 - Giving credit to staff members who did the work.
9 - Giving staff members the initiative and supporting them.
10 - Supporting things staff members are keen on.

Another staff member listed two techniques -

11 - Letting the national staff do the work but offering suggestions.
12 - Suggesting reading materials.

Two other staff members made one suggestion each -

13 - Ordering work done.
14 - Demonstrating by doing work oneself.

One staff member mentioned (1) (3) and (4) above, and one other staff member mentioned (6) above. Three staff members made no contribution to this list.

The techniques approved by Thai staff in the interviews were (1) (2) (5) and (11).

We realize that had these techniques been listed and experts asked to indicate the ones they used most experts would have marked most of those listed, and that as a matter of fact the experts do employ many of these techniques. However, the fact that the experts named so few indicates that they were not very conscious of their professional role.

Support for the Counterpart

Another aspect of the job of the expert which is not usually considered is related to the kind of changes occurring in the underdeveloped country. The external or technical changes for which the expert's special knowledge and skills are required are one kind of change. The other kind of change occurs within the people of the country.

This second kind of change is one which is given little consideration by experts working on technical assistance programs. Although studies have been made of the social implications of technical assistance, little on-the-job consideration is given to this phase of the work. However, it is one with which the expert should be greatly concerned because it is the internal changes within the leaders of the country, i.e. our counterparts, which determine whether or not the external changes will be continued and developed in useful and non-disruptive ways.

No real internal changes can occur within people unless they are willing and desire the change, and this factor should be kept in mind when projects are located and personnel are recruited. We should also give far more attention than we do to our personal relationships with our counterparts, since only on the basis of good personal relationships is it likely that we can do the interpretative work which should be one of our main concerns. This is particularly true in educational work since education is so intimately related to the culture and traditions of society.

The counterpart is usually under a good deal of stress. He has a new job which is also a new kind of job. Usually he is not very clear about what is expected of him on the job. In addition to this he is working with a foreigner who has a higher status, uses another language, has better living facilities and a much higher salary. Moreover, both he and his environment are changing.

All of this underlines the importance of getting as experts people who are themselves very secure so that they will not only be able to remain relaxed in the new country and the new job, but will be able to reassure and support their counterparts. It is often thought that the expert who is away from home should receive support and help from the counterpart, without reflecting that many of the changes for the expert are but temporary, whereas the changes the counterpart is being asked to undergo affect in profound ways his whole way of living and thinking. Probably it should be considered part of the expert's job to provide some of the support which will enable the counterpart to make these changes effectively and with minimal distress.

Methods of Working

Structuring work with counterparts

There are two kinds of structuring which we wish to recommend -- one, the structuring of work projects, and the other, the structuring of time spent with the counterpart.

We think it is desirable to have a firm routine for working with one's counterpart. By this we mean that times and days of the week are fixed and are adhered to, and that usually these working arrangements should include what might be called 'active' work sessions when a class is taught or a village visited, and 'discussion' sessions where work is evaluated and interpretations are made.

Here are three examples drawn from TUFEC and TURTEP:

A. A formula for the preparation of class sessions used in the preparation of the human relations class sessions.

(1) Preliminary discussion of what has happened, the objectives for the next session, and any ideas each person (expert and counterpart) has for the session.
(2) Each person takes some time to think about the next session and to get ideas for it. The reason for this is that the expert who has had previous training and experience is less likely to dominate the planning.
(3) Fairly full discussion and planning of the session, taking as much time as is required to clarify and come to an agreement on how the session is to be conducted.
(4) After this planning session the expert types up the plan for the class session in as much detail as is necessary. Usually this would be a full outline of the plan. This outline is important because even though both counterpart and expert have contributed to the plan the written outline firms up the ideas of the counterpart and gives him a feeling of security in the conduct of the actual class session for which he is responsible. The actual class session is conducted by the counterpart with the expert serving as a non-participant observer.
(5) Following the class session an evaluation of how the session has gone is conducted by both counterpart and expert. After-the-meeting evaluation forms are used in this meeting, and ideas about the next session are derived from these forms.

B. A formula used in planning supervisory visits to the village. These visits were made on Thursday by expert and counterpart for the purpose of supervising students who were doing practice teaching and participating in village projects, and for giving help to the teachers who were working with the students in the village.

(1) Each Tuesday the expert and his counterpart had a conference to (a) review what was seen and

done on the previous Thursday, (b) review and discuss with the counterpart what he has done on visits to the village when the expert was not present, (c) determine what will be done on the following Thursday, (d) discuss any other matters of interest to the counterpart. Time for the visit to the village was carefully blocked out.

(2) Following the conference the expert typed up a record giving a copy to the counterpart. This was a fairly full record, providing the counterpart with a written analysis of work done and occasionally additional notes of an interpretative kind.

C. A formula used to structure a section's work.

(1) The section staff met every Friday morning. The purposes of this meeting were to (a) discuss general policies and programs, (b) determine work for the following week, where this varies from the established routine, (c) lecture on some technical phase of the subject.

(2) Work with individual members of the section staff on lectures, programs, or other matters as determined by the staff.

The three preceding examples differ in setting, but in each case the work was clearly structured. It may be that some people will think that this would be the natural way to work and may assume that this is what always happens. As a matter of fact, it is relatively difficult to maintain such regularity and form in the work of the expert, because both expert and counterpart have many things to do. The normal working habits of the counterpart are not as regular as this suggests. A counterpart often appears to hope that the skills and knowledge of the expert can be passed over to him by some kind of magic which does not require hard work.

The other kind of structuring has to do with specific work projects. Planning is always necessary, but we mean here more precise and detailed listing of objectives and actions to be taken than is usual in most planning. It is not enough to go over what is to be done with the counterpart. The whole operation should be spelled out in precise detail -- what will be done, when it will be done, how it will be done, why it will be done, and who will do it.

The point is that if we are precise and detailed in our planning we bring about serious discussion of each step. This tends to bring into sharper focus the assumptions which underlie the expert's thinking, but which may not underlie the counterpart's thinking. It is these assumptions, in both the counterpart and the expert, that need to be clarified and discussed if the training by the expert is to take effective root in the counterpart. This is not merely a question of the expert explaining to the counterpart what he thinks, but a question of working out the most fruitful adaptation of the expert's ideas to the work the counterpart has to do.

Planning is always necessary if an operation is to be successful. It is all the more necessary when one party to the operation is inexperienced in the country where the work has to be done and where the other party is relatively inexperienced in the work itself. It is important that projects succeed because counterparts, like everyone else, learn most from successful projects. Not all projects will be successful, but where failures occur, it will be easier to spot the reasons if the original planning has been properly done.

A third reason for careful planning of projects is that in such discussion expert and counterpart have a chance to explore one another's ideas in a purposeful but relaxed manner. This is not a substitute for informal discussion of ideas but an important complement to it. Without it the expert may easily run into situations where misunderstanding or ignorance will leave him mystified and confused by his counterpart's behavior and unable to make a useful contribution to the program.

Working with groups

Working through either staff groups or other groupings was a method of training the national staff that was used on both projects, but it was difficult to tell with what effect. At both institutions staff meetings were held for the planning and discussion of the work of the projects. All of the staff were aware of the value of these staff meetings as a source of learning, but little formal effort was made to utilize the meetings for this purpose and we were unable to make any checks on the usefulness of the devices that were used. For what they were worth, however, we mention them here because we feel this is a method of providing technical assistance that has not been sufficiently explored or used. The advantage is that the discussions are about specific problems that must be dealt with in a reasonable time. The disadvantage is that the problems must be acted on fairly quickly and there may not be sufficient time for adequate discussion. We tried a number of devices recorded here.

Keeping the minutes of the staff meeting can be a help in training. So that the minutes would advance the training of the Thai staff the discussions were recorded in fair detail and always recorded in such a way as to throw as much light as possible on the underlying principles and ideas. The minutes were usually circulated quickly after the staff meeting so that all members of the staff would have a chance to read them while matters were still fresh in mind.

A difficulty that was never solved was that, since the international staff member was keeping the record, it necessarily appeared in English. The attempt to have the record translated and appear in both Thai and English was tried but the physical effort required of the Thai translator was too great. Although we often thought of checking on the effectiveness of the way the minutes contributed to training we were never able to do so.

Another device that was used was to prepare written documents on major matters, circulate them ahead of staff meetings or committee meetings, and base discussion on them at the meetings. Although Thai staff said they liked to have these documents and read them, we were never able to get much idea of how useful they actually were or how much training they actually supplied.

One of us was able to establish a formal group for somewhat more specific training. This was a regular weekly two-hour session for the training of the Thai staff responsible for the supervision of the students doing a village practium. At TUFEC there was a Village Work Committee responsible for the village work. This committee was concerned with questions of policy and methods of work, but the practical matters that had to be dealt with week by week made much discussion or training on methods of supervision impossible. It was therefore suggested that the staff members responsible for supervising the students meet for two hours each week to consider, not the daily business of the village program and its administrative difficulties, but the question of how the staff should work with the students so as to train them to be good community development workers.

There was some resistance from the senior Thai staff, not those actually involved in supervision, because they felt they had nothing to learn on this subject from the international staff. However, it was agreed that the sessions be set up and they continued for a period of 10 meetings. They were finally dropped because some members of staff thought that a possible food shortage in the area was more important and the time was surrendered to make plans for this threatened shortage.

The methods employed in the conduct of these sessions were:

1. To deal with specific problems or questions raised by the supervisors and based on the on-going village work.

2. To circulate a memo prior to the meeting indicating the area of discussion and suggesting preliminary thinking.

3. To keep full records and distribute these afterwards, in both Thai and English, to all the participants. These records organized the material discussed in such a way as to provide as much insight as possible into the problem. When the recorder added other material to the record this was clearly marked as additional. The expert in charge and his counterpart prepared the records and distributed the advance material.

Again it is difficult to estimate the value of this training procedure but we think it was worthwhile and certainly the method could be explored with advantage. An incidental, but important gain was the opportunity for the expert to demonstrate in practice to his counterpart how to work in a permissive situation and to discuss the problems presented in the discussion afterwards.

Although this is not the usual practice of expert counterpart contact, it would appear that this would be a valuable way of working in some situations and should be explored more fully. Ordinarily there is an uneasy balance between being dependent on the expert and resisting him, which a little more structure might help improve. The pressure for immediate results might be kept at a little further distance if more formal methods were employed on projects such as those we were working on. The formal methods would also help to keep clear the training role that is presumably the chief role of the expert. Another advantage of working with groups is that the knowledge and skills of the experts are made available to more members of the national staff than their immediate counterparts.

Suggestions

Planning

Without reviewing all the possible trouble that can flow from inadequate planning we have two suggestions.

Developing countries are not "developing" in one aspect only and planning to provide assistance in one area should take account of others. Of particular importance is the administrative structure involved. Consideration should be given to the fact that top administrators in developing countries many times are not professionally trained but have secured their positions for other reasons. However, senior members of staff usually do have some professional competence and should be drawn into the planning process.

Careful planning should also identify precisely what the expert may be expected to do, with whom he may be expected to work, and the necessary elements in the briefing of both expert and counterpart. This will make possible the most effective use of the expert's time.

Obviously, this kind of planning requires professionally competent staff in the agencies through which the aid is channelled.

Culture

The adverse effects of ignorance of the cultural backgrounds each of the other in the expert/counterpart relationship is readily acknowledged, but not much is done about it. In our study only one member of either staff had any suggestions on how the problem might be remedied, although the problem was identified by nearly every member of both staffs.

We would like to suggest the establishment of an ongoing international dialogue for both the national and international staff working together on projects. The briefing should be a formal exercise conducted in a regional center set up at a university or similar institution. Such a program should draw primarily on national resources for in struction and should provide an opportunity for the exploration by experts and counterparts of their cultural differences and similarities as these will affect and be affected by the project. Such briefing should be incorporated into the planning processes for the project and be expected to provide the opportunity for expert and counterpart to become acquainted with one another and make a beginning at setting up their working relationships.

Training

Experts are aware of the need to know about the culture and traditions of the people they are working with, They know they ought not to dominate. Most of them think that if they knew the language things would be much better. But when it comes to teaching or consulting skills most of them do not have these skills, and many of them do not even recognize that there are such skills or that the possession and use of them is the hallmark of the professional.

We think this is a point which can hardly be ignored much longer. The expert who comes on a technical assistance mission must, of course, know his technical field. It is also essential that he have some grasp of the skills that a good consultant or a good teacher must have if he is to make the most useful contribution to the people with whom he is sent to work.

Most of the experts come with enthusiasm and a good deal of eagerness. Some of the experts have had prior experience in teaching or in extension work. There is a good deal of understanding that there are cultural barriers and of the importance of working through them. We would like to suggest, however, that as part of the orientation and briefing course provided for experts, attention be given to methods of working with people. Such an effort would help those with prior training in extension or teaching to review and adapt their skills to the new situation and would provide some training for those experts who are relatively inexperienced in such matters.

To combine such training with the orientation course in which the national staff would be involved would also alert them to the problem of making the best use of the experts and the importance of setting up the most useful methods of working together. We think an inter-cultural dialogue and attention to the structure of work, with both national and international staff taking part, would do a great deal to strengthen, not only the immediate work of the expert but the whole complex operation of technical assistance.

10. Counterpart Training: The Implications for Scientific and Educational Policy in Emergent Scientific Communities

Thomas Eisemon

Overview

This paper examines the possible outcomes of counterpart training programs in relation to the scientific communities of developing countries. Most developing countries have given priority to science and technology, partly in the belief that scientific and technological innovation is fundamental to the process of modernization, partly in order to achieve a measure of control over the exploitation of their own human and material resources. With few exceptions, the scientific infrastructure of these nations -- scientific societies, scientific journals as well as scientific training -- has been neglected until very recently. This situation has changed as developing countries endeavor to become self-sufficient in science and technology. Paradoxically, to obtain a measure of self-sufficiency, many developing countries have relied on various forms of assistance from western scientific communities. An important focus of such assistance is the training of local counterparts to western scientists and technologists.

Throughout this paper I will be using the term counterpart training to describe two contexts in which such training can occur. In the first, the foreign scientists spends a year or longer in a Third World country helping to train local scientists in a university or national research center. The second context comprises travel overseas to western universities to receive post-graduate training, typically under the supervision of foreign scientists with professional experience in Third

World countries. Both involve the apprenticing of Third World scientists to western colleagues and the consequent communication (or attempt to communicate) the scientific and educational experience of individuals and of societies, generally. In a more restrictive sense, however, my remarks will be directed to counterpart relationships formed within the framework of assistance programs whose purpose is to develop the infra-structure for scientific work in Third World countries.

The importance of counterpart training in fostering the scientific capabilities of developing countries is difficult to quantify (see Claude Welch's paper on military counterpart elsewhere in this volume). Little information is available concerning the scope and the magnitude of the resources that have been committed to counterpart training programs in the scientific assistance rendered by different national and international agencies. Nor is much known about the long term 'effects' of counterpart training programs that have been evaluated. It is usually only the tangible short-term outcomes that are assessed, reflecting the need to provide practical guidance relating to the selection, training, and placement of foreign advisors and their local counterparts. The danger in this, as I see it, is the temptation to draw conclusions about the impact of counterpart training programs from the day-to-day frustrations experienced by participants. It is easy to be persuaded that counterpart training has been a success or failure if the programs themselves 'run smoothly.' A much more important measure of their success or failure is what has been left behind. Consider this example.

In the late 1950s, early 1960s, the United States Agency for International Development (A.I.D.) assisted India in expanding its system of engineering education. Several major (primarily mid-western) universities were contracted to provide graduate training for Indian professors of engineering and supply replacement staff to the Indian universities. The primary objective of this program was to enable India to develop graduate training and research programs sufficient for its technological needs. More than one hundred engineering institutions in India and the United States were involved. Most of the Indian professors sent abroad received master's degrees. A substantial number continued on for doctoral study, either in India or in the United States. American staff were usually assigned to Indian universities for one academic year. Given the scope of the program, especially the involvement of so many different layers of governmental and educational authority, and the 'cultural distance' between India and the United States, it is not surprising that there were many problems. Indian professors sent to American universities for graduate training 'adjusted' only with great difficulty. Encountering another educational system whose structure, organization and 'style' was substantially different, they experienced considerable anxiety. Entirely new coping skills had to be acquired. There was considerable anxiety on the part of American academics as well. Indian universities operate very differently than American ones as most American professors discovered. One American professor describing his frustrations, gave this pessimistic report:

> I have serious doubts about my accomplishments during the previous year...I doubt that real assistance could be given to the Mechanical Engineering Department at N- University for many reasons. First, the syndicate (governing board) controls the University to such an extent that school officials seem to have little or no control over the destiny of the school. This is particularly onerous at the department head level. The allocation of funds for equipment and setting of salaries are beyond his control. The slowness with which things move is discouraging. Second, there is little intelligent atmosphere. The offices, classrooms and laboratories are all closed at 4:30 p.m. I even had great difficulty obtaining a key. There is no encouragement for research and practically no equipment with which to conduct research. A few people have written papers recently, but such work is done almost surreptitiously. Third...the external examining system is detrimental not only in its effect on the morality of the classroom teacher, but also on any change in course content. The possibilities of establishing a sound graduate program are remote because the undergraduate program is too weak. This (is due to) student concentration on external examinations where they know pretty well what will be covered, rather than concentration on the body of knowledge necessary for competence in the field. (1)

The report prepared in 1962 goes on for several pages in this vein. It is fairly representative of many I read in connection with a study of American-educated Indian engineering professors in 1972. (2) During the course of the study I visited N- University and interviewed several members of the department of mechanical engineering who had been educated in the United States. A great deal had changed since the American advisors departed in 1965. The decision-making structure was no longer as hierarchical as it had been. Department heads, for example, had more responsibility for laboratory purchases and staff recruitment and promotion. In contrast to previous practice, the department headship was made a rotating, elective office. Research was being encouraged. Junior staff, many of whom held Ph.D's from American universities complained of a 'publish or perish' syndrome. The system of external examination whereby professors from other universities are invited to independently assess the written and oral work of graduating students, remained but, in 1972, internal examiners assigned more than 50 percent of the examination marks. Moreover, the structure of the undergraduate program had been transformed. Instruction was organized on a semester basis. Electives were introduced. In 1966, graduate programs were established and four years later the Ph.D. degree was offered. Doctoral and master's studies were based on course work as well as research. In short, the nature of academic life in this department had been substantially altered, largely, I think, under the influence of the American Assistance program.

The role of counterpart training in communicating professional and educational norms and practices from scientific communities in developing countries to those in the developing world is the focus of the present discussion. The first of the two following sections treat the impact of counterpart training on scientific and technological research among academics in emergent scientific communities. The second section explores the ways in which the organization of scientific and technological education in Third World countries may be influenced by assistance programs. It should be noted at the outset that this paper is explanatory in nature, intended to draw attention to the implications of counterpart training for emergent scientific communities.

The Impact of Counterpart Training on Scientific and Technological Research

The Third World's share of world scientific research has increased exponentially in the past two decades, (3) indicating the importance attached in the science policies of these countries, to stimulating scientific research. In order to develop their capabilities for scientific research, it has been noted, most developing countries have relied in varying degrees on foreign assistance and counterpart training. Such assistance has taken several forms: stipends to scientists for graduate study abroad; funds for purchase of scientific equipment and the establishment of laboratories; direct subsidies to local scientific journals and professional societies; the use of foreign scientists and technologists to organize and direct local research efforts.

The impact of foreign scientific assistance on Third World scientific communities will depend on many factors. Certainly the size, scope, duration, coordination, and degree of 'follow-through' of assistance programs are among the most aalient factors. (4) Equally important are the characteristics of the 'recipient' scientific community: its size, its recency, its scientific priorities, etc. (5) A great deal has been written about the distortions foreign scientific assistance may introduce insofar as the nature of scientific work in Third World countries is concerned. It is widely held, for instance, that foreign assistance promotes "inappropriate" scientific and technological research and perpetuates dependence--political and economic as well as scientific--on the developed world. (6) Let us examine some of the ways in which foreign scientific assistance, specifically counterpart training, may influence scientific activity in emergent scientific communities.

The communication of the normative obligation to contribute to scientific knowledge (7) is perhaps one of the most significant albeit most obvious outcomes of foreign assistance. Throughout many parts of the Third World, science and technology have been developed primarily through the structure of higher education. Universities extablished during the colonial period were seldom created to become centers of research. (8) Their primary and indeed often, only, function was instruction at the undergraduate level. Today universities in many developing countries are taking on new functions in the area of graduate training and research. (9)

Foreign training may play an important role in this connection by imparting the belief that scientific research is a necessary function of higher education and a professional obligation of those working in universities. The contribution of foreign scientists serving in advisory capacities to scientific research in many Third World countries is very visable. In Kenya, for instance, foreign scientists account for nearly a third of all scientific papers produced in that country in 1975 (most of these in collaboration with local colleagues). (10) Although the deference which expatriate scientists once automatically enjoyed has passed, the foreign scientist's membership in a scientific community of a more developed country still conveys prestige. In countries where the traditions of academic life have not favored research, the foreign scientist offers an alternative role model, potentially of much attractiveness to local counterparts seeking to relate themselves professionally to a 'world' scientific system.

The communication of research norms and skills is of course an explicit objective of study abroad inasmuch as, in science and technology at least, most foreign training is undertaken at the graduate level. But the exposure of the Third World scientists and technologists to Western universities is of a special kind. The institutions to which Third World scientists are sent for training generally are known internationally for their pre-emminence in scientific and technological research. Thus, contact with western science and technology is with those segments which best exemplify the tradition of the academic scientist as an active researcher. Since training abroad certifies the Third World scientist's competence vis-a-vis western science and to the extent that foreign certification carries with it prestige, those who return may promote scientific research by their example. Their status within the local scientific community and in the larger international context may be derived from and re-affirmed by their commitment to research. Like the foreign scientist, they may become professional referrants for others.

I examined the influence of foreign study on life-time research productivity in my study of Indian engineering professors. Over three-fourths of the American-educated engineers had published. (11) While the amount of published research was not prodigious by the standards of some American engineering institutions, most produced one publication a year. I compared this group to a sample of Indian engineering professors who had received all of their graduate training in India and were similar to the returnees with respect to age, highest degree and institutional affiliation. Interestingly, the lifetime productivity of the two groups did not vary significantly (although in absolute terms those who had received training in the United States were somewhat more productive). (12) The explanation for this, I felt, lay not in the 'demoralization' of American returnees but in the permeation of the Indian engineering community with American academic norms, among them, the normative obligation to conduct research. This explanation seemed to be supported by the high priority which both American- and Indian-educated engineering professors assigned to research. Both groups gave it the same importance accorded teaching. In light of the teaching tradition of Indian universities, this is a fundamental change in the way in which Indian academic engineers see themselves professionally. It is likely that one outcome of the American assistance program, therefore, was the introduction of research as an integral professional activity of the academic engineer, an activity that is still largely unrecognized in the allocation of 'rewards' in many Indian universities.

Foreign scientific assistance, in addition to instilling the normative obligation to conduct research, may be instrumental in transmitting certain notions regarding appropriate subjects of scientific inquiry and the most productive forms of organizing and conducting scientific research. This is a subject of much controversy. It is argued that foreign counterpart training in Third World countries has the effect of stimulating scientific work that is inconsistent with local needs, conditions, and priorities. (13) The influence of Western science on Third World scientific research is evident in many ways: in the amount of research published by Third World scientists that finds it way into Western scientific publications; the establishment of scientific research institutions with facilities on par with those existing in more developed countries; in the prevalence of teamwork as the predominant mode of organizing scientific research, etc. Yet the role of foreign assistance in shaping the nature of scientific activity in emergent scientific communities is not transparent for two reasons.

First, foreign study does not necessarily encourage attachment to the research concerns of developed countries. The training received by Third

World scientists abroad may be structured in recognition of the conditions they will encounter on their return. Such students may be discouraged from pursuing research interests which appear to be inappropriate or unsuited to scientific conditions in their country. Moreover, evidence of the preoccupation among foreign-educated Third World scientists with obtaining international recognition for their research is somewhat lacking. Most of the academic engineers I studied in India--those trained abroad as well as those trained in India--had published less than 20 percent of their research in international journals. (14) None had published exclusively abroad. It is thus difficult to conclude that among the long-term effects of foreign study is an obsession with international standards of scientific recognition.

Second, it is doubtful that many foreign scientists in developing countries make a serious effort to replicate the environment for scientific work to which they are accustomed. After all, few hope to advance their scientific careers in a developing country. From the point of view of western scientists, assignment abroad is often an impediment to professional advancement in a western scientific community. On the other hand, assignment abroad is often viewed as an unique opportunity to do a different kind of scientific work for different, possibly more meaningful, professional rewards. In my experience, it is the foreign scientist who is the most sensitive to local needs, conditions and aspirations, and the least concerned with carrying out research likely to obtain international recognition, and with procuring the latest, highly sophisticated laboratory equipment.

To the extent that foreign advisors may be instrumental in transmitting the research concerns of developed countries, I suggest that this is more often a latent outcome, inconsistent with the intentions of those providing assistance. From the point of view of local counterparts, foreign scientists encouraging their colleagues in developing countries to forsake recognition from abroad in favor of making a more tangible contribution to their country's development may be perceived as patronizing. The perhaps well-intentioned advice of foreign scientists is easily seen as advocacy of 'second class' science and technology. It is insensitive to the aspirations of Third World scientists for a greater share of international scientific recognition.

To summarize this discussion, foreign scientific

assistance may play a very important role in Third World scientific research. The influence of foreign counterpart training is probably most apparent in shaping the role of definitions of the Third World scientist, specifically, in imparting the normative obligation to conduct scientific research. Foreign scientists and those trained abroad may provide models to others in this regard. The influence of foreign assistance on the research concerns of Third World scientists is more ambiguous, however.

Foreign Scientific Assistance and Educational Transfer

In obtaining scientific assistance from abroad the purpose is often to enable a country to become self-sufficient in the training of its scientific and technological manpower. Assistance is generally organized on an institution to institution basis. In the language of assistance programs, collaboration between institutions in developed and developing countries is described in familial terms ('sisterhood', 'twinhood', etc.), implying that the intention is not merely to increase institutional capabilities but also to bring about more substantive changes in the structure, organization, and functions of the assisted institution; all that is summed up by the term 'institution building'.

Foreign scientific assistance to emergent scientific communities may have a considerable impact on the educational systems of developing countries. This impact may be anticipated by the recipient country and desired as a stimulus for educational change. In the example of foreign assistance to engineering education in India, it was the intent of the Indian government to stimulate change in its system of technical education through the establishment of new engineering institutions modeled after those in the United States and other Western countries. (15) It was also carried out, indirectly, through the assignment of American staff to older technical institutions, evolved on the 1850 University of London model, which were perceived to be dysfunctional in terms of independent India's technological and educational needs.

American advisors, most of whom were drawn from land grant universities, saw their assignment as a chance to apply American educational expertise to Indian educational problems. This report, written by an American professor of electrical engineering is, I believe, indicative of the missionary zeal which many of them brought to their assignment:

> It is something of a shock to an American professor to walk into a classroom and have their students come stiffly to attention until he greets them and nods an 'at ease'. This was my greeting in the classroom in India where I worked under the Indo-American technical cooperation program. My students were equally surprised when I sat at the edge of the table in the casual classroom manner that is typically American.
>
> As I became more familiar with the Indian educational program, it seemed to me that it might be characterized as more authoritarian and less experimental than American programs. This difference was not surprising to me, however, because the Indians have been a subject people for many generations and were accustomed to accepting authority...The daily program was filled with classes and laboratory work from 8:30 to 3:30 or even later, so only the evening remained for study-time. It was customary to allow almost a month for study before the final examinations. Many of the students didn't even start to study until after classes had ended! The staff soon realized the need for periodic examinations which we established on a school-wide basis.
>
> Previously, the final grade depended almost entirely on the final examination, so some adjustments in grading procedures were necessary to give weight to homework...More time was now being given for study during the year and...the extended 'cram' period before the final examination has been eliminated. (16)

The impact of American assistance on Indian technical education was considerable. The changes alluded to above had been introduced in the majority of technical universities which I visited in 1972: changes in the method of examination (more importance given to internal assessment); in curricula (widespread use of American textbooks as well as more emphasis on basic science and mathematics, the introduction of electives, social science, humanities, and business administration courses for engineers, etc.); in teaching methods (frequent use of quizzes, periodic homework, integration of lecture-and laboratory-oriented instruction, etc.); and in the organization of post-graduate training (towards a greater reliance on coursework). Indian professors returning from American universities were an important source of support for the introduction of educational changes inspired by American practices. Those sent to the United States for study returned impressed by many features of the American educational system and with a desire to carry out a 'modernization' of Indian technical education along the lines of what was practiced in the world's most technologically advanced society. The complimentarity between the American advisor's evaluation of the educational needs of Indian technical institutions and the assessment of American educational practices by Indian counterparts was striking, as a comparison of this commentary (from a returned Indian) with the preceeding one indicates:

> In my view, one of the most salient features of the American educational system is flexibility. The curriculum of studies in any particular course depends directly upon the teacher and the department concerned. The changes in courses to make them up-to-date with modern technological development can be easily incorporated. This flexibility is further strengthened by the fact that the teacher can devise his own method for examining students. He is not hampered by the fact that he is required to comply with the requirements of a rigid framework of the examinations. The system presents a constant challenge to the teacher to improve his techniques. It is this flexibility which makes a University an institution of learning rather than an examining body.
>
> To put it in one sentence, I must say on the whole the educational system of the United States is realistic and is based upon the faith on the part of the University in the integrity of the teacher and the student. (17)

The assessment of the American educational system by Indian engineering professors was not uncritical, however. Many complained, for instance, about the 'quiz system' then in vogue in American universities. Nevertheless, exposure to an educational system evolved along very different lines, stimulated a re-assessment of Indian educational practices. Returnees were supportive of many of the educational changes which American staff working in Indian universities were attempting to introduce. The educational outcome of American assistance was not the indiscriminate borrowing of American educational practices but an accommodation of what was perceived to be the best features of the American educational system with the best features of India's system of technical education. In the case of examinations, for instance, the system of external examination was not replaced, its best aspects from the Indian point of view, external maintenance of high standards, were combined with the best aspects of American examination practices, instructor autonomy and flexibility.

The educational outcomes of foreign counterpart training are of much consequence with respect to the scientific and educational priorities of developing countries. A major focus of scientific assistance to Third World universities is post-graduate training. In developing countries such as India in which the structure of higher education was established in the colonial period and little attention was given to post-graduate training, foreign-assisted institutions, oriented toward post-graduate training and research, consume a disproportionate share of the resources allocated for scientific and technological education. The needs of institutions whose role in the educational system emphasizes undergraduate training may be neglected although they train the bulk of scientific and technological manpower. Brighter students and more qualified faculty are attracted to institutions offering post-graduate programs, further impoverishing undergraduate education. (18)

In developing countries in which the expansion of graduate and undergraduate programs has occurred almost simultaneously, staff resources are spread thinly and an adequate 'foundation' for graduate training is difficult to develop. In such countries, the need for first degree scientists and technologists may be more urgent than the need for individuals with advanced degrees. Yet post-graduate training carries with it greater prestige and students may be motivated to continue from undergraduate to graduate training without an intervening period of practical experience. Because of the priority assigned to post-graduate programs, the doctoral degree becomes the qualification for admission into the academic profession. This is increasingly common in the scientific and engineering faculties in sub-Saharian African universities. (19) In short, foreign assistance may substantially alter a country's educational as well as scientific priorities. Though assistance may enable a country to become more self-sufficient in the training of scientific and technological manpower and though it may enable a developing country to achieve a measure of international recognition, it may also have the effect of producing scientific and technological capabilities inconsistent with scientific and technological needs.

Conclusion

To review, it is being argued that counterpart training in Third World countries may exert an important influence on the scientific development of these countries in regard to scientific research as well as scientific training. With respect to scientific research, I have suggested that counterpart training may be instrumental in communicating the normative obligation to conduct research. It may be effective in stimulating research productivity and in broadening the scientist's perception of his professional role. On the other hand, I have contended that the nature of scientific research carried out by Third World scientists is not necessarily influenced by foreign assistance. While foreign scientific counterpart assistance may provide reinforcement to individuals seeking scientific recognition from the developed world, it may not, in itself, be a significant factor in communicating the research concerns of Western scientific communities.

The educational implications of foreign scientific counterpart assistance, it has been observed, may be profound, contributing to the introduction of educational changes inspired by Western examples. This is possibly the most immediate and most direct outcome of counterpart programs.

The preceding sections of this paper have examined foreign scientific counterpart assistance as an instrument for developing science in the Third World countries; it is a lesson derived from the history of science in Western countries. Today's most advanced scientific communities were in varying degrees assisted by the scientific communities in other Western countries. There were no counterpart programs, *per se*, but, a circulation of scientists from advanced to less advanced scientific communities in the West. The reliance on foreign scientific counterparts among many Third World countries must be viewed in this perspective, I think. Inasmuch as foreign assistance has been relied on to develop scientific communities in Third World countries, it is necessary to study the nature of this influence and the long-term implications for science and technology. The success or failure of scientific counterpart programs, as noted earlier, ought not to be measured only in terms of their organizational efficiency, but in terms of what they have left behind. What has been the role of foreign scientific counterpart assistance in the evolution of science in Third World countries? Under what conditions is it effective in communicating the scientific and educational norms and practices of 'donor' scientific communities? To what extent are the outcomes of foreign scientific ounterpart assistance consistent with the national science policy goals and priorities of Third World countries? This paper will have performed a useful purpose if it serves to stimulate exploration of these questions.

NOTES

1. Unpublished correspondence, University of Wisconsin Archives, 1962.

2. Eisemon, Thomas, US Educated Engineering Faculty in India, Bombay: Tata-Popular Prakashan, 1974.

3. Rabkin, Yakov and Herbert Inhaber, "Science in the Periphery: A Citation Study", unpublished paper, 1976.

4. Eisemon, Thomas; "Educational Transfer: The Implications of Foreign Educational Assistance", Interchange, Vol. 5, No. 4 (1974), pp.53-61.

5. Ibid.

6. For a review of the literature on this subject see M. Moravcsik, Science Development: Toward the Building of Science in Less Developed Countries; Bloomington: Ind.: International Development Research Center, n.d.

7. For an elaboration of this concept see Gerald Platt and Talcott Parsons, "Decision-Making in the Academic System: Influence and Power Exchange," in C. Kruytbosch and S. Messinger, The State of the University. Beverly Hills,

Calif.: Sage Publications, 1968, pp. 133-180.

8. Ashby, Eric; *Universities: British, Indian, African*, Harvard University Press, 1966.

9. Eisemon, Thomas, "Changing Professional Outlooks of Engineering Faculty in Developing Countries", *Proceedings: Symposium of Staff Development in Engineering Education*. Paris: UNESCO, 1975, pp. 29-34.

10. From data available in Institute for Scientific Information, *Who is Publishing in Science*. Philadelphia: Institute for Scientific Information, 1975.

11. Eisemon, *US Educated Engineering Faculty in India*, *op. cit*, Ch. 4.

12. *Ibid*.

13. Moravesik, *op*. *cit*.

14. Eisemon, unpublished data re. *US Educated Engineering Faculty in India*, *op*. *cit*.

15. Eisemon, "Educational Transfer: The Implications of Foreign Educational Assistance," *op*. *cit*.

16. Humphery, F., "An Adventure in Engineering Education," *IIE News Bulletin*, Vol. 8, No. 6 (1968), pp. 32-36.

17. Unpublished correspondence, University of Wisconsin Archives, 1962.

18. Eisemon, Thomas, "Changing Professional Outlooks of Engineering Faculty in Developing Countries", *Proceedings: Symposium on Staff Development in Engineering Education*. Paris, UNESCO, 1975, pp. 29-34.

19. *Proceedings: Symposium on Staff Development in Engineering Education*. Paris: UNESCO, 1975.

11. Civilian Control, Military "Professionalism," and the Expert-Counterpart Relationship: Theory and Cases from Africa

Claude E. Welch, Jr.

The transfer of military equipment, technology, and expertise has become a booming international undertaking. In the decade 1963-1973, more than $2.5 trillion was spent on military security. (1) The graph below, with costs adjusted to compensate for inflation, shows a steady rise. Arms exports, in constant dollars, nearly doubled in the 1963-1973 period, from $4.423 billion to $8.725 billion; arms imports by developing countries leapt in the same span of years from $2.217 billion to $7.300 billion. (2) Sales by the Soviet Union and the United States in 1973 accounted for over $7.154 billion (3) -- and this figure has ballooned further. Since the early 1970's the largest market has been in oil-producing states; however, even states less blessed by natural resources have sought dramatic increases in military equipment. This arms traffic is not solely a result of the new international distribution of wealth, however. Many of the sales are initiated by developed countries wishing both to cement political alliances and to insure sufficient markets for technologically complex weapons systems. Not only are balance of payments issues eased, alignments on international issues seemingly can be safeguarded.

Important repercussions--political, economic, and social--stem from this redistribution of military technology. The monopolies on costly, sophisticated weaponry enjoyed by a few powers are being challenged by increased sales. Regional distributions of power are being skewed by the fortunes of oil revenues. Bipolarity has been challenged in the new international order. But the alterations must not be viewed only in terms of military materiel.

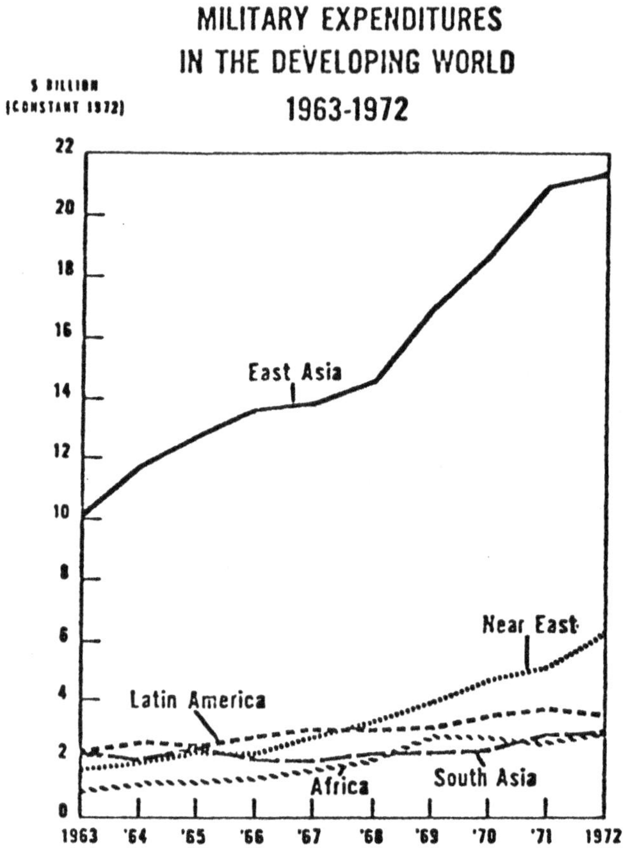

Source: World Military Expenditures and Arms Trade 1963-1973 (Washington: U.S. Arms Control and Disarmament Agency, 1975), p. 2.

Global dissemination of complex weapons systems entails alterations in officer training. New skills must be acquired--and, in the process, new attitudes and values may be developed. This chapter explores the ways in which officer training, as carried out through expert-counterpart relationships, influences values. To express briefly the arguments of this essay, a largely unanticipated consequence of military expansion in numerical and fiscal terms has been military expansion in "political" terms--that is to say, greater military influence within national political systems. The expert-counterpart relationship, intended by donor countries to enhance the professional skills and the subordinate political role of the armed forces, has led in fact to a definition of professional skills in which the military plays a predominant rather than secondary role.

I have selected officer training as the focus since its modalities and assumptions highlight a basic but relatively unexplored part of the expert-counterpart relationship. The relationship is intended, among other goals, to facilitate the acquisition of skills by specific individuals in the recipient state. High levels of skills obviously are required in contemporary military systems. Logistics, weapons maintenance, troop morale and deployment, and related issues are immensely difficult. Officers require extensive training and periodic reschooling. The more complex the armed forces, the greater the portion of the officers' time that may be absorbed by staff colleges, short courses, and the like. The usual locus of such training efforts are indigenous military academies. For the newer, more complex weapons systems, and for small states with relatively new armed forces, however, overseas training, or the short-term importation of specialist advisers, may be necessary. It is in the latter form of officer training that the expert-counterpart relationship is usually found. This relationship is intended to enhance the technological proficiency of individual officers; it may also influence their ideas.

It is difficult to distinguish clearly between acquisition of specific skills and the assimilation of particular attitudes. Skills and attitudes can be examined, or at least subsumed, under the general phenomenon of "modernization." Officer training, several scholars have asserted, enhances individuals' awareness of change, preparing them better for leadership in roles attuned to contemporary circumstances. The following quotations illustrate this general line of thinking.

In the words of a report submitted to the United States Senate Committee on Foreign Relations,

> It is possible for the army to develop a group of confident officers with modern attitudes and modern skills, operating within a reasonably orderly modern institution administered on relatively modern lines.... In all the new armies attempts have been made to introduce specialized training schools and advanced techniques of personnel and procurement. Inevitably, then, a certain number of officers and men are being trained in industrial skills more advanced than those common to the civilian economy (in developing countries).(4)

An M.I.T. scholar believed impact of armed forces would benefit change:

> ...the armies created by colonial administration and by the newly emergent countries have been consistently among the most modernized institutions in their societies. The fact that army leaders, particularly the younger and more ambitious, generally come from those trained in staff positions means that they are extremely sensitive to the needs of modernization and technological advancement...the revolution in military technology has caused the army leaders of the newly emergent countries to be extremely sensitive to the extent to which their countries are economically and technologically underdeveloped. (5)

Finally, modernization within the military inevitably has and will continue to affect politics, as Halpern argued for the Middle East:

> The more the army was modernized, the more its composition, organization, spirit, capabilities, and purpose constituted a radical criticism of the existing political system. Within the army, modern technology was eagerly welcomed and its usefulness and power appreciated. By contrast, the political system showed greater inertia, inefficiency, skepticism, and greed in utilizing the products of modern science.

> Within the army, merit was often rewarded. In civilian politics, corruption, nepotism, and bribery loomed much larger. Within the army, a sense of national mission transcending parochial, regional, or economic interests, or kinship ties seemed to be much more clearly defined than anywhere else in society. (6)

Certain underlying assumptions should be noted in these writings.

1. Officers trained in "western" technology could exercise responsibilities not narrowly confined to their military specialization, but could readily move into political action;

2. those benefiting from "western" training were presumed to hold attitudes more generally favorable to "western" objectives;

3. the political objectives of the donor state thus presumably would be well served by the provision of officer training;

4. officer training could take any of several forms, counterpart training being one. (7)

To provide focus to a complex, multi-faceted issue, I shall examine the impact of officer training, including the expert-counterpart relationship, on attitudes toward civilian control of the military. "Civilian control," as Huntington has pointed out, means governmental control over the activities of the armed forces. (8) It is a relationship in which the most powerful coercive branch of the state apparatus serves objectives set elsewhere within the government. In another publication, I have defined this relationship in the following terms:

> The key issue in civilian control is one of setting limits within which members of the armed forces, and the military as an institution, accept the government's definition of appropriate areas of responsibility. Put in this perspective, civilian control means that the military lobbies as do other parts of the government; seeks to carry out a relatively specific set of policy objectives; and employs channels of decision-making within the military that do not breach its integrity as an institution, or, alternatively, ensures that this organizational integrity is subordinated to

> political institutions such as parties. The armed forces thereby accept subordinate roles in the political system. (9)

The overwhelming bulk of military assistance to Third World countries is furnished by states marked by civilian control over the armed forces, as defined above. The specific modalities may differ--but few would disagree with the proposition that the United States, the Soviet Union, Great Britain, or France typify subordination of the armed forces. Officers appear (despite the 1958 exception in France, occasioned by the extraordinary strains of the Algerian war of independence) to have accepted circumscribed political roles. They achieve professional fulfillment through and within a framework ultimately responsible to civilian leaders. Should it be assumed that, in undertaking advisory roles overseas, such officers would seek to implant or encourage similar political outlooks? Can they? Should they?

Certain types of officer training by expatriate specialists have been explicitly political. The major example comes in colonial armed forces. Intended to uphold the power of an external government, militaries in colonial possessions were not viewed as representative of their putative states' composition and outlook. The chief objective was, simply put, to maintain external control. Several consequences flowed, and continue to flow, from this definition. The rank-and-file were recruited from "martial races," to use the British term, whose loyalty could be maintained against the lures of indigenous nationalism. Such groups--usually located in less developed areas of the colonial possession or even (as in the Nepalese Gurkhas serving in the Indian army) drawn from outside it--gave their support to the imperial presence. Indigenous officers would be recruited from social sectors whose outlook, demeanor and political and social predelictions grouped them with the European overlord. For example, those drawn into the Indian army prior to World War I were, in Cohen's' judgment, "grossly unrepresentative," in which "most soldiers were middle-class peasants; the camp followers, menials and porters, were composed entirely of the depressed classes and untouchable castes." (10)

Direct colonial relationships do not apply in most of the contemporary world, however. The civilian control of the military officers now accept is <u>not</u> control by individuals external to their political system. Their loyalty and pledge of allegiance are given to the government on the spot. To see how these are ensured, it is appropriate to look briefly at major means of civilian control.

Dahl and Lindblom differentiate three means by which superiors can affect the behavior of their subordinates. The simplest, and most obvious, is control by means of command: fear leads to obedience; compliance results "exclusively by virtue of a penalty prescribed by the controller for non-performance..." (11) Within certain constrained settings, control by means of command works, and works well. It would not appear, however, to be directly relevant to seconded officers serving in advisory capacities. They stand outside the usual chain of command and, as foreign nationals, may risk negative consequences by emphasizing penalty.

Contemporary civil-military relations and the role of the alien expert are marked more by what Dahl and Lindblom deem direct field control and spontaneous field control. The latter involves unintended manipulation of the wants, desires, gratification and deprivation of officers; the former involves conscious manipulation of these. Explicit promotion of those favoring government policies constitutes direct field control; a belief by officers that promotion will be provided only those who faithfully execute official policies, and consequent conscious alterations of behavior, constitute spontaneous field control. Once again, an expert-counterpart relationship does not lend itself readily to these forms of control. The foreign adviser, often on short-term contract, may have little impact on promotions and other rewards.

Spontaneous field control can be linked to reference group theory, applied to politically active Ghanaian officers by Robert Price. (12) Price examined the writings of Generals Afrifa and Ocran, both prominent in the 1966 coup d'etat. The two men, in Price's view, absorbed an attitude inculcated by British advisers and in the Royal Military Academy (Sandhurst) that "politics is not for soldiers." (13) In the face of major provocations from civilians, these officers remained politically inert, finally stirring into action only when the President of Ghana had left the country on an international peace-making mission. Could the deposed President Nkrumah have precluded his ouster? In the words of the last expatriate commander to have served in Ghana, "Given a little more time, President Nkrumah could have had a thoroughly reliable, efficient corps of officers..." (14) This statement suggests that duration and intensity of contact may be key variables in ensuring government oversight of the armed forces. Foreign advisers, in the presence of propitious conditions, might be able to encourage among their counterparts an acceptance of civilian control over the military. But time--a great deal of it--may be necessary. Further, the political consequences and risks of retaining an alien presence may seem too great. To complicate the matter even further, a hasty transition from command by expatriates to command by indigenes may backfire against those making the decision. Again to cite an example from West Africa, the effect of haste may be severe weakening both of civilian control and of the armed forces as an institution subordinated to civilian control. Luckham describes the 1966 coup d'etat in Nigeria in the following terms: "It was the pace at which military institutions were transferred and the structure of the situation in which this took place, rather than the failure of African officers to internalise their roles, or the lack of vitality of modern organizations in contexts, which were largely responsible... for the apparent breakdown of military institutions which took place in Nigeria in 1966." (15)

The expert-counterpart relationship and civilian control over the military should also be considered from the perspective of military "professionalism." A seconded officer is intended to transfer skills and attitudes that mark a "professional" military man; the political subordination of the armed forces is directly affected by the ways in which the military conceives of its "professional" responsibilities. But what, precisely, is "professionalism"?

Huntington identifies three constituent elements: expertise, corporativeness, and social responsibility. Expertise would appear to be a self-evident part of "professionalism." In the military context, an officer attends command schools or staff colleges, works with expatriate advisers, participates in regular maneuvers and exercises, competes for promotion (which, after all, is intended to recognize something more than seniority), and seeks to enhance his technological competence. The corporate nature of the military profession finds expression in many ways: in uniforms and insignia, special signals of recognition and deference such as the salute, barracks or cantonment life, recruitment and training that instill corporate pride. Social responsibility, as defined by Huntington, leads directly to civilian control of the military (or, more accurately, to governmental control of the military). Professional officers, in his rhapsodic description, have little taste for politics, but willingly accept a subordinate, advisory role. "The military leaders are professional expert advisers to the civilian political leaders who make the decisions.... Civilian control is thus achieved not because the military groups share in the social values and political ideologies of society, but because they are indifferent to such values and ideologies. The military leaders obey the government not because they agree with its policies but simply because it is their duty to obey." (16)

These declarations have drawn considerable academic attack. Finer, for example, notes that "professionalism" whets the political appetites of armed forces. Expertise better equips them to seize control, corporateness leads to strong group identity and cohesion, social responsibility might in fact lead the military to conceive of itself as the guarantor of the entire political system. The consequence is a "disposition to intervene" that can be translated, under certain conditions, into an "opportunity to intervene." (17) The upshot may well be another military junta installed in office. Related concerns have been voiced by Abrahamsson, whose careful analysis of what he terms "professionalization" leads to the conclusion that the greater the cohesion, the greater the potential political involvement of the armed forces. (18) Finally, Perlmutter has emphasized the corporate nature of military professionalism. Military intervention, in his view, stems largely from threats to the armed forces' bureaucratic or professional roles. Both are likely to be increased as modernization occurs. (19)

It would thus seem that what is militarily "professional" in one country may involve displacement of the government; what is "professional" in another state would be full acceptance of civilian control. What the expert had learned in his own education may be inappropriate for transplantation elsewhere. Although certain institutions may be physically transferred from one setting to another (for example, the officers' Mess), the ethos that pervades them will differ. (20) The expert can transfer technological skills with relative ease, but can transfer politically relevant attitudes only with extended time and a favorable setting.

In applying these general observations to contemporary Africa, one must also consider the circumstances under which African armies were created. The militaries of most tropical African states are lineal descendents of forces established to maintain colonial control. (21) Prior to independence, their primary duties were those of internal "pacification" and supplementation of metropolitan forces in major international conflict. Recruitment of the rank-and-file was concentrated on the loyal, obedient, and usually illiterate peoples of certain supposed "martial races," as was previously noted. Rarely were educated Africans recruited for military service, until late in the colonial period; with but few exceptions, metropolitan officers (Belgians, British, French) filled all positions in the establishment. And, even as independence approached, it was assumed that Europeans would continue both to hold major command positions and to play significant advisory roles for extended periods.

These metropolitan officers regarded themselves as "professional"--and included in their belief systems a generalized acceptance of the notion "politics is not for soldiers." They sought, consciously and unconsciously, to transfer this idea to indigenous officers and, it seems plausible, to indigenous politicians as well. (22) This essentially anti-political view could have been continued in tropical Africa only under two conditions: 1) had the boundaries of the military as an institution remained integral, thereby isolating the armed forces from pressures of ethnicity, regionalism, political favoritism, and the like; 2) had the recruitment and socialization of indigenous officers proceeded at a relatively slow pace, permitting the fuller inculcation of non- or anti-political norms. Neither condition was met. Rapid programs of Africanization were undertaken even at the cost of efficiency. Rates of promotion were exceedingly high, in the process perhaps fueling unrealistic expectations. The boundaries of the armed forces were quickly broached, as in (for example) attempts to insure political loyalty through selective promotion or dismissal of officers, utilization of the military to suppress domestic dissidence, and alterations in budgets. The patterns of civil-military relations in tropical Africa thus came dramatically to differ from those of India, where a slow, careful process of professionalization and dextrous civilian leadership maintained an anti-political view within the armed forces. (23)

Expatriate officers serving as experts confront markedly different situations than expatriate officers serving as commanders. Important qualitative differences exist between short-term experts recruited to provide technical assistance, and expatriate officers holding command positions. Until recently, the heritage in tropical Africa has been of the latter, not the former, of aliens controlling the armed forces for imperial objectives. Although some metropolitan officers won respect for their impartiality, efficiency, and willingness to serve duly-constituted political authority (whether indigenous or imposed), others were viewed by African officers as obstacles to promotion and by African politicians as uncertain servants in their quest for power. This residue of distrust has diminished, but not disappeared. It has diminished for the obvious reasons that expatriates in the past were imposed by a colonial government, and that those recruited in the present and future will be approved by self-governing states.

The growing coercive might of African states has increased the need for technical advisers. Military expenditures in some instances absorb a quarter or more of governments' budgets. Interstate conflict in Africa, despite the principles of the Organization of African Unity, has flared among and between such historic antagonists as Morocco, Algeria and Mauritania, or Ethiopia and Somalia. Increasing military pressure in southern Africa--especially if exerted against the sophisticated armaments of the Republic of South Africa--will likely expand the role of expatriate military experts.

Major changes in the source of such experts can be foreseen. The closeness of the colonial connection (including equipment provision) made the former metropolitan powers the usual initial sources of advisers--save, of course, in cases of grave political rupture. But there were political costs involved, and by the 1960s officers from Canada, India, Pakistan and (until 1972-3) Israel supplemented the efforts of the former colonial countries. United States military aid has widened far beyond Ethiopia and Liberia, to which the overwhelming portion of assistance was given well into the 1960s; on the other hand, American reaction to the Vietnam war has considerably slackened willingness to embark on extensive military involvement south of the Sahara. (Arms sales, as contrasted with assistance, pose issues for consideration beyond the scope of this paper.) Socialist countries have furnished few advisers, to African states with the exception of Angola, Ethiopia, Mozambique, and (to late 1977) Somalia; on the other hand, intensified military pressure against South Africa may well result a more prominent role for Communist officers.

Irrespective of the source of the advisers or experts, they cannot expect to transfer what they in their home countries consider "professional" behavior to counterpart officers with whom they are working. The resolves and responsibilities of military leaders can be defined only within particular cultural and political contexts. Civilian control over the armed forces exists in most countries providing experts to tropical Africa--but civilian control is not itself readily transferable. Counterparts can readily imbibe technical information; but what they learn in terms of military corporativeness and social responsibility may in fact turn them toward greater rather than lesser political involvement.

NOTES

1. World Military Expenditures and Arms Trade 1963-1973 (Washington: U.S. Arms Control and Disarmament Agency, 1975), p. 2.

2. Ibid., p. 72.

3. Ibid., pp. 114, 119.

4. United States Foreign Policy: Economic, Social and Political Change in the Underdeveloped Countries and Its Implications for United States Policy, a report submitted to the United States Senate Committee on Foreign Relations by the Center for International Studies, Massachusetts Institute for Technology, 1960; reprinted in Claude E. Welch, Jr., ed., Political Modernization (Belmont: Duxbury Press, 1971), pp. 38-9.

5. Lucian W. Pye, "Armies in the Process of Political Modernization," reprinted in Pye, Aspects of Political Development (Boston: Little Brown, 1966), pp. 174-8.

6. Manfred Halpern, The Politics of Social Change

in the Middle East and North Africa (Princeton: Princeton University Press, 1963), p. 258.

7. There appears to be a surprising lack of attention in the literature to the direct impacts of advisors or experts on their military counterparts. One exception is a brief technical paper, "The Military Advisor as Defined by Counterparts," by Dean K. Froelich, presented in 1969 at the 15th annual Army Human Factors Research and Development Conference (Fort Ord, California). Based on a pilot study carried out in the Republic of Korea, Froelich emphasized the importance of motivations, knowledge and skills of advisors that elicit cooperation from their counterparts. Among the factors identified were trustworthiness, enthusiasm, competence, social sensitivity, thoughtfulness, and sincerity. Presumably the identification of such qualities would facilitate selection of efficient American officers for MAP (Military Assistance Program) advisors.

8. Samuel P. Huntington, "Civilian Control of the Military: A Theoretical Statement," in Heinz Eulau, Samuel J. Eldersveld, and Morris Janowitz, eds., *Political Behavior: A Reader in Theory and Research* (Glencoe: Free Press, 1956), p. 380.

9. Claude E. Welch, Jr., *Civilian Control of the Military* (Albany: State University of New York Press, 1976), p. 2.

10. Stephen P. Cohen, *The Indian Army: Its Contribution to the Development of a Nation* (Berkeley: University of California Press, 1971), p. 54-5.

11. Robert A. Dahl and Charles E. Lindblom, *Politics, Economics, and Welfare* (New York: Harper & Row, 1953), p. 106.

12. Robert M. Price, "A Theoretical Approach to Military Rule in New States: Reference Group Theory and the Ghana Case," *World Politics* XXIII, 3 (April 1971), pp. 399-430.

13. Sharp criticism for Price's theory can be drawn from the case of Nigeria. In the first coup d' etat of 1966, the overwhelming majority of the inner circle of conspirators came from the same

group trained at Sandhurst. The links forged by the two-year course in England were, in Luckham's words, "especially powerful." What was accepted by British officers in their own domestic context may not, in the views of Nigerian officers back home, have been equally applicable. For details, see Robin Luckham, The Nigerian Military: A Sociological Analysis of Authority and Revolt 1960-67 (Cambridge: Cambridge University Press, 1971), esp. pp. 132ff. From Luckham's careful work, it seems obvious that by far the most reference group is not expatriate officers but peers in age, rank and ethnic/national background.

14. Major-General H.T. Alexander, African Tightrope: My Two Years as Nkrumah's Chief of Staff (London: Pall Mall, 1965), p. 22.

15. Luckham, The Nigerian Military, p. 4.

16. Huntington, "Civilian Control of the Military," p. 381.

17. S.E. Finer, The Man on Horseback (London: Pall Mall, 1962).

18. Bengt Abrahamsson, Military Professionalization and Political Power (Beverly Hills: Sage, 1972).

19. Amos Perlmutter, The Military and Politics in Modern Times: On Professionals, Praetorians, and Revolutionary Soldiers (New Haven: Yale University Press, 1977), p. 281.

20. See, as examples, Luckham, The Nigerian Military, pp. 83-197 and Valerie Plave Bennett, "The Intransferability of Patterns of Civil Military Relations: The Case of Ghana" (Buffalo: Council on International Studies, State University of New York at Buffalo, 1973).

21. W.F. Gutteridge, The Military in African Politics (London: Methune, 1969).

22. A major example of such a view came in President Nkrumah's passing-out speech to cadets of the Ghana Military Academy in 1961:

> You must have confidence that the Government is doing what is best for the country, and support it without question or criticism. It is not the duty of a soldier to criticise or endeavour to interfere in any way with the political affairs of the country; he must leave that to the politicians, whose business it is. The Government expects you, under all circumstances to serve it and the people of Ghana loyally.

All circumstances obviously could not be foreseen! For detailed historical analysis, see Bennett, "The Intransferability of Patterns of Civil-Military Relations," and Jon Kraus, "Arms and Politics in Ghana," in Claude E. Welch, Jr., ed., Soldier and State in Africa (Evanston: Northwestern University Press, 1970), pp. 154-221.

23. For details, see Stephen P. Cohen, "Civilian Control of the Military in India," in Welch, Civilian Control of the Military, pp. 43-64.

Part IV Alternative Perspective of the New International Order

12. The Process of Technical Assistance and the Expert-Counterpart Relationship

Khairy Abdul Kawi

The previous articles approach the subject of the counterpart system from diverse points of view and reflect different scholarly backgrounds. They discuss the subject from managerial, economic, philosophical, political, and communicational viewpoints, and reflect the authors specialization in Political Science, Economics, Education, Law, and Sociology. This notwithstanding, there are common characteristics of thought reflected in the article. Some of these are worth noting.

The purpose of this article is twofold. First, it is to identify some of these general characteristics which unite the articles, and second, to present a counter viewpoint of the relationship between expert and counterpart based on an analysis of the process of technical assistance. By the process of technical assiscance I mean all the steps taken from project initiation through implementation and evaluation, including negotiating technical assistance agreements.

The viewpoint expressed here adds yet another area of academic specialization - public administration - to the list mentioned above. In addition, it reflects special personal experiences of this author. While most of the previous authors may have served as experts in technical assistance projects in Third World countries, this author is the only one who has had the rather unique opportunity to serve both as an expert and a counterpart. Furthermore, this author, by personal life history, is also the only one to bring the combined perspective of both developed and developing countries to bear on the discussion. It is thus my hope that this will add a fresh dimension to the subject.

Common Characteristics of the Previous Papers

First. There is general agreement that there is little scholarly attention paid to the counterpart relationship, as evidenced by the dearth of literature and the absence of organized research. What little literature is available deals almost exclusively with the expert. (1) Accordingly, some papers identified areas worthy of further investigation. Some outlined, even though briefly, possible approaches to the study of aspects of the counterpart system. Collectively, the papers may have provided a reasonable list of areas where further research is needed. What is needed at this point, however, is the development of a comprehensive view of the subject, one which organizes and classifies it for further investigation, or organizes the shopping list of research topics into a rational comprehensive cohesive whole. It would be useful if this methodological problem was tackled.

Second. The term "counterpart system" has been widely used throughout the papers. The term, however, is not quite accurate given the implications of the concept of system. What is actually under consideration here is the expert-counterpart relationship. Thus, as used in this chapter, the "counterpart system" means the relationship between expert and counterpart in an international technical assistance situation.

In addition, there is little agreement on the nature, let alone definition, of the counterpart system. The system obviously means different things to different authors. Furthermore, the role or roles played by expert and counterpart were not spelled out. The result is that the counterpart system takes on extremely broad dimensions and an all encompassing scope and nature. The implication of Eisman's article, for example, is that professors from a developing country attend U.S. universities under an organized AID program as "counterparts". "Counterpart" was even used to refer to both expert and counterpart as the following quotation from Altbach's article shows:

> The recruitment and training of counterparts often reinforces the psychological implications of the system. Most counterparts are in technical areas and are individuals who have not been selected for their sensitivity to the Third World and its cultures, but rather

for their technical skills in the narrowly defined sense of the term. With the exception of certain programs like the U.S. Peace Corps and some academics who function as counterparts in the university context, most Western counterparts are motivated to participate in counterpart programs because of economic advantages to themselves. This combination of circumstances means, in many cases, that the counterparts have little understanding of the cultures in which they are working and little systematic orientation to the adaptation of their work to local conditions.

Needless to say, this is a serious terminological problem, one which deserves closer attention. For the purpose of this discussion, I suggest that we follow the common usage. Accordingly, an "expert" is a person who has the knowledge and skill to be transferred to the "counterpart". Experts come from developed countries, although in recent years a growing number of experts came from developing Third World countries. Counterparts, on the other hand, are always from recipient developing countries.

Third. It is the general view of the papers that the counterpart system is an instrument for the transfer of skills from the industrial technologically advanced countries to Third World Countries. It is not clear, though, what kind of skills are to be transferred, or what techniques for skill transfer are successful.

A more important question was suggested indirectly by Welch's paper, but left unresolved. The question is important not only in terms of the relations between experts and counterparts, but also in terms of the relations between developed and developing countries, and the whole philosophy of technical assistance. Is it the duty of the expert to attempt to transfer his beliefs and values, or should he be limited to the transfer of technical skills? More fundamentally, is the counterpart system and the whole technical assistance effort a vehicle to change the value systems of Third World countries? Or, is it merely to develop in these countries the necessary skill and capacity to do certain jobs on their own and by their own manpower.

It is not the expert's job to seek to influence the values of societies, primitive or different as they may be. Third World countries do not tolerate assistance which assumed the right of the expert to meddle in their value systems. This lesson was learned the hard way early in the post World War II technical assistance game, when U.S. "experts" sought to transplant American values, governmental institutions, solutions to problems as well as technical skills to developed countries only to find these transplanted systems rejected as the body rejects an unsuitable heart.

Having said that, I must add that this is undoubtedly a very difficult question. It requires, among other things, a precise definition and understanding of what we mean by values and beliefs. This then is another area where more needs to be done in identifying what is appropriate for the expert to insure his effectiveness and the success of his mission.

Fourth. With probably one exception, the papers reflect an outmoded ethnocentric view of the relations between developed and developing countries. Discussions of foreign aid, technical assistance, and the counterpart system, are presented in terms of the relations between the industrialized West and Third World countries. The authors' conclusions and lessons are generalizations based primarily on U.S. experience with foreign aid and technical assistance. No attempt was made to study, in a scientific organized fashion, the experiences of other Western or Eastern countries to find out if they do or do not confirm the American experience.

Furthermore, this ethnocentricity seems to have ideological overtones. How else can one explain the absence of any reference to the experiences of experts from non-capitalist industrialized countries. The only modest exception is Altbach's paper where, in trying to prove that foreign aid is tied to the donor country's policy goals, he say that:

> the governments of capitalist countries will not usually be interested in supporting public sector projects where private sector efforts are available.... By the same token, foreign aid provided by the Soviet Union or China generally goes to public sector enterprises...

Parenthetically, Altbach's conclusion is not supported by actual practice. For decades, AID provided technical assistance for various areas of public administration and administrative development activities in governments of developing countries. In fact, AID was a champion in support of aid to public administration and public enterprises in Third World countries.

Fifth. Most of the papers subscribe, directly or indirectly, to the notion that the colonial relationship of decades past still play a dominant role in today's foreign aid and technical assistance. The main difference apparently is that it now takes on the name of "neo-colonialism."

While there may be something to that, the papers in general fail to realize the radical change in international relations which has taken place at least since the quadruple increase in oil prices and the oil embargo. Ignored is the new awareness of global "interdependence" and the dawning of a "new realism" in the sense of "a broader community of national states working together for a new global order". (2) I will have more to say about this later. Suffice it to say now that this change, symbolized by the call for a new international economic order, rendered obsolete many of the old notions and concepts used to explain the relations among nations.

Sixth. Central to all issues considered in all papers is the question of cross-cultural communication and how effective it is in the context of technical assistance. This undoubtedly is an important element in the success or failure of any interpersonal relationships. It is, as such, important in the relations between expert and counterpart. Nonetheless, the papers seem to have exaggerated the significance of this element in present day technical assistance.

Fundamental change has occurred in international negotiations of technical assistance between developed and Third World countries and in the management of technical assistance which has reduced considerably the importance of this issue. In a recent panel discussion of the subject at the annual conference of the International Studies Association, Mr. Gordon Hawkins of UNITAR noted that the counterpart or the learner is today much more secure and much less dependent on the industrialized West. He has other sources of learning provided by the principle of self-reliance which means the reliance of Third World countries on their own resources and their own experts. A conscious effort is being made by international organizations and Third World countries to (1) increase the number of experts from developing countries, and (2) achieve a more effective utilization of the principle of Technical Cooperation among Developing Countries (TCDC).

Modest progress has been made. For example,

UNDP reports an increase in the number of experts from developed countries between 1970 and 1975 from about 23% to 29%. (3) In other words, close to 30% of all experts provided by the United Nations system during 1975 came from developing countries.

As mentioned, this is a modest degree of progress. It does indicate, however, one kind of change in the technical assistance field which undoubtedly has a far reaching effect on the questions of cross-cultural communication and colonialism.

As the above clearly indicates, the previous articles share a number of characteristics and basic assumptions. They also bring differing perspectives on the subject of the counterpart system. This is useful, given that the field is yet to be systematically organized for further research and exploration. Toward that end, the next part of my paper will present another perspective on the expert-counterpart relationship.

The Process of Technical Assistance and The Expert-Counterpart Relationship

Rather than focus attention on the relationship between expert and counterpart, as was done in the previous papers, I suggest that we place this relationship in its proper perspective. The expert-counterpart relationship has meaning only when we truly understand its larger context: the process of technical assistance. The following analysis, thus, looks at the nature of the technical assistance process, and considers the counterpart system as an instrument for the achievement of its goals.

I will deal primarily with technical assistance relationships between developed and developing countries. Reference will be made to the growing size of technical cooperation among Third World countries, a development of extreme importance to this whole discussion. No reference will be made, however, to cooperation among the industrialized countries. It falls beyond the scope of our concern.

Harari's definition of technical assistance, quoted earlier in Kerr's papers, reveals that technical assistance is based on the assumption that: (1) a problem exists in a developing country; (2) native knowledge, skill experience, financial resources are either non-existent or are inadequate to deal with it; and (3) the developing country imports are expert(s) whose job description may include (a) doing the job, (b) training someone to do the job, sible to their own government and have sole loyalty to it. They report to the donor government which in turn may transmit these reports to the recipient government.

The recipient country on the other hand, would also be guided by its national interests educated by a background of political and economic relations with the donor country. It fully realizes the contributions to be made by the donor and the conditions of such aid. More importantly, it realizes that receipt of this aid depends on the will of the donor, and that a change in the political climate between the two countries could place in jeopardy the aid projects agreed to.

It is in this kind of situation, I believe, that most of the discussions of the previous papers were cast. It is also in this context that issues of colonialism, neo-colonialism, and equality will have the heaviest impact on the effectiveness of the counterpart system, if used.

The above statement is true in case of a bi-lateral agreement between an industrialized country and a Third World country. However, this is not the only kind of bi-lateral agreement. Such agreements can take place between two developing countries, one of whom may have an excess of skill or resources needed by the other. This is becoming a popular Third World response to their technical assistance problems with developed nations. India, Egypt and Sri Lanka are examples of developing countries with an abundance of highly educated professional people. Their supply is undoubtedly larger than their economies can absorb. This resource is used to aid countries in short supply of such skills. For years, Egypt fulfilled the need for teachers badly needed by many Arab countries, including some that are more prosperous.

Bi-lateral technical assistance agreements among Third World countries is a relatively new but rapidly growing phenomenon. Third World countries are gradually becoming less than totally dependent on the industrialized West. They have found financial aid and technical assistance available through the Technical Cooperation among Developing Countries (TCDC) movement. This is evidence by the growing number of regional development banks such as The Kuwait Development Bank, The Asia Development Bank, etc. In addition, as Table II indicates, an increasing share of the financial resources available to developing countries now comes from developing countries.

and/or (c) defining the nature of the problem and recommending ways of solving it.

Thus, the nature of the problem facing the developing country defines the role of the expert, the need for a counterpart(s), and the kind of relationships likely to develop. As such, the counterpart relationship can really be understood only as a tool for the achievement of a specific goal. It is an instrument of technical assistance, and its utility, role, and potential are determined very much by the nature of the specific technical assistance process which called for it.

It is important that we distinguish between different kinds of technical assistance agreements. Discussions of the counterpart system and technical assistance in the previous papers reveal a simplistic overview which lumps different types of technical assistance situations together and treats them as one kind. This naive approach to a rather complex subject ignores important differences between technical assistance agreements.

There are several ways for classifying technical assistance agreements. The one most suitable for this discussion identifies three major groups:

1. Bi-lateral agreements.
2. Regional agreements.
3. International agreements.

In addition, given that multi-national corporations are heavily involved in skills transfer and were discussed at some length in the previous articles, they will be discussed here as a fourth, though separate category.

Bi-Lateral Agreements for Technical Assistance:

These are agreements between two countries: a donor of financial resources, equipment, and/or experts, and a recipient. Bi-lateral agreements are entered into by the governments of both countries and are, as such, governed by the foreign policies and relations between them. Agreements are heavily affected by national interests, and by what each seeks to gain from it. (4)

It is natural that the donor would want to maintain control and supervision over the implementation of the agreement. Accordingly, where experts are needed, they are almost exclusively recruited by the donor country from its own natives. Experts are then given briefings and operational instructions intended to ensure their understanding of what their government aims to accomplish. Experts are respon-

Bi-lateral technical assistance agreements could also be between countries where the elements of colonialism have little if any reason to exist. I imagine that a technical assistance agreement between Sweden or Norway, for example, and a developing country would be little burdened by the heavy shadow of colonial relationships.

All this notwithstanding, it is within this bilateral type of technical assistance agreements that the most undesirable outcomes of technical assistance and the counterpart system, as described in the seven papers, may be expected to emerge.

Regional Agreements of Technical Assistance

While bi-lateral agreements bind two countries to a program of technical assistance, regional agreements are between an international regional organization, such as the Organization of American States, and one of its member nations.

Under such an arrangement, there is no donor country. The regional organization, on behalf of its collective membership, is the donor. Accordingly, the agreement will be motivated by the collective interests of the community. Needless to say, a specific member may well have a disporportionate influence which ensures that the agreement favors its own national interests.

Implementation of such an agreement is the responsibility of both the regional organization and the recipient country. The former appoints the experts, who most likely come from more than one member state, pays their salaries, supervises their work, and commands their loyalty.

The recipient negotiates the agreement with a relatively greater sense of independence. Being a member of the regional organization, it will be exercising a right guaranteed all members, supported by resources to which it presumably contributed. It should feel no heavy sense of indebtedness or obligation to a specific country, no fear that the agreement may easily be broken, and presumably can refuse to accept terms that conflict with its best interests. In dealing with experts, counterparts are likely to feel a sense of kinship with the experts, which offsets feelings of inferiority generated under bi-lateral agreements.

A great deal of technical assistance is conducted under agreements between the United Nations and developing countries. (5) This mode of aid delivery is undoubtedly the most favored by Third World countries.

Fundamental differences exist between this type and the previous two. For one thing, the parties to the agreement are the UN and one of its member states who enjoys rights and privileges guaranteed by the UN Charter. Member nations have the right to apply for technical assistance and to have their applications considered on equal footing with those from other countries. They also expect their applications to be considered with the highest possible objectivity and the least influence by a non-sympathetic country, or one with whom it is on poor political terms.

Another fundamental difference is that UN funds for technical assistance are general international resources received from donor countries, put into a general fund(s) and used as resources of the international organization itself. No country can claim to have directly financed a specific project in a developing country. (6) The recipient country is thus under no obligation to any donor country.

Under the circumstances, there is a greater degree of objectivity in conducting technical assistance agreements of this sort. Projects are prepared and reviewed by staff of the international organization whose loyalty, at least legally, is assumed to be solely to the organization. Approvals are made by international boards where the recipient country is directly or indirectly represented. Implementation is also carried out by an international civil service representing all member nations. A developing country thus deals with the international organization from a position of greater independence than is possible under the two previous types.

International technical assistance agreements are rid, to a large extent, of the self-serving interests of one country dictating to the other. Agreements are guided by the best interests of the recipient country and the international community as a whole. (7) Resources are allocated from the general revenue of the international organization, on the basis of decisions made by boards representing all member states, and supported by a bureaucracy international in profile.

Furthermore, where experts are called for, recruitment is conducted world-wide. More importantly, actual appointment depends on the will of the recipient country, and experts remain on the job only at the will of the recipient country.

Experts are appointed by the international organization, and their salaries are paid by it. They are required to take a loyalty oath to the organization committing themselves to take orders from no government, even their own. Their work is supervised by the organization to which they are responsible.

While the above may represent the ideal, and while there are of course exceptions, the above safeguards reduce to a minimum the chances of the expert being a tool of his own government. It almost eliminates the impact of bi-lateral power politics and other foreign policy conflicts from affecting the goals of technical assistance. It also eliminates, to a large extent, the significance of the issues of colonialism and inequality.

There remains, of course, the human relations and interpersonal communication problems between expert and counterpart. Experts bring to their job patterns of thought and action which determine their ability to deal with interpersonal-intercultural conflicts with the counterpart. Proper selection, carefully planned orientation, and length of international service would help improve the chances of an effective expert-counterpart relationship.

Multi-national Corporations and Technical Assistance

Multi-national corporations, in my view, should not be included in this discussion. Since several papers referred to them, however, it would be appropriate to point out some of their distinguishing characteristics.

Our discussion so far has centered on relations between sovereign governments entering, directly or indirectly, into technical assistance agreements. Agreements between governments and multi-national corporations, are between two non-equals a sovereign government and a profit making business organization.

The primary purpose of the multi-national corporation is to maximize its profits by working in a developing country. Any developmental activity in which it is engaged would have to be either part of its overall business strategy, or a condition imposed upon it by the government as an element in the price the corporation has to pay for the privilege of doing business in that country. Developing countries are becoming increasingly wiser in the use of this bargaining tool in dealing with the multi-nationals.

The government can, and in many cases does, change the conditions of life and the circumstances under which the corporation may do business. In addition, many changes in the contractual relationship are imposed on the corporation. The corporation of course can pull out of that country; a decision made primarily on economic grounds.

Another important difference in the multi-national situation is that both expert and counterpart work for the same employer. They are paid by the multi-national, and are responsible to it. In addition, they are expected or required to perform a job, to produce work, and in the process effect the transfer of skill. Experts and counterparts share the responsibility for productivity, with the expert assuming primary responsibility. The expert is usually hierarchically superior and the counterpart his subordinate.

Clearly, the above does not represent the normal pattern of expert-counterpart relations in technical assistance. This is a unique situation where skill transfer takes place under totally different circumstances. Probably the only element in common with the previous three types of technical assistance agreements is that the expert and counterpart come from different countries, which would cause the human relations problems and intercultural conflicts mentioned before.

One final comment needs to be made in reaction to the previous papers. It is clearly evident that, in general, these papers reflect notions of technical assistance and international relations of at least a decade ago. The letter and the spirit of these papers give the distinct impression that the conditions of the 1960's prevail. One is drawn back to days when the U.S. was the only political and economic power in the world, able to persuade needy countries to follow its will. It was a world of dependence of almost the whole world on the might and wealth of this great country.

Fundamental changes swept the world in the last decade or so which generated an awareness of international inter-dependence symbolized by the demand for a new international economic order.

Interdependence is more than just a word. It is a fundamental principle of a reality which "was embraced by many academic theorists and free-trade partisans back in the early Sixties, but it became gospel in October 1973. The four-fold rise in oil prices and the Arab oil embargo after the Yom Kippur War exploded old myths and brought the need for a new world economic order into glaring light." (8)

From this beginning, a period of "New Realism" in world affairs was ushered in. (9) "Industrialized nations found they could no longer wield their capital as in the past to exploit cheap raw materials from developing countries. Wealthy, non-oil producing Europe was suddenly in the same boat with poor, non-oil producing nations of the Third World." (10) Efforts to organize the industrial West and Japan into a common front to challenge OPEC failed. Finally, though reluctantly, former Secretary of State Henry Kissinger declared, before a UN Special Session, his faith in interdependence and the U.S. willingness to cooperate with OPEC and Third World countries.

In a span of only three or four years, "cooperation between industrial nations and the rapidly advancing countries of the Third World is entering a new phase - a phase of constructive realism" accoring to Maurice Williams, Chairman of OECD's Development Assistance Committee. SID's Survey of International Development, summarized Mr. Williams' views, expressed in his Annual Report as follows:

> The period 1974-76 will be viewed in retrospect as one of transition to a 'New Realism' in world affairs, a turning point in the evolution of a broader community of national states working together for a new global order." .... He observed that "one of the salient political developments of the last few years has been the emergency of the Third World countries as full participants in areas of global decision-making which affect them -- and this in a period when interstate consultation in the management of global economic affairs has assumed greater importance. There is occurring a "new realism in the recognition of nations that they share responsibility for the maintenance of global economic stability, for the removal of constraints to a more just international economic system and for a sustained economic expansion in order to meet the urgent needs of the world's expanding population." What is now "fully understood between developing and industrial countries is the importance

> of longer term structural change in the world economy and their shared responsibility for the on-going process of reform."

While there may be full agreement among nations on their independence, the "new realism" has yet to be translated into operational terms to guide the New International Order. The nature of the "structural change in the world economy" has yet to be defined, although it is understood to be based on justice among all nations. Problems of "management of interdependence" are still under serious deliberate consideration. The new realism necessitates "participation by developing countries in the international councils which affect their economic affairs." It also creates the need for a:

> "concerted effort for self-reliant development on the part of poorer countries, in mature partnerships with the world community....There must be full respect for the dignity and sovereignty of developing countries," and there must be recognition on part of "all countries -- industrial as well as those on the way to further industrialization -- that economic progress and stability can only be assured from within." While alternative development strategies and an improved strategy for international development co-operation are essential, they are "no substitute for appropriate domestic policies and programmes.... It is the policies of nations which determine the success or failure of their own development."

Conclusion

The previous articles have agreed that the counterpart system is an important instrument of technical assistance. They have concluded that many factors impact negatively on the system's effectiveness as a tool for skill transfer. They have argued that basically this is due to the impact of colonialism, neo-colonialism, and inequality between rich technologically advanced industrial West, and Third World countries.

It appears, from the previous discussion, that the world may be changing at a much faster pace than scholars are able to follow, observe and comprehend. The image of a world divided into dependent and dependent-upon is being replaced by a new picture of an international system of interdependence. This drastic change makes Third World countries equal partners in the international decision-making process, and fully responsible for world stability, security, and development.

Granted all this is happening so fast that its implications are difficult to imagine. However, there is little doubt that it will have significant impact on the counterpart relationship. The view now must be that both expert and counterpart are partners in handling a problem which is geographically located in one country, but is likely to bear on the international community as a whole. Their success or failure requires mutual understanding, cooperation, and a global perspective on the objective of their mission.

NOTES

1. It is not clear why it is that the field, important as it is to the mission of technical assistance, has not attracted more attention. Hopefully, this effort by the Counterpart Group would at least serve to highlight the importance of this area of human activity and stimulate further research.

2. Society for International Development, "DAC Chairman Finds that Cooperation between Industrial and Third World Nations is Entering a New Phase of 'Constructive Realism'." Survey of International Development. Vol XIV, No. 1, January-February, 1977.

3. Tables I a, b, and c provide a comparative numerical analysis of the number of experts provided by the UN system from both developed and developing countries over the years 1970-1975.

4. In discussing the U.S. initiatives for world development, the Department of State's Special Report No. 28 states that:

> While the U.S. aid program, with its current emphasis on the poorest countries, can properly be called more "humanitarian" than it has ever been before, it is not a charitable undertaking. The United States, like other donor countries, does look for

certain things in return -- in particular, an international economic system that runs well, in which mutual obligations are observed, and in which developing countries assume greater obligations as they become more prosperous. It is only natural, moreover, that the United States, in assisting other countries, should take into account the degree to which they share such values as a respect for human rights which are prized in American society.

5. The UN and the International Organization are used in this discussion to refer to the UN system as a whole or any part of it.

6. Except probably in case of projects financed through funds-in-trust accounts.

7. It is recognized that certain countries exert undue influence on the International Organization thus forcing its actions in directions most suited to its own interests. Examples of this abound from both developed and developing countries. This power is usually exercised in what each country would consider most serious matters of political and/or security nature. U.S. withholding its financial contribution to UNESCO a few years ago is a case in point.

8. Drozdiak, William, "North/South Dialogue: Paris Conference Tests 'Economic Independence'." European Community, No. 200, March-April, 1977, p. 11.

9. Society for International Development, ibid.

10. Drozdiak, ibid, p. 12.

Table I a

Number of Experts and Consultants Provided by the United Nations System, 1970-1975

A. UNDP-financed programme

Year	Total all countries	Total developing countries	% to total
1970	8848	1866	21.1
1971	10139	2173	21.4
1972	10237	2251	22.0
1973	9644	2228	23.1
1974	9809	2424	24.7
1975	10788	2903	26.9

B. Programme Financed from Regular Budget

Year	Total all countries	Total developing countries	% to total
1970	2037	660	32.4
1971	2029	650	32.0
1972	2081	723	34.7
1973	1982	687	34.7
1974	2028	761	37.5
1975	1904	710	37.4

Table I a Cont'd.

C. Programme Financed from Trust and Other Funds

Year	Total all countries	Total developing countries	% to total
1970	1598	316	19.8
1971	1755	339	19.3
1972	1756	295	16.8
1973	1858	335	18.0
1974	2250	371	20.9
1975	2394	582	24.3

D. Grand Total

Year	Total all countries	Total developing countries	% to total
1970	12483	2842	22.8
1971	13923	3162	22.7
1972	14074	3269	23.2
1973	13484	3250	24.1
1974	14087	3656	26.0
1975	15086	4199	27.8

Source: Division of Management Information Services of UNDP.

Coverage: United Nations, ILO, FAI, UNESCO, WHO, World Bank, ICAU, UPO, ITU, WMO, IMCO, IAEA, UNIDO, UNCTAD, ADB, IDB, ASDB, UNDP

Table I b

Developing countries with highest number of experts and consultants in 1975

(by region)

Regions as covered by the Regional Bureaux of UNDP	Countries	
Africa	Ghana	6
	Nigeria	5
Asia and the Pacific	India	636
	Pakistan	74
	Philippines	18
	Sri Lanka	17
	Thailand	9
Europe, Mediterranean and the Middle East	Egypt	247
	Yugoslavia	98
	Jordan	14
Latin America	Chile	298
	Argentina	219
	Colombia	106
	Uruguay	11
	Brazil	10

Source: Response to UNDP statistical enquiry.

Coverage: FAO, WHO, UNESCO, UNIDO, United Nations, ILO, ITU, UNCTAD, ESCAP, ICAO, UNDP, IAEA, ECLA, WMO, ECA, World Bank, UPU and IMCO.

Table I c

Other countries with highest number of experts and consultants in 1975

Countries	Total
United Kingdom	1,782
United States	1,772
France	1,164
Netherlands	421
Belgium	321
Canada	194
Germany, Federal Republic of	190
Sweden	185
USSR	58
Japan	33
Austria	33
Norway	28
Australia	14

Source: Response to UNDP statistical enquiry

Coverage: FAO, WHO, UNESCO, United Nations, ILO, World Bank, UNIDO, ITU, ICAO, IAEA, UNCTAD, UNDP, ECLA, IMCO, WMO and UPU.

Table II

Net Flow of Resources Received by Developing Countries

$ billion

	1970-72 average	1973	1974	1975
I. Bilateral flows (total net)	16.9	23.5	29.1	39.1
-DAC countries	15.3	21.7	25.0	33.8
of which: ODA	6.2	7.1	8.3	9.8
other official flows + private	9.1	14.6	16.7	24.0
-OPEC countries	0.4	0.6	2.9	4.4
-Centrally Planned Economies	1.1	1.2	1.2	0.9
II. Flows from multilateral institutions, net (1)	2.1	3.3	4.6	5.8
III. Estimated Euro-currency, borrowing, net	2.1	8.5	8.0	9.5
IV. Total I to III	21.1	35.3	41.7	54.4
IMF Oil Facility	-	-	1.1	2.4
Grand Total	21.1	35.3	42.8	56.8

(1) DAC Members provided $ 3.8 billion to multilateral agencies as ODA in 1975

Counterparts and Advisors—A Selected Bibliography

Graham B. Kerr

For this bibliography I have selected items written in English from a larger bibliography prepared for the 15th World Congress of the Society for International Development.

The literature about advisors and counterparts is scattered and not well organized. Articles tend to be repetitious, listing many times over the personal qualities and professional qualifications required of good technical advisors. Most writers view the exchange process from the advisor's point-of-view, some discuss the importance of the advisor-counterpart relationship, and the counterpart's role, but few deal in any meaningful way with the counterpart himself.

The situation is improving, however, with the recent publication of Focus in the International Development Review. Each issue serves as a forum where articles concerning advisors and counterparts can be presented and discussed by the people working in technical assistance and scholars studying the process. Recent articles appearing in Focus recognize the importance of the role performed by the counterpart and suggest that more research should be focussed in his direction. This volume is also testimony that we are beginning to recognize the equal role of the counterpart and that a more balanced conceptualization of the process may enhance the New International Order.

Those interested in specific aspects of the counterpart system are directed to the following selected sources.

The Advisor -- Qualifications, Selection, and Training

Foster, R.J. Dimensions of Training for the Overseas Assignment. Technical Report 69-11 (Washington, D.C., Human Resources Research Office, George Washington University, 1969).

Johnston, M.B. "Training Needs of Overseas Americans as seen by Their National Co-workers in Asia." International Development Review/Focus, No. 4, 1974, pp. 21-25.

Lindholm, S. Appointment with the Third World: Experts and Volunteers in the Field: Their Work, Life and Thoughts. (Stockholm, Sweden, Dag Hammarskjold Foundation, 1974).

Mathiasen, K. Personal Qualities Required in Technicians. (Washington, D.C., AID, 1962).

Trail, T.F. Education of Development Technicians: A Guide to Training Programs. (New York, Praeger, 1968).

The Advisor's Role

Bass, Bernard M. "The American Advisor Abroad." Journal of Applied Behavioral Science, Vol. 7, No. 3, 1971, pp. 285-308.

Benveniste, G. and Ilchman, W.F. (Editors) Agents of Change: Professionals in Developing Countries. New York, Praeger, 1969.

Byrnes, F.C. "Role Shock: An Occupational Hazard of American Technical Assistants Abroad," The Annals of the American Academy of Political and Social Science, Vol. 368, 1966, pp. 95-108.

Harari, D. The Role of the Technical Assistance Expert, (Paris, OECD, 1974).

Jun, J.S. Ambiguity in the Professional Role: Perceptual Differences among AID Advisors. (Los Angeles, California, Ph.D. Dissertation, University of Southern California,

1969).

Linton, N. "The Role of the Expatriate in Developing Countries." International Development Review, No. 2, 1970, pp. 24-27.

Rigney, J.A. "Optimum Role for U.S. Overseas Advisors," in Strategies in Technical Assistance. (North Carolina State University, pp. 17-36, 1968).

Sanders, I.T. American Professionals Overseas. (New York, Ford Foundation, 1965).

Useem, J. "Work Patterns of Americans in India." Annals of the American Academy of Political and Social Science, Vol. 368, 1966, p. 146.

The Counterpart-Advisor Relationship

Ascroft, J. "A Conspiracy of Courtesy." International Development Review/Focus, No. 1, 1975, pp. 8-11.

Brasseur, R.E., "Constraints in the Transfer of Knowledge", International Development Review/Focus, No. 3, 1976, pp. 12-18.

Chaput, M.J. "Consultant-Client Problems in Africa," International Development Review, No. 1, 1971, pp. 23-25.

Fiks, A.I. "The importance of 2-way communication for volunteers in international service." International Development Review, No. 3, 1970, pp. 23-24.

Globerson, A. "Interaction Between Foreign Personnel and Local Counterparts", in Spitzberg, I. (ed.), The Exchange of Expertise: Counterparts and the New International Order. (Boulder, Colorado, Westview, 1978).

Jesse, M., and Smith, D., "Experts and Counterparts: A professional Problem", in Spitzberg, I. (ed.), The Exchange of Expertise: Counterparts and the New International Order. (Boulder, Colorado, Westview, 1978).

Glaser, W. "Some Preliminary Conclusions about Social Roles in Technical Assistance," in Kumar, K. (ed.) (in press) Experts and Counterparts in Technical Assistance (Honolulu, Hawaii, East-West Center Press).

__________ "Improving Communication in the Technical Cooperation Relationship," International Development Review/Focus, No. 3, 1975, pp. 10-14.

__________ "The Performance of Expert-Counterpart Dyads in Technical Assistance," (Mimeo, New York., Bureau of Applied Research, Columbia University, 1974).

__________ "Making Better Use of Technical Assistance Experts," International Development Review /Focus, No. 2, 1975, pp. 21-25.

Grabowski, T. "Cooperation between Experts and Counterparts," International Development Review/Focus, No. 2, 1976, pp. 20 & 32.

Jacobson, J. "Pitfalls for Consultants and Their Clients in Developing Countries," International Development Review, No. 2, 1971, pp. 2-8.

Kerr, G.B. "Communication and the Advisor-Counterpart Relationship in the Technical Assistance Process." Amsterdam, the Netherlands, Paper presented at the 15th World Conference of the Society for International Development, Nov. 29-Dec. 3, 1976.

Lindholm, S. Appointment with the Third World: Experts and Volunteers in the Field: Their Work, Life and Thoughts. (Stockholm, Sweden, Dag Hammarskjold Foundation, 1974).

Raman, N.P. "A framework for effective interaction between national and international personnel." International Development Review/Focus, No. 2, 1974, pp. 23-24.

Storm, W.B. and Jun, J.S. "The Counterpart Relationship and the American Professional Overseas." Public Personnel Review, Vol. 29, No. 1, 1968, pp. 7-12.

Winter, D.K. American Professors in West Pakistan: A Study in Cross-Cultural Relations. Ph.D. Thesis, Michigan State University, East Lansing, Michigan, 1968.

The Counterpart: Qualifications, Selection and Training

Eisemon, T. "Counterpart Training: The Implications for Scientific and Educational Policy in Emergent Scientific Communities." Paper presented at the 15th World Conference of the Society for International Development, 29 November-December 3, 1976, Amsterdam, The Netherlands.

Green, J.W. "Success and Failure in Technical Assistance: A Case Study," Human Organization, Vol. 20, No. 1, 1961, pp. 2-10.

Sahba, H. and M. Scott Myers, The Iranian Counterpart Role in Technical Development. (Tehran and Paris, University of Tehran and UNESCO, no date).

The Counterpart's Role

Kerr, G.B. "Communication and the Advisor-Counterpart Relationship in the Technical Assistance Process." Amsterdam, The Netherlands, Paper presented at the 15th World Conference of the Society for International Development, Nov. 29-Dec. 3, 1976.

Lindholm, S. "Should language training be compulsory?" International Development Review/Focus, No. 2, 1974, pp. 13-16.

Sahba, H. and M. Scott Myers. The Iranian Counterpart Role in Technical Development. (Tehran and Paris, University of Tehran and UNESCO, no date).

For Product Safety Concerns and Information please contact our EU representative GPSR@taylorandfrancis.com Taylor & Francis Verlag GmbH, Kaufingerstraße 24, 80331 München, Germany

Batch number: 10726011

Printed by Printforce, the Netherlands